# HUME'S
# PHILOSOPHICAL
# DEVELOPMENT

# HUME'S PHILOSOPHICAL DEVELOPMENT

*A Study of his Methods*

BY

JAMES NOXON

OXFORD
AT THE CLARENDON PRESS
1973

*Oxford University Press, Ely House, London W. 1*

GLASGOW  NEW YORK  TORONTO  MELBOURNE  WELLINGTON
CAPE TOWN  IBADAN  NAIROBI  DAR ES SALAAM  LUSAKA  ADDIS ABABA
DELHI  BOMBAY  CALCUTTA  MADRAS  KARACHI  LAHORE  DACCA
KUALA LUMPUR  SINGAPORE  HONG KONG  TOKYO

*Printed in Great Britain*
*at the University Press, Oxford*
*by Vivian Ridler*
*Printer to the University*

TO

CATHERINE BEATTIE

# PREFACE

FOR several years McMaster University has generously supported my work by Summer Research Stipends which it is a pleasure to acknowledge.

This book has been published with the help of a grant from the Humanities Research Council of Canada, using funds provided by the Canada Council.

I am grateful to my friend and colleague, Professor Albert Shalom, for his generous interest in my work, helpful discussion of certain problems, and perceptive comments on the first draft. I am also greatly indebted to Mr. J. L. Mackie, of University College, Oxford, for criticisms which proved invaluable in the preparation of the final version.

I am pleased to acknowledge here numerous academic debts of long standing owed to Lela Noxon, whose assistance in the past far exceeded the bounds of maternal duty. I am equally grateful to my father for tolerating with patience and good humour many inconveniences occasioned by my work.

J. N.

*McMaster University*
*February 1972*

# CONTENTS

x                    *Contents*

# ABBREVIATIONS

*For the reader's convenience, references to Hume's works are cited in parentheses immediately after quotations, the abbreviations used being explained in the table below. References to other works, and supplementary citations of Hume, appear as footnotes.*

T      *A Treatise of Human Nature*, ed. L. A. Selby-Bigge (Clarendon Press, Oxford, 1888). (Page references for passages which are *quoted* are given in the form (T 101) or, in the case of those taken from Hume's Introduction where pagination is by lower case roman numerals (T xix). In the case of topics which are *mentioned*, the reader is directed to Book, Part and Section by a note of the form (T I iii 14), which means *Treatise*, Book I, Part iii, Section 14.)

A      *An Abstract of a Treatise of Human Nature*, eds. J. M. Keynes and Peter Straffa (Cambridge University Press, Cambridge, 1938).

E₁      *An Enquiry Concerning Human Understanding*
                          and

E₂      *An Enquiry Concerning the Principles of Morals*
                          from

E      *Enquiries* . . ., ed. L. A. Selby-Bigge (Clarendon Press, Oxford, 2nd ed. 1902). ('E', without subscript, is used only for reference to the 'Editor's Introduction'.) (Both of Hume's *Enquiries* are divided into Sections, some of which are divided into Parts. In addition to the usual page references for quotations, (E₁ 101), for example, topics may be located by notes of the form (E₁ VII ii), which means first *Enquiry*, Section VII, Part ii.)

G & G      *David Hume: The Philosophical Works*, 4 vols., ed. T. H. Green and T. H. Grose (London, 1886). Cited in all references to Hume's *Essays, Moral, Political, and Literary, A Dissertation on the Passions*, and *The Natural History of Religion*. (The capitalized roman numeral indicates the volume, the arabic number the page.)

D      *Dialogues Concerning Natural Religion*, ed. Norman Kemp Smith (L. L. A., Bobbs-Merrill, New York, 2nd. ed., 1947).

H      *The History of England from the Invasion of Julius Caesar to the Revolution in 1688*, 6 vols. (John B. Alden, New York, 1885). There appears to be no modern, standard edition of Hume's *History*, and I have not had access to his final revised edition of 1778. Since I cannot expect many readers to have a copy of the edition that I happen to own, I have referred simply to chapters which in the above edition are numbered without break throughout. (Duncan Forbes's recent edition of Hume's *History of Great Britain, Volume One, containing the reigns of James I and Charles I* (1754) (Penguin, Harmondsworth, 1970), is a most welcome publication which one hopes may be enlarged in future to include the whole of Hume's *History*.)

L      *The Letters of David Hume*, 2 vols., ed. J. Y. T. Greig (Clarendon Press, Oxford, 1932). (The capitalized roman numeral indicates the volume, the arabic number the page.)

# INTRODUCTION

MEN of David Hume's time who were primarily interested in psychology, society, and political science were encouraged by the dramatic accomplishments of natural philosophers. The rapid advances in knowledge of the physical world were recognizably dependent upon the scientific method, a complex form of intellectual activity which had not been invented but had evolved, and which was still imperfectly understood even by those who were using it with brilliant effect. The prospect of adapting this method to the study of human nature was enticing. It had already, fifty years before, attracted Thomas Hobbes, a towering figure whose shadow falls across the greater part of the eighteenth century. It seemed that morality, society, and political life could at last be based upon a sound, scientific understanding of human nature. What had appeared in the eighteenth century to be a glorious opportunity reappears in the twentieth as a last desperate chance. Anyone wishing to take that chance will learn from the eighteenth century some lessons which have been forgotten and also find that some roads which are still being travelled today were even then discovered to lead nowhere.

Eighteenth-century optimism was not justified. Confidence in the methods of natural science to solve human problems was misplaced. Sooner or later applied science would supply the means of securing almost any end which men might choose. But on questions of the wisdom of the choices science must remain for ever mute. The magnitude of the failure to realize the eighteenth-century ideal of a rational, humane social order is now manifest in the gothic paradox of power which men create but cannot control. But even in Hume's day it was becoming evident that the attempt to introduce scientific method into moral and religious subjects would misfire. Bitter unresolved controversies about human motives, about the grounds of moral judgement and obligation, the basis of sovereignty, the supporting evidence for religious belief, and so on, could have persisted only if the issues involved were immune to scientific treatment. When a reader moves from the natural to the moral philosophy of the eighteenth century he enters an area of uncertainty where almost every shade of opinion is defended by arguments of roughly equal plausibility. The torrent of pamphlets, usually written neither for fame nor profit, but anonymously, and often at the risk of legal prosecution, testifies to the susceptibility of the age to cortical stimulation by a moral concept, a religious dogma, an abstruse point of critical or political theory. In the no man's land of beliefs and values, satirical weapons were the most tactical ones. Polemicists could overrun positions by parody, by carrying them to unintended logical conclusions. An intense concern with issues which could not be settled by logic or evidence created perfect conditions for breeding satirists. It is little wonder that a question about the limits of the human understanding came to dominate the philosophical investigations of so resolute a thinker as David Hume.

The aim of the following study is to trace the development of Hume's thinking about two profound and intimately related problems. From the beginning he was equally concerned with determining the lawful limits of human knowledge and belief and with understanding human preferences, relationships, and institutions. He started with the conviction that experimental psychology would yield a theory of human nature from which solutions to the problems of epistemology and of aesthetics, ethics, and politics could all be derived. The difficulties which he encountered forced a change of tactics which accounts for the main differences between his early and his mature philosophy. My intention is to examine these difficulties in depth, for they are, I think, intrinsically interesting and important, as well as being the keys to the evolution of Hume's thought.

# PART I

## Hume's Intentions and How They Changed

### Section 1. *The Science of Man*

HUME began his *Treatise of Human Nature* in his twenty-third year, having already in the previous three years 'scribled many a Quire of Paper' (L I 16). After spending three years in France in this first 'Attempt to introduce the experimental Method of Reasoning into Moral Subjects', Hume came to London with the first draft of his book. After another eighteen months of revising, he published in 1739 the first two volumes, 'Of the Understanding' and 'Of the Passions', and in the following year the third, 'Of Morals'.

Hume's admirers have been understandably curious about his choice of La Flèche in Anjou, where Descartes had spent the nine years of his college life, as the scene of his first and most ambitious philosophical work. The only extant letter written by Hume from La Flèche, published twenty years ago by Ernest Campbell Mossner,[1] gives no support to the natural supposition that Hume was attracted to the town and to the Jesuit College there on account of their Cartesian associations. While commending the 'Buildings and Gardens', Hume makes clear that he had no interest in studying at that College, nor at any other. He recommends La Flèche to his young friend for its pleasant site on the banks of the Loire, for its proximity to 'some of the most celebrated Country Towns in France', for the friendliness of its inhabitants, and for 'The Cheapness of it'. He does not mention Descartes, a disappointing omission which need not be explained by the implausible conjecture that he had no interest in the great French

---

[1] 'Hume at La Flèche, 1735: An Unpublished Letter', *Texas Studies in English* 37 (1958), 30–3.

sceptic. The slight and inconclusive evidence of this single letter
does suggest that Hume did not go to La Flèche on a pilgrimage.
The philosophy that he wrote there strongly suggests that he was
joining in the critical reaction that had already displaced Descartes
in favour of Locke and Newton at home.

At least one perceptive commentator[2] has noticed the militantly
anti-Cartesian programme announced by Hume in the Introduction to his *Treatise*. Descartes also had been interested in the
foundations of science, and had written hopefully of bringing
ethics within the scope of his universal science. However, these
foundations crumbled as he probed them, and Descartes ended the
first sceptical phase of his work in a state of doubt and despair
which anticipates the mood of the Conclusion to the first book of
the *Treatise*. But Descartes, of course, struck bed-rock certainty in
his own existence as a thinking being. Scepticism is blocked by
the indubitable proposition, 'Cogito, ergo sum', and Descartes
started to build with supreme confidence in pure reason upon that
unshakeable logical foundation. Hume will reject this solution
as a fraudulent manœuvre and, concluding that scepticism 'is a
malady, which can never be radically cur'd' (T 218), have to find
his own remedy for a chronic disability in order to get on with
his construction. The metaphysics which Descartes depicted as
rooting the tree of knowledge in reality consisted of a few simple,
indubitable principles whose rational strength could support all
branches of human knowledge. The Cartesian ideal of certainty
to be realized through the pure objectivity of logical thinking is
quietly set aside by Hume at the outset. A presupposition of his
attempt to ground the sciences in human nature is that all knowledge is humanly conditioned. Unlike Descartes, he does not aim
to vindicate scientific knowledge, to supply a metaphysical
guarantee of its veracity, but to examine the foundations of
science in order to determine 'the extent and force of human

---

[2] J. A. Passmore, *Hume's Intentions* (Cambridge, 1952), 12: ' "Philosophy",
wrote Descartes, "is like a tree whose roots are metaphysics, whose trunk is
physics, and whose branches, which arise from this trunk, are all the other
sciences." Hume sets out to show that the theory of human nature, not metaphysics, is the roots and that the moral sciences, not physics, are the trunk. That
is the principal intent of his positivism.'

understanding' (T xix). The limits he fixed measure the scepticism which opponents have always found unduly restrictive. When the problems involved in his attempt to introduce the method of natural science into the study of human nature are raised in Part Three, however, the *Treatise* will appear as a work of unwarranted methodological optimism.

In 1739 Hume prefaced the first two volumes of his *Treatise* with an Advertisement of works on morals, politics, and criticism to follow, should this first venture succeed. '*My design*', he announces there, '*is sufficiently explain'd in the* introduction.' In that Introduction Hume declares his intention of establishing an empirical science of man which will serve as the foundation—'the only solid foundation' (T xx)—of both the practical sciences in which he was particularly interested, '*Logic, Morals, Criticism, and Politics*', and of the theoretical ones 'which are the objects of pure curiosity' (T xx), '*Mathematics, Natural Philosophy, and Natural Religion*' (T xix). The announcement of his programme is clear—on the surface. But as soon as one attempts to get an unobstructed view of this science of man, the apparently limpid text becomes cloudy indeed. Hume is emphatic enough in stressing its importance, but regrettably ambiguous in fixing its place within his system. His failure to present complete and careful specifications for the work to be done excuses some of the unflattering misconstructions put upon his 'design'.

Hume tells us that 'the science of man is the only solid foundation for the other sciences' (T xx), that 'Even *Mathematics, Natural Philosophy*, and *Natural Religion*, are in some measure dependent on the science of MAN' (T xix), and that 'those sciences, which more intimately concern human life' (T xx) can be mastered only after we have taken command of the science of man. Thus his proposal for 'a compleat system of the sciences, built on a foundation almost entirely new' (T xx) would seem to require the science of man as the groundwork upon which the particular moral sciences, logic, morals, criticism, and politics, are to be raised immediately, the sciences of mainly theoretical interest following 'at leisure'. However, there are equally strong suggestions that the science of man consists of the four moral sciences, rather than being an independent fundamental science supporting them. 'In these four sciences', Hume announces, 'of *Logic, Morals, Criticism, and Politics,* is comprehended almost everything, which it can in any way import us to be acquainted with' (T xx), and adds, half a page later, 'There is no question of importance, whose decision is not compriz'd in the science of man. . . .' Hume's statement in his anonymously published *Abstract* of the *Treatise* that 'it may be safely affirmed that almost all the sciences are comprehended in the science of human nature' confirms this suggestion, but immediately cancels it out in the subordinate clause, 'and are dependent on it' (A 7). He proceeds to quote verbatim the *Treatise* specification of the subject-matter of the four moral sciences: '*The sole end of* logic *is to explain the principles and operations of our reasoning faculty, and the nature of our ideas*; morals and criticism *regard our tastes and sentiments; and* politics *consider men as united in society, and dependent on each other*' (A 7).

How can these sciences be both included within the science of man (or 'science of human nature'—he uses the terms synonymously) and be dependent on it? The paradox can be resolved on the assumption that Hume uses the expression 'science of man' or 'science of human nature' ambiguously, referring at times to the whole set of moral sciences, at other times to one member of the set upon which the others depend. The heir apparent for that position is logic, whose 'end' as just defined coincides with that specified for the 'science of MAN', viz., 'to explain the nature of the ideas we employ, and of the operations we perform in our reasonings' (T xix).[3]

In the Advertisement to Books I and II of the *Treatise*, Hume explains that '*The subjects of the* understanding *and* passions *make a*

---

[3] It should be pointed out in confirmation of my view that when Hume is about to close his discussion of Book I, 'Of the Understanding', in the *Abstract*, he says, 'I shall conclude the logics of this author . . .' (A 24). It is true that later in the *Treatise* itself (I iii 15), Hume uses 'logic' in a much narrower sense to refer to a set of general rules governing causal judgements. Having formulated eight 'Rules by which to judge of causes and effects', Hume adds, 'Here is all the Logic I think proper to employ in my reasoning . . .' (T 175). But these rules of inductive inference do not constitute the logic whose function was defined in his Introduction, and which later came to be called 'epistemology'.

*compleat chain of reasoning by themselves . . .'* This remark suggests that his theory of the passions—psychology—is to be given equal standing alongside logic—the theory of the understanding—as consolidating the foundations of the moral sciences. Despite his negligent omission of the theory of the passions from the list of moral subjects, or even of any mention of it anywhere in the Introduction, the role suggested here for psychology accords, I am sure, with Hume's intention. Some months later he went even further in advertising his psychology as fundamental for the works to come; in the *Abstract* he says, speaking first of Book I and then of Book II, 'The author has finished what regards logic, and has laid the foundation of the other parts in this account of the passions' (A 7).

The relations between Hume's theories of the understanding and of the passions are complicated. As empirical explanations of mental and emotional phenomena respectively, they are collateral. Hume intends the 'logic' of Book I to include psychological explanations of imagination, memory and inductive inference, generalization, judgement, belief, and other such processes, all on associationist principles. The psychology of Book II, his 'accurate anatomy of human nature' (T 263), is intended to explain pride and humility, love and hatred, envy, benevolence, malice, sympathy, and other passions, on the same basis. Thus the first two books of the *Treatise* together supply a psychology of both the intellective and the affective life, and in this sense they '*make a compleat chain of reasoning by themselves*'. One obvious link in the chain is supplied by Hume's concern with the respective roles of reason and passion in human experience. The main epistemological doctrine of Book I, that the fundamental natural beliefs of men are grounded in instinct and enforced by feeling, has its counterpart in Book II, where Hume argues that men are motivated to act by feeling, not by reason. This celebrated conclusion of Book II, that 'Reason is, and ought only to be the slave of the passions' (T 415), provides in turn a major premiss to reach a principal conclusion of Book III, viz. that moral distinctions are not derived from reason, but from a moral sense, i.e. from feeling or sentiment.

However, the psychology of the emotions is also in a sense
dependent upon the logic. For Hume's intention in Book I is not
only 'to explain the principles and operations of our reasoning
faculty' (T xix), but also to defend in advance the empirical
method which is to be used in Book II. When Hume wishes to
stress the methodological implications of his logic, rather than its
intrinsic value as a positive contribution to mental psychology, he
characterizes it as a prelude to his main business. ' 'Tis now time',
he says, just before the formal Conclusion to Book I, 'to return
to a more close examination of our subject, and to proceed in the
accurate anatomy of human nature, having fully explain'd the
nature of our judgement and understanding' (T 263). By a
nautical metaphor extended throughout the opening paragraph
of the Conclusion itself, he pictures the whole of his logical work
as a hazardous embarkation manœuvre which has merely brought
him to the point of launching 'out into those immense depths of
philosophy, which lie before me' (T 263).

As Hume's system evolves, logic and psychology each take on
independent roles. Morals, criticism, and politics are based directly
upon the theory of the passions. In Book II of the *Treatise*, in
other words, Hume formulates the psychological principles from
which explanations of moral, aesthetic, and political phenomena
are to be derived. In Book I he develops the theory of meaning
and knowledge which is to be applied directly in the analysis of
the concepts and methods of natural philosophy, mathematics,
and natural religion. His interest in these latter three disciplines is
critical, not constructive. He does not intend to advance these
theoretical sciences by working within them, but rather to
determine the logical character and limits of the knowledge
available from them. He undertakes to do this by a genetic
inquiry, supposing, as a good Lockian would, that if he can discover how men do in fact acquire knowledge and belief, he will
be able to show which objects and methods conform to the natural
principles of the human understanding and which do not. It seems
that Hume originally conceived this problem as one of empirical
psychology to be resolved by an adaptation of the experimental
method, to which he was reputedly attracted through his admira-

tion for Newton. Throughout his attempt to apply the experimental method to the investigation of thought processes, he was plagued by technical difficulties. Just how serious these were will appear from the reflections of Part II below on the workings of this method in the hands of Newton and from the comparative study of Hume's own theory and practice of scientific method in Part III.

The critical aspect of Hume's philosophy comes to dominate the argument completely in the final part of Book I, where he examines a set of traditional metaphysical doctrines. Although these lengthy analyses may appear digressive, Hume considered them relevant to defending the empirical method he intends to use for constructing his system. His succinct reason for extending the experimental method of natural philosophy to moral subjects is that the essence of mind is as unknowable as the essence of matter, and therefore the *a priori* deductive method must be superseded in the human sciences as it had been over a century before in the physical sciences. The credibility of empirical science derives from a method which is simply a refinement of the means by which men learn from experience in everyday life. The 'chimerical systems' of metaphysics, on the other hand, are logically akin to ideal constructions in pure mathematics and violate the principles men naturally follow when exploring the real world. The vindication of experimental philosophy and the elimination of metaphysics are thus corollaries, equally dependent upon fixing the nature and limits of human understanding. Fortunately the realization of Hume's critical aims, the exclusion of certain theories and doctrines from the domain of attainable knowledge, did not depend upon a psychological 'System of the Mental World' which determined the limits of human understanding. The explanation of human behaviour is the proper business of psychology, and there are powerful logical objections to any attempt to convert psychological facts and principles into epistemological rules and standards. The psychology of the understanding belongs to the constructive side of Hume's programme. It is part of his science of man. But psychological theory is not, as I shall argue against prevailing criticism in Part IV, the basis of

his philosophical analysis, nor even an integral part of it. Psychological explanations of conceptual confusion are subsidiary to the
analyses of philosophical terms, and they are not, however
interesting in themselves, indispensable to Hume's sceptical
critique of metaphysical and theological procedures and doctrines.
At the root of Hume's eventual divorcing of his critical work from
his constructive philosophy is the actual logical independence of
psychological theory and philosophical analysis. When Hume
publicly disowned *A Treatise of Human Nature* toward the end of
his life, he tacitly confessed that he had failed to integrate his
critical and his constructive designs within a unified system. It is
with the various forces, logical, methodological, and metaphysical,
which ensured this failure that I shall be concerned throughout
this book, which concludes, in Part V, with a study of the reconstruction of Hume's philosophy in his later works.

## Section 2. *Scepticism: Cartesian and Humean*

It is well known from Hume's own testimony that he was driven
by the analytic spirit into scepticism—'the barren rock', he calls
it—where he is reduced 'almost to despair' upon realizing 'the
impossibility of amending or correcting . . . the wretched condition, weakness, and disorder of the faculties' (T 264). At the
conclusion to Book I, surveying the wreckage behind him, he
admits that he has no reason to believe in the existence of anything
except the perceptions of which he is momentarily conscious—no
reason even to believe in the 'wreckage': 'After the most accurate
and exact of my reasonings, I can give no reason why I shou'd
assent to it . . .' (T 265). Hume has struck no rational grounds even
for maintaining the reality of the external world, which he
*imagines* to exist, nor for his habit of generalizing upon experience,
although all of his professed empirical knowledge depends upon
that. Is it not an outrageous paradox to lay down this debilitating
scepticism as 'the only solid foundation' of the sciences? Even 'the
barren rock' begins to shatter; for by settling on scepticism 'you
expressly contradict yourself', he explains, 'since this maxim must

be built on the preceding reasoning, which will be allow'd to be sufficiently refin'd and metaphysical' (T 268). Who could bear the discouragements of trying to build on this crumbling basis? Hume, at one moment, thought that even he could not. 'The *intense* view of these manifold contradictions and imperfections in human reason has so wrought upon me, and heated my brain, that I am ready to reject all belief and reasoning, and can look upon no opinion even as more probable or likely than another' (T 268–9). And he adds a coda with Cartesian overtones:

Where am I, or what? From what causes do I derive my existence, and to what condition shall I return? Whose favour shall I court, and whose anger must I dread? What beings surround me? and on whom have I any influence, or who have any influence on me? I am confounded with all these questions, and begin to fancy myself in the most deplorable condition imaginable, inviron'd with the deepest darkness, and utterly depriv'd of the use of every member and faculty. (T 269)

Although Hume's philosophy develops in opposition to Descartes's at almost every point, the *animus* of its ruthless questioning of assumptions, beliefs, and principles is indelibly Cartesian. The sceptical movement in the *Meditations* is deft and polished, recording the quintessence of metaphysical thinking. Descartes quickly reaches the dramatic climax of doubt, then resolves it with a brilliant stroke. The elegance and economy of the proof suggest a work thought through completely and in fine detail before a single word was put to paper, and the reader feels confident of following an argument that is moving inexorably toward a well-planned denouement. Hume, by contrast, drags his reader unsteadily around every turn of his tortuous thought, and when in the end he admits that his doubts cannot be excised by logical means, it is far from sure that he had foreseen that conclusion. Beneath the differences in style, there is in Descartes and Hume the same sense of obligation to test the power of reason. There is no doubt in my mind that it was Hume who pressed the questions harder, far beyond the point where reason could re-establish itself by claiming intuitive certainty of an existential truth.

From the impasse Hume had reached there was no way out

except to retreat, to return to the old uncertified beliefs, to agree to think and to decide, to reason, argue, predict, and explain according to the natural principles of the understanding. These principles upon which unreflective men habitually act in the affairs of everyday life seemed to Hume a good deal more reliable than any artificial ones the metaphysician might hope to devise. To Hume it seemed madness to renounce those principles, the Principle of the Uniformity of Nature, for example, or the Law of Causality, simply because the fraudulence of all claims for their rational validity had been exposed. If such principles expressed logically unjustifiable assumptions, they also represented psychologically necessary ones for imposing order and intelligibility upon the world in which men have to think in order to survive. The healthy response to sceptical disillusionment is to consent to work with instruments which are less than perfect. While never deceiving himself about their imperfections, the sceptic must in consistency have some reservations about doubts inspired by subtle and recondite reasoning. 'A true sceptic will be diffident of his philosophical doubts', Hume remarks, 'as well as of his philosophical conviction . . .' (T 273). In practical affairs, stubbornness at this point would be suicidal; in theoretical matters, it would result in the extinction of all science. 'I may, nay I must yield to the current of nature, in submitting to my senses and understanding; and in this blind submission I shew most perfectly my sceptical disposition and principles' (T 269). 'The conduct of a man, who studies philosophy in this careless manner, is more truly sceptical than that of one, who feeling in himself an inclination to it, is yet so overwhelmed with doubts and scruples, as totally to reject it' (T 273). Once the philosopher has learned to live with uncertainty, then he 'might hope to establish a system or set of opinions, which if not true (for that, perhaps, is too much to be hop'd for) might at least be satisfactory to the human mind, and might stand the test of the most critical examination' (T 272).

When Descartes became dubious about some of his opinions, he decided to put them all in question, even the highly probable ones. Before coming upon one absolute certainty, he found the voluntary suspension of judgement taxing, requiring constant vigilance. 'But this is a laborious task', he confessed, 'and insensibly a certain lassitude leads me into the course of my ordinary life . . . so insensibly of my own accord I fall back into my former opinions.'⁴ This tendency to relapse into the uncritical acceptance of pre-philosophical opinions is a troublesome problem for Descartes at the beginning of his metaphysics; for Hume it is the only hopeful resolution at the end. For once the philosopher chooses to put his natural beliefs and habits of thought into question, the further he probes, according to Hume, the more deeply they are undermined: 'As the sceptical doubt arises naturally from a profound and intense reflection on those subjects, it always encreases the farther we carry our reflections, whether in opposition or conformity to it. Carelessness and inattention alone can afford us any remedy' (T 218). Even Descartes had been careful to point out that he could risk his self-conscious suspense of judgement only because he was 'not considering the question of action, but only of knowledge'.⁵ In order to live one must act, and actions presuppose certain beliefs; after these beliefs have been discredited by what Hume calls 'reflections very refin'd and metaphysical' (T 268), they return, surreptitiously, as the agents of survival, for, as Hume says of himself, one is 'absolutely and necessarily determin'd to live, and talk, and act like other people in the common affairs of life' (T 269) and, as Locke had said before him, 'He that will not eat till he has demonstration that it will nourish him; he that will not stir till he infallibly knows the business he goes about will succeed will have little else to do but to sit still and perish.'⁶ Whoever professes strict scepticism has to contend not only with the embarrassment of having to violate his

⁴ *Meditation I, The Philosophical Works of Descartes*, tr. Elizabeth Ross and G. R. T. Haldane (Dover, New York, 1955), i. 149.

⁵ Ibid. 248.

⁶ *An Essay Concerning Human Understanding*, ed. A. C. Fraser (Dover, New York, 1959), ii. 360. Cf. *An Enquiry Concerning Human Understanding* 160, where Hume observes that the Pyrrhonian must acknowledge 'that all human life must perish, were his principles universally and steadily to prevail. All discourse, all action would immediately cease; and men remain in a total lethargy, till the necessities of nature, unsatisfied, put an end to their miserable existence.' Then he adds, significantly and characteristically, 'It is true; so fatal an event is very little to be dreaded. Nature is always too strong for principle.'

theoretical principles to meet practical demands, but also with the natural compulsion to break out of the intolerable mood of 'philosophical melancholy and delirium' (T 269) which possesses the sceptic after a bout of metaphysical indulgence. If the sceptic cannot be defeated on his own grounds, neither can anyone work from his philosophy, nor live by it, nor even believe it; it is characteristic of sceptical arguments, as Hume mentioned apropos of Berkeley, *'that they admit of no answer and produce no conviction'* (E₁ 155n).

As all serious commentators have come to realize, the term 'scepticism' is too imprecise to fix Hume's position. There is no doubt that he claims to be a sceptic, a distinction to which his undermining of many dogmas entitles him. But on the other hand, he is often concerned with showing the futility of scepticism, and more than once even denied the very existence of any true sceptic. On the one hand he tells us that the only result of scepticism is 'momentary amazement and irresolution and confusion' (E₁ 155n), and on the other that 'if we are philosophers, it ought only to be upon sceptical principles' (T 270). He explains how 'nature breaks the force of all sceptical arguments' (T 187), but advises that 'In all the incidents of life we ought still to preserve our scepticism' (T 270). These warring statements have often been diagnosed as symptomatic of an unresolved conflict within Hume. At some moments he is bent upon showing that a sceptical conclusion on one metaphysical issue or another is absolutely irrefutable; at others that a sceptical opinion on the same issue is incredible. At one time he leads the sceptical assault upon a certain dogma, at another insists that we have no choice but to take the dogma for granted. And sometimes he stands outside both positions, commenting on the futility of the debate between dogmatists and sceptics, which he finally characterized as a verbal dispute expressing a difference in 'habit, caprice, or inclination' (D 219n). Hume has proved to be a moving target, and in retaliation many frustrated critics have denounced him as a charlatan, having no seriously held principles at all. Others have made elaborate and ingenious attempts to pin him down, and by the subtlety of their arguments at least proved how elusively he moves. And still others have taken the discord in his writings to reflect dialectical tensions for which he refused any cheap and easy resolution. Presumably all would agree with André Leroy that the question of Hume's scepticism is 'the ultimate question'. Any serious attempt to answer that question, which has proved to be crucial for evaluating Hume's quality as a philosopher, pre-supposes intimacy with the details of his work and a steady view of the direction in which his thinking evolved. At this point I shall simply state without much argument a few obviously relevant points about Hume's sceptical intentions.

By showing that certain problems which had traditionally preoccupied metaphysicians were absolutely insoluble, Hume hoped to promote his aim of 'giving in some particulars a different turn to the speculations of philosophers' (T 273). At the same time he would be able to disclose the limited sphere of demonstrative reasoning, and thus promote the empirical method—recommend, in short, his 'attempt to introduce the experimental method of reasoning into moral subjects'. After showing that certain com-pelling universal beliefs found no rational justification, although sanity and even survival depended upon them, he could in good conscience develop a theory of human nature based upon experience.

The Pyrrhonian spirit presides over Hume's proceedings against ontologists who devise theories to vindicate our natural belief in the substantial reality of the external world and of the mind. This excessive scepticism is mitigated by reflection on the practical necessity of holding on to these natural beliefs which cannot be proved. The beliefs, although temporarily shaken, are not permanently abandoned; for that degree of scepticism ('total') would be self-destructive, even if it were psychologically feasible. It is only the dogmatic attempt to demonstrate the truth of the beliefs that is given up. Explanations of how these beliefs come to be held are, in contrast, expected of a theory of human nature. Such explanations will be based upon empirical investigation ('a cautious observation of human life'); accompanied by no claims to apodictic certainty, they will be submitted to the reader to verify by his own introspection. When the principles upon which depend men's natural beliefs and customary ways of reaching conclusions from experience have been discovered, it will be possible to ground science upon them, and quite properly, for 'philosophical decisions are nothing but the reflections of common life, methodized and corrected' ($E_1$ 162).[7]

It is thus misleading to allege without qualification that Hume attempts to build his system on a sceptical foundation. It is true but irrelevant to remark with J. A. Passmore that 'Hume could not succeed in the impossible—a science founded on scepticism no degree of ingenuity can successfully construct'.[8] Certainly Pyrrhonian or excessive scepticism could not bear that weight, for it cannot even sustain itself against the natural force of human credulity. The 'only solid foundation' of the sciences is therefore not Pyrrhonian scepticism, which has only to clear the ground of the sophistries and illusions of irresponsible metaphysics, particularly of the illusory hope of striking bed-rock certainty upon which to secure logically any existential theory. When Pyrrhonism has done its work, it is supplanted by mitigated or academic scepticism which recognizes both the limits of the human understanding and the necessity of working within them. These limits define the sphere of legitimate operations as the realm of sense-experience and prescribe the empirical method as the appropriate one. The foundation of Hume's moral science is laid in human nature, upon the natural principles of the human understanding, and mitigated scepticism consists in acquiescing in them.

As I have already mentioned, the style of the *Treatise* suggests that Hume was thinking his way through to this position while he wrote. Not only did he express dismay at the outcome in the Conclusion to Book I, but he also published disquieting second thoughts about his analysis of personal identity in an Appendix to the third volume a year later. His eventual disowning of the *Treatise* may have resulted from the realization that he had failed to define his position clearly in his first book. The notion of

---

[7] Cf. *Dialogues Concerning Natural Religion*, Part I, p. 134, where Hume has Philo remark that 'To philosophize on such subjects ['either on natural or moral subjects'] is essentially nothing different from reasoning on common life . . .'

[8] *Hume's Intentions*, 151.

mitigated or academic scepticism as a clear alternative to Pyrrhonism does not appear explicitly in the *Treatise* at all, although he does at one point identify the position of 'true philosophers' with 'moderate scepticism' (T 224). Looking back from the *Enquiry Concerning Human Understanding*, which is perfectly clear and unequivocal on the point, it appears that mitigated scepticism was the position to which Hume was tacitly committed in the earlier book, or at least the one toward which he was moving. But in the *Treatise* itself he seemed at times to hold that the philosopher was condemned to shift between two hopeless positions—Pyrrhonism, which ruined every prospect of constructive work, and Dogmatism, which discredited every achievement. What Hume intended, of course, was to secure a vantage point from which he could block the metaphysicians in their efforts to reach knowledge of super-sensible realities, particularly in the theological field, and yet still himself advance in psychology, morals, aesthetics, and politics. Although the *Treatise* meticulously logs his approach, it does not, so to speak, give a very clear report from the summit. Nine years later, Hume is perfectly familiar with his strategic position and reports it exactly and with great confidence:

Another species of *mitigated* scepticism which may be of advantage to mankind, and which may be the natural result of the Pyrrhonian doubts and scruples, is the limitation of our enquiries to such subjects as are best adapted to the narrow capacity of human understanding. The *imagination* of man is naturally sublime, delighted with whatever is remote and extraordinary, and running without control, into the most distant parts of space and time in order to avoid the objects, which custom has rendered too familiar to it. A correct *Judgement* observes a contrary method, and avoiding all distant and high enquiries, confines itself to common life, and to such subjects as fall under daily practice and experience; leaving the more sublime topics to the embellishment of poets and orators, or to the arts of priests and politicians. To bring us to so salutary a determination, nothing can be more serviceable, than to be once thoroughly convinced of the force of the Pyrrhonian doubt, and of the impossibility, that anything but the strong power of natural instinct, could free us from it. Those who have a propensity to philosophy, will still continue their researches; because they reflect, that, besides the immediate pleasure, attending such an occupation, philosophical decisions are nothing but the reflections of common life, methodized and corrected. But they will never be tempted to go beyond common life, so long as they consider the imperfection of those faculties which they employ, their narrow reach, and their inaccurate operations. While we cannot give a satisfactory reason, why we believe, after a thousand experiments, that a stone will fall, or fire burn; can we ever satisfy ourselves concerning any determination, which we may form, with regard to the origin of worlds, and the situation of nature, from, and to eternity?

This narrow limitation, indeed, of our enquiries, is, in every respect, so reasonable, that it suffices to make the slightest examination into the natural powers of the human mind and to compare them with their objects, in order to recommend it to us. We shall then find what are the proper subjects of science and enquiry. ($E_1$ 162–3)

## Section 3. *First Intentions and Second Thoughts*

Before Hume could write his first *Enquiry* and the philosophical works that followed, he had to recognize his failure to create in the *Treatise* the coherent, integrated system which he had planned. He had set out to construct 'a compleat system of the sciences, built on a foundation almost entirely new' (T xx). 'This treatise, therefore, of human nature', he wrote in the *Abstract*, speaking anonymously of his own performance, 'seems intended for a system of the sciences' (A 7). Throughout the *Treatise* itself he repeatedly refers to the work as 'the present system'. However, the system which he projected is only half finished; the Logic and Morals are there; the Criticism or Aesthetics is missing, and so is the Politics, except for certain concepts treated in Book III which, since Plato, have been the common concern of ethical and of political theory. Many of the most important differences in content and stress between the *Treatise* and the later works reflect Hume's decision to forgo his original ambition of forging a comprehensive, unified system in favour of a series of relatively independent works treating separately the several topics announced in the Introduction to the *Treatise*.

Few critics, friendly or hostile, have acceded to Hume's request to ignore 'that juvenile work', the *Treatise*, and to grant that the later ones should 'alone be regarded as containing his philosophical sentiments and principles'.[9] Comparisons of each Book of the *Treatise* with the two *Enquiries* and *A Dissertation on the Passions* raise numerous questions of comparative merit, about style, clarity, complexity, and depth of thought, about wealth of ideas and consistency of argument, and overriding all particular points, about Hume's intellectual probity in youth and maturity. Even, or perhaps especially, those who resist most vehemently the principles and arguments of Book I of the *Treatise* have disparaged the first *Enquiry* as a vulgar pandering to superficial tastes. To realize a quick popular success, they allege, Hume sacrificed metaphysical seriousness to literary elegance; sweeping the profound ontological problems out of sight, he chose to join in a slick and provocative manner in the public debate about miracles, providence, and a future state. In the opening Section of the first *Enquiry* Hume wrote perceptively and candidly about his own desire to strike a balance between 'the easy and obvious philosophy' and 'the accurate and abstruse', and I shall say nothing here to defend him against the charge of having lowered his early

[9] From the 'Advertisement' to the second volume of the 1777 edition of *Essays and Treatises on Several Subjects*, which contained the two *Enquiries*, *A Dissertation on the Passions* and *The National History of Religion*. The Advertisement reads in its entirety as follows: 'Most of the principles, and reasonings, contained in this volume, were published in a work in three volumes, called *A Treatise of Human Nature*: A work which the Author had projected before he left College, and which he wrote and published not long after. But not finding it successful, he was sensible of his error in going to the press too early, and he cast the whole anew in the following pieces, where some negligences in his former reasoning and more in the expression, are, he hopes, corrected. Yet several writers, who have honoured the Author's Philosophy with answers, have taken care to direct all their batteries against that juvenile work, which the Author never acknowledged, and have affected to triumph in any advantages, which, they imagined, they had obtained over it: A practice very contrary to all rules of candour and fair-dealing, and a strong instance of those polemical artifices, which a bigotted zeal thinks itself authorized to employ. Henceforth, the Author desires, that the following Pieces may alone be regarded as containing his philosophical sentiments and principles.' Hume accompanied the draft of this advertisement with a note to his publisher: 'It is a compleat answer to Dr. Reid and to that bigotted silly Fellow, Beattie' (L II 301).

high philosophical standard. At this point I am committed to the drier task of contrasting the early and the later Hume only with respect to his lost ambition to be a systematic philosopher.

On first inspection, the *Enquiry Concerning Human Understanding* differs most strikingly from Book I of the *Treatise* in omissions and abbreviations.[10] The analysis of space and time (T I ii) disappears, as do the distinction between ideas of memory and of imagination (T I i 3 and iii 5), the discussion of complex ideas (relations, modes and substances) (T I i 5–6), of the idea of existence, (T I ii 6), and of philosophical relations (T I i 5 and I iii 1). The Section on abstract ideas (T I i 7) is paraphrased in a footnote ($E_1$ 158), and that on the association of ideas (T I i 4) is reduced by half ($E_1$ III). The psychological explanations of many forms of belief, credulity, and self-deception (T I iii 13) are excluded, along with the analysis of the conditioning of opinion (T I iii 9) and of the imaginative response upon which the verisimilitude of fictions depends (T I iii 10). The study of probability that occupied thirty consecutive pages of the *Treatise* (T I iii 11–13) in addition to scattered, incidental discussions shrinks to three pages in the *Enquiry* ($E_1$ VI). The sceptical critique of the Law of Universal Causation (T I iii 3) and the rules of causal judgement (T I iii 15) are both dropped. Part iv of the *Treatise* is subjected to the most drastic economizing; reduced to less than a fifth, it survives as the concluding Section XII of the *Enquiry*. Hume's theory of belief in the reality of the external world (T I iv 2) is thereby sacrificed, and his critical analyses of

---

10 My debt to L. A. Selby-Bigge will be obvious in this paragraph. In the Editor's Introduction to his edition of *Hume's Enquiries*, the differences in content of the *Treatise* and the later works which I shall mention have been set forth by him in a more thorough and systematic manner, and he has supplied an invaluable set of tables comparing, topic by topic, the contents of the three Books of the *Treatise* with those of the later works corresponding to each Book. In an 'Appendix: The Recastings' to his book *The Moral and Political Philosophy of David Hume* (Columbia U.P., New York and London, 1963), 325–39, John B. Stewart covers the same ground, adducing some vigorous arguments against Selby-Bigge's view that between the *Treatise* and the second *Enquiry* Hume's moral philosophy underwent a significant change. The significance of these differences between the first and later versions for understanding Hume's philosophical development has been exhaustively explored by Antony Flew in *Hume's Philosophy of Belief* (Routledge and Kegan Paul, London, 1961).

the doctrines of material (T I iv 3, 4) and immaterial (T I iv 5) substance and of personal identity (T I iv 6) are lost in silence.

Throughout Book I of the *Treatise*, Hume conducts two different performances which are never harmonized into a balanced, unified programme. He develops a critical theme which is introduced at the outset with his principle that ideas copy impressions. This 'copy principle' ('the first principle . . . in the science of human nature') is the basis of Hume's empiricist criterion of meaning and it is relentlessly applied in the destructive analysis of a succession of concepts, principles, and doctrines. Counterpointing this sceptical movement, a set of psychological theories 'to explain the principles and operations of our reasoning faculty' (T xix) is elaborated from the principle of the association of ideas, also announced early in the book as one of 'the elements of this philosophy' (T 13). Now if one tries, in accordance with Hume's expressed intention, to view Book I *in toto* as a sustained effort to build a foundation for the projected system, the impression of discord and irrelevance is overwhelming. One would expect, for example, the constructive side of the argument to yield a concept of mind or self which Hume could use in his study of the passions in the following Book. But his study 'Of personal identity' is dominated by the analytical, critical mood, and the result appears to be purely sceptical, purely negative. Perhaps nothing that Hume wrote can make a stronger, purer appeal to the philosophical intellect than the sceptical critique of metaphysical concepts and doctrines in Part iv of Book I. But it is not apparent that these long, subtle, abstruse investigations are germane to Hume's stated intention of laying foundations for the human sciences. Nor does his critical attack upon certain dogmas in the foundations of mathematics in Part ii appear any more relevant to that end.

The variety, density, and complexity of Book I of the *Treatise* are the results of Hume's mixed intentions. He aims to work out a theory of the understanding which, together with his theory of the passions presented in Book II, will supply the psychological basis for reconstruction in moral, social, and political philosophy. He is also interested in diverting the attention of philosophers from metaphysical questions to problems concerning human nature. This aim of giving 'a different turn to the speculations of philosophers' (T 273) he thought could be furthered by discrediting the method which metaphysicians were driven to use when trying to handle questions to which no imaginable sense experience could suggest an answer. It seems that in the beginning Hume supposed that his psychology of the understanding could be made to serve both his constructive and his subversive ends: it would do as a theoretical basis for the social sciences and also for the elimination of metaphysics. If this had been so, then Hume might have satisfied his ambition to create an integrated philosophical system in which his constructive and his destructive intentions were realized in concert. For reasons to be explored (reasons incessantly invoked by Hume's critics), psychological explanations of knowledge cannot be automatically converted into criteria of knowledge. Fortunately for Hume, whatever may have been his first thoughts, his effective instrument for analysis, the copy principle, is not logically dependent upon the strength of any psychological theory whatever. Nor, as Hume will later decide, is experimental psychology 'the only solid foundation' (T xx) for the social sciences. Principles of ethics, society, and politics are immanent in human history, in the history of social arrangements and of political organization. When Hume in his search for the principles of human nature turns from the science of man to the history of man, the intentions which were to be realized through the system projected in the *Treatise* have altered.

The *Enquiry Concerning Human Understanding* would be a baffling work if read as a revision of Hume's original effort to lay the foundations of the system projected in the *Treatise*. Outside the discussion of freedom and determinism (S. VIII, 'Of Liberty and Necessity'), where instances of moral behaviour and judgement must enter as examples, there is no suggestion of any interest in moral philosophy or aesthetics. Apart from an appeal in the opening Section to the practice of moralists and critics, to justify his own search for general principles in mental philosophy, the sole reference to these subjects occurs on the final page, where Hume remarks, 'Morals and criticism are not so properly objects of the understanding as of taste and sentiment'. On the other hand, he indulges his interest in theological issues, in miracles and the argument from design, over a full quarter of the book. Here he can exploit the devastating power of his empiricist principles as instruments of analysis, having realized that their use is critical, not constructive, and as effectively demonstrated in popular controversy as in the 'dreary solitudes, and rough passages' (T 270) of abstruse metaphysics.

The relaxed stress on associationist theory is similarly consistent with the pre-eminently critical aims of the first *Enquiry*. In the *Treatise*, Hume suggested a comparison between his principles of association and the law of universal gravitation (T 12–13) and in the *Abstract* declared that 'if anything can intitle the author to so glorious a name as that of an *inventor*, 'tis the use he makes of the principle of the association of ideas, which enters into most of his philosophy' (A 31). In the *Treatise*, Hume heeded his own advice to examine the effects ('extraordinary' and 'various') rather than the causes of his principle, and relied upon it to account for the formation of complex ideas, and to explain the mechanics of emotions in general and, in particular, of the sympathetic response which is fundamental to the moral theory of the third Book. In the early editions of the first *Enquiry*, as Norman Kemp Smith has pointed out, the theory of association still commanded sufficient space for Hume to illustrate its workings in aesthetic contexts and in emotional experiences. But in the last edition (1777) which Hume prepared, this illustrative development is struck out, and only a dry two-page paraphrase of the theory remains. The distinction between simple and complex ideas is not mentioned in any edition of the first *Enquiry*, nor are impressions of reflexion—viz. passions, desires, and emotions, which, he said early in the *Treatise*, 'principally deserve our attention' (T 8). On the single occasion on which Hume recurs to the associative theory in the first *Enquiry*, it is not to probe any operations of the understanding at depth, but simply to show how objects (e.g. pictures and relics) enliven the ideas with which they are associated.

Hume's analysis of causal inference is recast in the first *Enquiry*, its prominence accentuated by the pruning of other doctrines that originally surrounded it. Both accounts agree with the words of the *Abstract* that "'Tis evident that all reasonings concerning *matter of fact* are founded on the relation of cause and effect' (A 11). Since the two books share the common aim of determining the conditions and limits of empirical knowledge, the question of the logical status of the causal principle remains of undiminished concern. The aim stated in the Introduction to the *Treatise* of becoming 'thoroughly acquainted with the extent and force of human understanding' (T xix) is confirmed in the opening Section of the first *Enquiry*, with foreknowledge of the limitations and exclusions that will result:

> The only method of freeing learning, at once, from these abstruse questions, is to enquire seriously into the nature of human understanding, and show, from an exact analysis of its powers and capacity, that it is by no means fitted for such remote and abstruse subjects. We must submit to this fatigue, in order to live at ease ever after: And must cultivate true metaphysics with some care, in order to destroy the false and adulterate. (E₁ 12)

The early and the later Hume are compatible as analysts; the criterion of significance is unchanged, and its destructive intent fully realized in both books, although against different victims. The confident, bantering tone of the later work suggests that Hume had learned 'to live at ease ever after' the intellectual trauma of the *Treatise*; the former sense of deep personal involvement is missing; there are no expressions of metaphysical agony comparable to those which conclude Book I of the *Treatise*. Hume has realized that the works he has yet to write—or to rewrite—can be done independently of the theory of knowledge which underlies his philosophical analysis, although, of course, in conformity with its empiricist principles. The elegant, forceful line of the second argument reflects the simplification effected by his decision to separate the critical and the constructive elements of his philosophy.

The elaborate ingenuity of Hume's detailed psychological studies in Book II of the *Treatise* was commensurate with his intention of laying 'the foundation', as he explained in the *Abstract*, 'of the other parts [of his system] in his account of the

passions' (A 7). His extension of the theory of association formulated in Book I to his investigation 'Of the Passions' in Book II
constituted Hume's most forthright move to bind together the
elements of his system. The most fruitful psychological conception for later construction was, undoubtedly, the doctrine of
sympathy upon which his ethical theory heavily depends.

Hume used the sympathy principle effectively in Book III of
the *Treatise*, where his principal aim was to discover the grounds
or origin of moral feelings and judgements. His skill at detecting
the vein of truth in positions falsified by overstatement yielded a
theory which nicely balances the rival claims of the 'low' and the
'sentimental' views of human nature. His distinction between the
artificial and the natural virtues allows him to reconcile the con-
ventionist view of morality, founded on the presumption of
absolute egotism, with the moral sense theory which counted
optimistically, even naïvely, upon the natural benevolence of
mankind.

The cursory summary of Book II of the *Treatise* offered in the
*Dissertation on the Passions* (1757), appearing six years after the
publication of *An Enquiry Concerning the Principles of Morals*,
reflects in its tardiness, vastly reduced scale, and uninspired
dryness Hume's loss of confidence and interest in psychological
theory as a foundation for his philosophy of values. He concluded
the *Dissertation* by remarking:

I pretend not to have here exhausted this subject. It is sufficient for
my purpose, if I have made it appear that, in the production and conduct of the passions, there is a certain regular mechanism, which is
susceptible of as accurate a disquisition, as the laws of motion, optics,
hydrostatics, or any part of natural philosophy. (G & G 166)

This suggestion that Hume intended this recapitulation of the
main points of his study 'Of the Passions' merely to show the
possibility of a scientific psychology of the emotions, not as an
integral part of a philosophical system, is borne out in the opening
Section of *An Enquiry Concerning the Principles of Morals* where
Hume proposes 'to reach the foundation of ethics' ($E_2$ 174) by
observing and comparing 'particular instances' of moral, not
psychological, phenomena.

The other scientific method, where a general abstract principle is
first established, and is afterwards branched out into a variety of inferences and conclusions, may be more perfect in itself, but suits less the
imperfection of human nature, and is a common source of illusion and
mistake in this as well as in other subjects. Men are now cured of their
passion for hypotheses and systems in natural philosophy, and will
hearken to no arguments but those which are derived from experience.
It is full time they should attempt a like reformation in all moral
disquisitions; and reject every system of ethics, however subtle or
ingenious, which is not founded on fact and observation. (E₂ 174-5)

Allowing that Hume is here, as earlier, repudiating rationalistic
ethical systems, this passage, when so discounted, still contrasts
strikingly with the intention to create a unified system declared
on the opening page of Book III of the *Treatise*: 'I am not, however, without hopes, that the present system of philosophy will
acquire new force as it advances; and that our reasonings concerning *morals* will corroborate whatever has been said concerning
the understanding and the passions' (T 455). Consistently with
his revised intention of presenting his moral philosophy in an
independent, self-contained work, the sympathy principle, which
had supplied both the basis of unity of Book III and its essential
link with Book II, declines from a genuinely explanatory psychological principle to an unanalysable ('original') quality of human
nature, indistinguishable from benevolence or the sentiment of
humanity.

The evolution of Hume's political philosophy shows a comparable change of intention. His attempt to base politics upon the
science of man is given up one year after being partially realized
in the third Book of the *Treatise*. The political thinking recorded
in the *Essays Moral and Political* of 1741 is informed by reflections
on constitutional history, not by empirical investigations of
human psychology. Hume's argument in the third essay 'That
Politics may be reduc'd to a Science' depends solely upon a study
of political phenomena recorded in the annals of history. Here
'universal axioms' or 'general truths' in politics are not derived
from principles of psychology but from observations of what
have in fact been the consequences of various types of political

organization. It may be that these consequences are understood to be the natural effects of human character responding to various sets of social, economic, and legal conditions; and it may also be that Hume did not really change his view of man's moral nature in the way suggested by the Hobbesian pessimism of many passing comments. But these are not the relevant points here. The point is that Hume has come to realize that political theory, which in his practice includes economic theory, can be based directly upon the historical study of political events without involving any intricate psychological investigations. What the social and political philosopher needs to know about human nature can be learned from the recorded observations of men's behaviour in various historical circumstances.

With the publication of *Political Discourses* in 1752 the metamorphosis of the experimental psychologist into the philosophical historian was already complete, two years before the first volume of Hume's great *History* appeared. Hume's *Essays and Treatises on Several Subjects* conclude the constructive part of the programme announced at the beginning of his career. But the ethical, aesthetic, and political theories they contain are logically independent of the system of which he originally intended to make them integral parts.

The critical side of Hume's programme was conducted rather unevenly. The decisiveness with which he distinguished between the truths of pure mathematics and those of empirical science, and the clarity of the explanation he gave of this logical difference were permanent contributions of immense importance. But his struggle with the concepts of space and time and his efforts to give geometry an empirical grounding have been generally recognized as unavailing. His attempt to fix the scope and limits of natural philosophy by exploring the experiential grounds of its method produced the analyses, particularly of causation, upon which his reputation has been mainly questioned and defended in modern times.

The devastating power of Hume's empiricism is most apparent when he applies its principles in the examination of natural religion. Absolutely decisive refutations of propositions, principles or theories are unusual in philosophy; the annihilation of an entire discipline which engaged some of the best minds of the time was a prodigious feat requiring rare powers of analysis, firm principles, resolution, and perfect control of argument. Hume dealt with all the issues that figured prominently in the religious controversies of his day. Despite his eleventh-hour choice of reticence in the *Treatise*, the theological implications of his analyses of existence, causation, substance and self for the ontological and cosmological arguments and for doctrines of soul and immortality are inescapable. Even before starting the *Treatise*, Hume had become interested in the effect of religious belief on morality, and in 'Of Superstition and Enthusiasm', included in the first edition of *Essays Moral and Political*, he viewed it with a detachment and disfavour which in later treatments hardened into animosity toward a malign influence. The *Natural History of Religion* (1757) advances disquieting hypotheses about the psychological bases of religious belief and aims to discredit claims for the moral superiority of monotheism. In the essay 'Of Miracles' in *Philosophical Essays Concerning Human Understanding* of 1748, re-titled *An Enquiry Concerning Human Understanding* in the fourth edition of 1758, Hume assailed the stronghold of Christianity, Revelation, by arguing that no miracle can be a fit object of a rational man's belief. In *Dialogues Concerning Natural Religion* (1779) Hume deployed his mature philosophical and literary talents with brilliant effect against the argument from design, the keystone of eighteenth-century theology. The painfully difficult effort he had made at the beginning of his career to determine 'the extent and force of human understanding' (T xix) was repaid at the end when the most lavishly embellished but baseless theological construction of all time collapsed under the strain of his sceptical probing. The critical, analytical side of Hume's intellect was fully realized in this graceful, witty, dramatic work of philosophical art. One may hope that when Hume was adding the final touches to it a few months before his death, he felt amply compensated for the loss of the comprehensive philosophical system which he had intended to compose forty years before.

# PART II

# The Use and Abuse of Newton

## Section 1. Hume: 'The Newton of the Moral Sciences'?

HUME began to write philosophy as a young man only three or four years after the death of Sir Isaac Newton. The research and speculation inspired by Newton was gathering the momentum throughout Hume's century that would carry it almost to the end of the next. The *Mathematical Principles of Natural Philosophy*[1] was the consummation of the scientific revolution which had begun officially with the publication of *De revolutionibus orbium coelestium* in 1543. The Copernican hypothesis of the earth's motion, Kepler's laws of planetary motion and his discovery of the elliptical orbits of planets, Galileo's experimental investigations of the motions of terrestial objects, involving his realization of the fundamental significance of inertia, his analysis of the concepts of force, mass, and acceleration, and the revelations of his telescope, Huygens's mathematical solutions to problems of the conservation of momentum and his theory of centrifugal forces, were the main elements combined in the Newtonian synthesis. Two and a half centuries of observing, experimenting, and theorizing about motion, terrestial and celestial, supplied Newton with the material to be transmuted by process of mathematical deduction into a system of universal mechanics. The orbiting of the moon and the flow of the tides, the earth's motion, the courses of comets

[1] *Philosophiae Naturalis Principia Mathematica*, London, 5 July 1686. A second, revised edition, edited by Roger Cotes, was published in 1713, and a third, edited by Henry Pemberton, in 1728. The work was translated by Andrew Motte in 1729. The standard twentieth-century English edition is *Sir Isaac Newton's Mathematical Principles of Natural Philosophy and His System of the World*, tr. Andrew Motte, 1729, revised Florian Cajori (University of California Press, Berkeley, 1946).

and of planets and their satellites, the swing of pendulums, the free fall of bodies near the earth's surface, and the flight of projectiles were explained as the intimately related mathematically derivable consequences of three simple laws and the principle of universal gravitation. The *Principia* was in every sense a monumental work, magnificent in proportion, an intellectual *tour de force* whose extreme demands threatened the mind of its creator, an enduring testimony to the efforts of generations of scientists, and a total vindication of the method of experimental science. By contrast, Newton's other great work, the *Opticks*,[2] was a pioneering work, a work of exploration. Of course, it too was an experimental work which submitted observational data to mathematical analysis and demonstrated certain firm conclusions, and it was a systematic work, also, which co-ordinated twenty years of Newton's own research and took account of the main contending theories. But his investigations of the properties of light and of the structure and behaviour of matter were pursued there beyond the limits of what was mathematically demonstrable or empirically verifiable. The *Opticks* opened up exciting possibilities of new discoveries to be made in physics and chemistry, and even in the biological sciences. It proved to be a tremendously stimulating and encouraging work for experimentalists, some of the greatest of whom, like Benjamin Franklin, were not up to the formidable mathematics of the *Principia*. Thus in Hume's day an entire generation of natural philosophers were inspired by Newton to apply the empirical method to the whole range of scientific problems. It is not surprising, therefore, that Hume's first work is represented on the title page as 'BEING AN ATTEMPT to introduce the experimental Method of Reasoning INTO MORAL SUBJECTS'.

John Passmore's observation that 'it was Hume's ambition to be the Newton of the moral sciences' states the official view of the scientist's influence upon the philosopher. 'And this in two respects,' he continues: 'first, by working out a bold general theory of the mind—his associationism—comparable to Newton's

---

[2] *Opticks, Or A Treatise Of The Reflections, Refractions, Inflections & Colours of Light*, Based on the Fourth Edition, London, 1730 (Dover, New York, 1952).

theory of attraction, and secondly, . . . by extending the Newtonian method to the moral sciences.'[3] Although Kemp Smith
regarded the waning stress on associationism as evidence that the
Newtonian influence was, in the first respect, a recessive factor in
the evolution of Hume's thought, he agreed that Newton's
influence with respect to method remained dominant. 'Newton's
conception of method . . . is precisely the method which Hume
claims to be following in his own thinking',[4] he remarked, confirming Charles Hendel's judgement that 'His own book [the
*Treatise*] was itself a venture in applying the "experimental
method" of Newton to the mental world.'[5] In his Introduction
to the Modern Library anthology, *The Philosophy of David Hume*,
V. C. Chappell states, in the same vein, that 'Hume . . . had been
tremendously impressed by the achievement of Newton in the
natural sciences, and he recognized how much Newton's success
depended on his employment of "the experimental method".
Hume thought the time had come to apply this same method to
"the moral subjects" . . .'[6] Having remarked that 'It was through
this principle [of association] that ideas—the atoms of the mind—
were to be connected into a comprehensive and truly Newtonian
system of mental mechanics',[7] Antony Flew later borrowed
Passmore's aphorism that Hume's 'ambition was . . . to become
the Newton of the moral sciences'.[8] Observing as a sign of Hume's
'chastened' Newtonian ambitions that the final version of
associationist theory was 'little more than a dwindled relic of a
young man's vision',[9] Flew continues throughout his perceptive

[3] *Hume's Intentions*, 43.

[4] *The Philosophy of David Hume* (Macmillan, London, 1941), 57.

[5] *Studies in the Philosophy of David Hume*, New Edn. (Library of Liberal Arts,
Bobbs-Merrill, New York, 1963), 366.

[6] (Random House, New York, 1963), xv.

[7] *Hume's Philosophy of Belief*, 18.

[8] Ibid. 94. One year later Flew took the opportunity to stress the same point
in his Introduction to an anthology, *David Hume on Human Nature And the
Understanding* (Collier, New York, 1962), 7: '. . . Hume's ambitions were to lay
the foundations for a would-be Newtonian science of man . . .' Cf. P. L. Gardiner,
'Hume's Theory of the Passions', in *David Hume: A Symposium*, ed. D. F. Pears
(Macmillan, London, 1963), 41: '. . . Hume tried to construct a psychological
science in parallel with Newtonian physics.'

[9] Op. cit. 18.

study of *Hume's Philosophy of Belief* to detect evidence of the
influence of Newtonian methodology. The doctrinal as well as the
methodological aspect of Newton's influence on the *Treatise* had
been stressed by T. E. Jessop almost a decade earlier, in the same
year that John Passmore published *Hume's Intentions*:

> Hume . . . felt himself inspired by a novel idea—that just as Newton
> had shown that the fundamental changes in the physical world can be
> explained by the principle of 'attraction' (gravitation), so the processes
> of knowing, so far as they consist in inferring presumed fact from actual
> fact, can be explained by the principle of association. . . . He was sure
> that he had found a comprehensive law, and what further kindled his
> enthusiasm was that the law satisfied his empirical scruples: like Newton
> with gravitation, he could exhibit association as a fact of experience,
> without any pretence of formulating for it an occult cause.[10]

Thus Newton's scientific work has been widely recognized as
a formative influence upon the development of Hume's philosophy, especially upon that of his method. What Hume scholars
call the 'Newtonian method' was not the invention of Newton;
it was the resolutive/compositive (or analytic/synthetic) method
which had its fifteenth-century origin in the University of Padua
and had been perfected by the mathematical and experimental
genius of Galileo. The most important discovery of the early
modern scientists was the discovery of science itself, i.e. of the
scientific method. Granting that certain spectacular discoveries
might have been made unsystematically, by chance, especially in
astronomy—e.g. the mountains of the moon, or the satellites of
Jupiter—given the lucky accident that led to the invention of the
telescope, they would have remained isolated curiosities, instead
of the elements of a new coherent model of the universe. This
powerful method generated a procession of discoveries of fact
and creations of theory whose momentous significance clearly
appeared only when they were systematically deployed by
Newton in the *Principia*. Even if Hume had studied none of the
works which we would today call scientific, he would have

[10] 'Some Misunderstandings of Hume', *Revue internationale de philosophie* 20
(1952); reprinted in *Hume*, ed. V. C. Chappell (Doubleday, Garden City, 1966),
46–7.

learned from the philosophers that the paramount fact about his age was that men's conception of the physical universe was being transformed by empirical science. He would also have been impressed with the fact that philosophers from Bacon onward were virtually obsessed with the subject of scientific method, with articulating its principles, promoting its use, questioning its scope and validity, probing its logical, psychological, and ontological foundations. And he would have been stimulated to find that some of the most ambitious of those thinkers had been trying to project that method (or their various conceptions of it) into the domain of the human sciences where he planned to work.

Although Hume follows Newton in qualifying the method as 'experimental', there was nothing uniquely modern in experimentation, as the history of alchemy shows. The verifying function of experiments was clarified and strengthened, but what was really novel was the application of mathematics to empirical data. In the hands of a truly modern scientist like Galileo, resolution or analysis (*metodo resolutivo*) reached a mathematically simple statement of the relations between the quantifiable features of phenomena, as illustrated by his law of falling bodies formulated in terms of uniform acceleration ($S = vt/2$) and by the even more important derivative law which states that a body falling from rest will travel a distance proportional to the square of the time of the fall ($S = t^2 \times g/2$). In the compositive or synthetic stage of the method (*metodo compositivo*), Galileo supplied geometrical deductions of the consequences of his laws and then devised experiments to verify their actual occurrence. Here was the logical essence of the method of Newton who, like Galileo, was prepared to analyse untidy empirical reality into radically simplified ideal models whose basic workings were mathematically expressible—even to the extent of presenting as the object of his very first Axiom or Law of Motion an entity which is never experienced and which, given the truth of a fundamental principle of the system (universal gravitation), could not possibly exist, viz. a body which continues in a state of uniform motion in a straight line. If Galileo contented himself surprisingly often with 'thought experiments' (which dutiful followers like Mersenne sometimes found physically impossible to perform or at other times turning out awry when actually conducted), Newton insisted that the logically possible world created by mathematical inference be brought into comparison with the actually experienced one.

There was a powerful incentive to adopt this superb method in the psychological and social sciences, especially since the practical benefits of the new science had been constantly stressed by Bacon, Hobbes, Descartes, and Spinoza, and had already been demonstrated in mining, medicine, and metallurgy, in the arts of warfare, navigation, and architecture. But at a time when scientists were just beginning to search for ways to subject magnetic, electrical, and chemical phenomena to mathematical analysis, would not the obstacles to applying mathematical principles to 'moral subjects' appear insuperable, or at least very discouraging? And if some other way were found to reach fundamental principles in psychology, ethics, politics, and criticism, would not the prospect of verifying them experimentally be ruined not only by technical problems but by the operation of an indeterminacy principle recognized by Hume himself? And after the mathematics and the experimenting dropped out, what was left of the great new method for the eighteenth-century moral philosopher but the bare abstract form of the pre-Galilean resolutive/compositive method with which Hobbes had struggled along in the previous century? Might not Hume's change of intentions documented in the previous chapter be, therefore, connected with some disturbance in his relations with Newtonianism, be, perhaps, a result of discouragements met in attempting 'to introduce the experimental Method of Reasoning into Moral Subjects'? And would not his change of direction be accelerated by the exploitation of Newtonian science at the hands of philosophers committed to advancing the cause of natural religion?

Serious discussion of these questions must be conducted against a background of first-hand acquaintance with the works of Newton and of at least some of his followers. Nor is it enough merely to pick out those familiar passages in which Newton issued his proclamations on scientific method. For wider acquaintance with his work shows that his professed principles must be qualified in the light of his scientific practice. If the character of Hume's philosophy was actually shaped by Newtonianism, then it is of paramount importance for the interpreter of Hume to examine the founding works of that movement. So much has been made of the influence of Newtonian science upon Humean philosophy, that a careful examination of their relations is now imperative. Even if it should turn out that Hume was not a faithful Newtonian, his work could hardly have remained untouched by the dominant intellectual movement of the day. Rather than attempting to reconstruct the conceptual world in which Hume did his philosophical thinking by a general survey of the scientific and religious thought of the period, I shall concentrate upon the writings of the man who consolidated the scientific world view and prompted the theological reconstruction which was to inspire the finest work of Hume's maturity.

Readers who are well versed in the history of Newtonian science and theology may not profit greatly from the following study of Newton. They can afford to proceed immediately to Part III, which contains sufficient references to Newton's work to make the comparison of his method with Hume's drawn there intelligible. Readers who have never concerned themselves very much with the scientific thought of the period may regard such a detailed consideration of scientific work as an intrusion into a book about a philosopher. My view, on the contrary, is that acquaintance with the era's natural science is indispensable for understanding its philosophies. More particularly, acquaintance with Newton, the dominant intellectual force of the day, is indispensable for appreciating Hume's ambitions, difficulties, and development.

## Section 2. *Newton's First Publication*

Newton's first published paper,[11] reporting his discovery that spectral colours are invariably connected with differing degrees of

---

[11] *Philosophical Transactions* 80 (19 Feb. 1671/2), 3075–87: 'A letter of Mr. Isaac Newton, Mathematick Professor in the University of Cambridge, containing his

refrangibility of light rays, is rightly regarded as a landmark in the history of experimental science. The opportunity for this theoretical advance was, typically, provided by a technical difficulty in the way of improving a scientific instrument, the refracting telescope. The convex lenses which were beginning to replace Galileo's concave eyepieces yielded images distorted by spherical aberration, but also, Newton observed, blurred at the edges by a coloured outline ('chromatic aberration'). In the hope of getting clearer images, he acquired a triangular glass prism, set it up in a darkened room before a small hole in the window shutter and studied the beam of sunlight refracted through it on the opposite wall. Given a round aperture admitting the light and 'the received laws of Refraction', he would expect the spectrum of colours to appear circular, whereas, in fact, it showed an oblong form, in length five times the breadth. In order to determine whether this unexpected phenomenon was caused by some incidental circumstance, he set about varying the experimental situation and was able to exclude as irrelevant such factors as the position, imperfections, and uneven thickness of the glass, the size of the aperture, the varying angles of incidence of rays emitted from different parts of the sun, and to dispose of the hypothesis ('suspicion') of varying degrees of curvature in the solar rays leaving the prism. Resolving his problem into a quantitative one as a matter of course, he discovered by a series of measurements that the divergence of rays emerging from the prism (sine of refraction) is disproportionate to the differences in the angles of incidence of converging rays emitted from opposite sides of the sun. The phenomenon, he infers, is attributable to some unknown property of light, and he devises an ingenious '*experimentum crucis*' to discover it.

He projected the light from the prism through a small hole in a board toward another similar board twelve feet away with another prism behind it. By rotating the first prism he was able to pass each of the coloured rays of the spectrum one by one

New Theory about Light and Colors . . .'; reprinted in fascimile in I. Bernard Cohen, ed., *Isaac Newton's Papers and Letters On Natural Philosophy* (Harvard U.P., Cambridge, Mass., 1958) 47–59.

through the opening in the second board and observe where each was refracted on to the wall through the second prism.

And I saw, by the variation of those places, that the light tending to that end of the Image, towards which the refraction of the first Prism was made, did in the second Prism suffer a Refraction considerably greater than the light tending to the other end. And so the true cause of the length of that Image was detected to be no other, than that *Light* consists of *Rays differently refrangible*, which, without any respect to a difference in their incidence, were, according to their degrees of refrangibility, transmitted towards divers parts of the wall.[12]

Concluding that his original practical problem of eliminating the distortions of convex lenses is insoluble because the object glass focuses the various rays at different points on its axis and the eyeglass can focus upon only one of these at a time, Newton turned to the construction of a reflecting telescope which earned him membership in the Royal Society. The report of his experimentation and its theoretical significance—'the oddest, if not the most considerable detection, which hath hitherto been made in the operations of nature', he announced—were communicated to Henry Oldenburg, then Secretary of the Royal Society, in appreciation of his election. The main points of his 'New Theory of Light and Colours' were that white light is a heterogeneous mixture of rays of every colour, that colours are 'original and connate properties' of light rays, and that colour differentiation is a function of varying degrees of refrangibility of different rays.

In this letter of a dozen pages Newton not only advanced optics by overturning established views of the composition of light, and laid the basis for spectroscopic analysis, but also, of comparable importance for the scientific revolution, he displayed a model of the experimental method and of reporting research. With the exception of the power of synthesis displayed in his systematic works, all the essential features of the Newtonian method are present in his first published paper. Firmly committed to the principle that general laws must be confirmed by phenomena, securely in possession of contemporary theory and a clear-sighted observer, he was alert to the significance of any unpredictable

[12] Ibid. 3079; Cohen, op. cit. 51.

occurrence. Newton was ingenious in bringing natural phenomena under experimental control, isolating for study possibly
relevant factors one by one until by a process of exclusion he
moved steadily toward the cause of the problematic event.
Mathematical analysis of observational data was an integral part
of his procedure and the statement of results in quantitative terms
a natural mode of expression. With his analysis (resolution)
completed by his discovery of the cause of the problematic
phenomenon, he proceeds in the synthetic (compositive) phase to
deduce what must happen when white light is refracted through
a spherical lens.

'A New Theory of Light and Colours' was turned over for
experimental verification to Robert Hooke, the willing experimenter and demonstrator of the Royal Society (officially its
Curator), and a copy was sent to Christiaan Huygens. Soon these
and other scientists were submitting their opinions of the theory,
and for several years Newton was involved in a running defence
of his method and conclusions. The logical pivot of this controversy was Newton's distinction between hypotheses on the one
hand and, on the other, particular propositions descriptive of
phenomena, general propositions or conclusions reached by
induction, and first principles—experimentally confirmed axioms
or laws. This distinction, on which Newton's own grasp sometimes relaxed, was not appreciated by critics who were for ever
patronizing as hypotheses conclusions presented as definitive, or
alleging that his theories depended upon hypotheses—required,
that is to say, logically possible assumptions for which incompatible alternatives might be substituted. Newton invited the very
criticism which he found most intolerable by tentatively pro-
posing the answers to still undecidable questions suggested by his
findings. There was a perfectly obvious difference, he thought,
between what he stated as firm conclusions settled by empirical
evidence and what he conjectured about more fundamental truths
which, as the logical possibilities narrowed, seemed likely to be
uncovered in the wake of theoretical advances. Having shown
colour to be a quality of light, it followed that light itself could
not be a quality, but must be a substance, and '*perhaps*' a material

one. Hooke was right to say that the hypothesis of the materiality of light had not been proved (which Newton had not claimed), and that the phenomena described were explicable by other hypotheses (which Newton was prepared to admit). But Hooke was wrong to infer that therefore Newton's conclusions about the properties of light remained problematic. Since whatever general conclusion Newton had truly established would be logically derivable from remoter truths about the nature and cause of light when discovered, it is understandable that he was accused of presupposing or affirming these to support his more particular claims. That Newton's pride in his accomplishment was soon embittered by misdirected criticism suggests his lack of insight into minds tending towards *a priori* constructions and naïveté about what to expect from seekers of truth whose hypothetical designs he threatened.

## Section 3. *'Hypotheses non fingo'?*

Undeniably, hypotheses were spawned in Newton's own scientific work in astonishing abundance—imaginative, ingenious, insightful, fruitful working hypotheses to guide his experimentation. In his earliest paper he called them 'suspicions'; in the closing pages of the *Opticks* he called them 'Hint's'. Bolder hypotheses which went beyond even his experimental resources were of enormous importance for stimulating scientific research in the eighteenth century, as I. Bernard Cohen shows with impressive erudition in *Franklin and Newton*.[13] Such hypotheses as the corpuscular nature of light and of the aether as the medium through which gravitational, electrical, and magnetic forces worked and whose vibrations would account for colour differentiation were suggested in order to explain the underlying mechanisms of phenomena whose properties and laws had been already established. The optical papers[14] sent to the Royal Society over the years between

13 American Philosophical Society (Philadelphia, 1956).
14 Reproduced in facsimile in *Isaac Newton's Papers and Letters* from the *Philosophical Transactions of the Royal Society* and Thomas Birch, *The History of the*

1672 and 1676, advancing substantially the theories assembled in the treatise *Opticks* of 1704, are adorned with speculative hypotheses, and one of the most important of these communications is frankly entitled, 'An Hypothesis explaining the Properties of Light, discoursed of in my several Papers'.[15] On this occasion, as usual, Newton expressed his distaste for hypotheses and the 'vain disputes' they provoke, and denied having earlier assumed the hypothesis of the corporeity of light ascribed to him by Robert Hooke. Still insisting as he had three years before[16] that his discovery of the properties of light stands independently of any of the numerous mechanical hypotheses which might explain his findings, for the sake of those who cannot understand them without some illustrative model, he agrees 'to proceed to the hypothesis' (of the aether) . . . 'not concerning myself, whether it shall be thought probable or improbable'.[17]

However opposed in principle to advocating hypotheses for which experimental confirmation was unavailable, Newton did allow a place for them, if not 'in experimental philosophy', at least on the frontiers. In a letter written to defend his first scientific paper against Pardies, he defined that position exactly:

For the best and safest method of philosophizing seems to be, first to inquire diligently into the properties of things, and establishing those properties by experiments and then to proceed more slowly to hypo-

*Royal Society of London* (Millar, London, 1757). The optical papers are briefly but interestingly introduced by Thomas S. Kuhn, 'Newton's Optical Papers'.

[15] *Isaac Newton's Papers and Letters*, 178–90.

[16] *Philosophical Transactions* 88 (1672), 5084–5103; reprinted in Cohen, op. cit. 118–19: 'But I knew, that the *Properties*, which I declared of *Light*, were in some measure capable of being explicated not only by that, but by many other Mechanical *Hypotheses*. And therefore I chose to decline them all. . . .' Ibid. 123: 'But whatever the advantages or disadvantages of this *Hypothesis*, I hope I may be excused from taking it up, since I do not think it needful to explicate my Doctrine by any *Hypothesis* at all.'

[17] Ibid. 178–9: 'And therefore, because I have observed the heads of some great virtuosos to run much upon hypotheses, as if my discourses wanted an hypothesis to explain them by, and found, that some, when I could not make them take my meaning, when I spoke of the nature of light and colours abstractly, have readily apprehended it, when I illustrated my discourse by an hypothesis, for this reason I have here thought it fit to send you a description of the circumstances of this hypothesis as much tending to the illustration of the papers I herewith send you.'

theses for the explanation of them. For hypotheses should be sub-
servient only in explaining the properties of things, but not assumed in
determining them; unless so far as they may furnish experiments. For
if the possibility of hypotheses is to be the test of the truth and reality
of things, I see not how certainty can be obtained in any science; since
numerous hypotheses may be devised, which shall seem to overcome
new difficulties. Hence it has been here thought necessary to lay aside
all hypotheses, as foreign to the purpose, that the force of the objection
should be abstractly considered, and, receive a more full and general
answer.[18]

The sort of hypothesis which Newton categorically rejects
here Cohen labels 'philosophical romance', a seventeenth-century
expression used of purely speculative theories, particularly of
Descartes's system of vortices, connoting an imaginative construction negligent of observational data and maintained in the
face of conflicting experimental evidence. Critics who failed to
distinguish between a logically possible explanation and an
experimentally confirmed law irritated Newton by confusing his
conclusions 'deduced from the phenomena' with hypotheses
suggested for higher level explanation. The whole point of
observation and experimentation was lost upon critics who
exercised their imaginations in contriving alternatives not only to
his hypotheses but to conclusions as firmly established as any in
empirical science can be. These arbitrary and gratuitous hypotheses are the ones he says it is 'necessary to lay aside'.

It was many years before Newton became so morbidly sensitive
to the damaging connotations of this sense of 'hypothesis' that he
refused to apply the term even to his admittedly speculative
theories or conjectures. Only one year before completing the
*Principia* he was content to refer to its 'Axioms, or Laws of
Motion' as 'Hypotheses' in *De Motu*,[19] a precursor of the great
treatise, sent to the Royal Society at Halley's instigation in order

18 *Philosophical Transactions* 85 (1672) 5014; *Isaac Newton's Papers and Letters*, 106.
19 *Isaaci Newtoni Propositiones de Motu* (1685), reprinted in Stephen Riguad,
*Historical Essay on the First Publication of Sir Isaac Newton's Principia* (Oxford U.P.,
1838), Appendix. Presumably it is to this work that Alexandre Koyré refers in
*Newtonian Studies* (Chapman and Hall, London, 1965), 16, n. 9, where he says,
rather misleadingly, 'in the first edition of the *Principia* the axioms or laws of
motion are called *hypotheses*'.

to register claim to certain crucial proofs. Three years after publication of the *Principia*, as Professor Cohen reminds us, he again sets out the Laws of Motion as 'Hypotheses' in a paper sent to John Locke, entitled 'A Demonstration, That the Planets by their Gravity towards the Sun, may move in Ellipses'.[20] And in the first edition of the *Principia* itself no fewer than ten entries are clearly labelled 'Hypothesis', and three such survive in the second and third editions which conclude with the dictum, '*hypotheses non fingo*'.

Anyone attempting to reconcile Newton's principle of excluding hypotheses with his practice of including them would be likely to consider that the source of the apparent discrepancy might be located in the ambiguity of the term 'hypothesis'. Following this approach with a scrupulous examination of Newton's usage and that of his contemporaries, Cohen has distinguished nine senses of the term then current.[21] After Cohen's brilliantly illuminating research, it is as clear that hypotheses in some of these senses were perfectly acceptable to Newton as that in at least one other sense they were utterly unacceptable. Evidently Newton had no methodological objection to the hypothesis of the earth's motion, of which his *Principia* was received by the Royal Society as the triumphant vindication, and he customarily referred to the Copernican system as the Copernican hypothesis. Nor could he, as a geometer, have wished to exclude hypotheses in the sense of suppositions premised in the demonstrations of theorems or the resolutions of problems.

Since throughout the first two Books of the *Principia*, Newton is concerned with demonstrating mathematical principles, reserving until the third Book questions of their applicability to physical reality, he is free to explore the consequences of hypotheses concerning forces: 'In mathematics', he observed in a Scholium well along in Book I, 'we are to investigate the quantities of forces with their proportions consequent upon any conditions supposed . . .'[22] Thus he is prepared, for example, to adopt the hypothesis

[20] Mentioned in *Franklin and Newton*, 583–4, where Peter King, *The Life of John Locke*, new edn. (London, 1830), i. 388 is cited.
[21] *Franklin and Newton* ch. 5 and app. 1.                [22] p. 192.

that 'elastic fluids' (gases) consist of mutually repellant particles in order to demonstrate that 'the centrifugal forces of the particles will be inversely proportional to the distance of their centres',[23] thereby validating Boyle's Law mathematically without committing himself to any categorical claim regarding the physical nature of gases. In the third Book, he is no longer concerned with the logically possible world of pure mathematics, but with the actual world of physical science: 'then', he continues the procedural statement quoted above, 'when we enter upon physics, we compare those proportions with the phenomena of Nature, that we may know what conditions of those forces answer to the several kinds of attractive bodies.' At this point he is no longer free to suppose 'conditions' or hypothetical situations ('If several bodies revolve about one common centre, and . . .'), but must apply his mathematical principles to the explanation of observed phenomena ('That all bodies gravitate towards every planet; and . . .'). Of course he may still, even in *Newton's System of the World*,[24] assume a hypothesis in the form of a contrafactual conditional in order to render a proof general, demonstrating that 'The circumterrestrial force decreases inversely as the square of the distance from the earth', first 'on the hypothesis that the earth is at rest' and then 'on the hypothesis that the earth moves', thus proving the truth of theorem to be independent of either hypothesis. A somewhat similar explanation can be given of the 'HYPOTHESIS' concerning the proportionality of the resistance of a fluid to the velocity of a body moving through it which is used to disconfirm the Cartesian theory of vortices in the concluding Section of Book III.[25]

The mechanical hypotheses of Book III are less easily accommodated. In order to prove that the centre of gravity of the solar system is immovable and the centre of the world, Newton relied upon the unprovable premiss ('HYPOTHESIS I') 'That the centre of the system of the world is immovable'.[26] 'HYPOTHESIS II'

[23] Book II, Prop. xxiii, Th. xviii, p. 300.

[24] First translated from Latin to English in 1728 (by Andrew Motte, Cajori thinks), reprinted in the Cajori edition of the *Principia* following Book III. The proofs mentioned are given in Sections 10 and 11, pp. 559–61.

[25] p. 385.            [26] p. 419.

(proved a century later by Laplace) was required 'To find the
precession of the equinoxes'.[27] One may, like Hermann Weyl,
lament 'a discordant note in the middle of the cogent inductive
development of his system of the world in the *Principia*'.[28] Or one
may, like Cohen, simply acknowledge yet another class of
hypotheses tolerated in the *Principia*: 'Propositions which Newton
was unable to prove.'[29] At least Newton was posthumously
vindicated in his conviction that Hypothesis II was in principle
demonstrable. 'Hypothesis I' might have been stated as an
'Axiom' or 'Postulate' accepted by proponents of the geocentric
and heliocentric systems alike. The 'discordant note' would have
been silenced (or at least muffled) conformably to Newton's own
former usage in which the terms 'Axiom' and 'Law' were
synonymous with 'Hypothesis': and of course those 'Axioms, or
Laws of Motion' are 'Hypotheses'—or they were before being
elevated to the peerage. But they were not, of course, the empirically vacuous hypotheses which Newton said he declined to frame.

Commentators stress Newton's aversion to controversy, a trait
upon which Newton himself commented often enough. The
same point might be made more precisely by saying that Newton
resented criticism. He could not bear to be contradicted. His
initial response to criticism of his first paper was a threat to resign
from science, or at least from scientific publication. He was
annoyed by Oldenburg's involving him in polemics, and complained to him that 'a man must either resolve to put out nothing
new, or to become a slave to defend it'.[30] And he wrote to
Leibniz, 'I was so persecuted with discussions arising out of my
theory of light, that I blamed my own imprudence for parting

[27] Prop. xxxix, Prob. xx, p. 489: 'HYPOTHESIS II: If the other parts of the earth
were taken away, and the remaining ring was carried alone about the sun in the
orbit of the earth by the annual motion, while by the diurnal motion it was in the
meantime revolved about its own axis inclined to the plane of the ecliptic by an
angle of $23\frac{1}{2}$ degrees, the motion of the equinoctial points would be the same,
whether the ring were fluid, or whether it consisted of a hard and rigid matter.'
[28] *Philosophy of Mathematics and Natural Science*, tr. Olaf Helmer (Princeton
U. P., Princeton, 1949), 100; quoted in Cohen, *Franklin and Newton* 133.
[29] *Franklin and Newton* 139 and 579.
[30] Letter of 18 Nov. 1676, reprinted in Louis Trenchard More, *Isaac Newton*
(Scribner's, New York, 1934), 91.

with so substantial a blessing as my quiet to run after a shadow.'[31] Whether his reluctance to publish was a corollary of his consuming passion for solitary research which made intolerable every intrusion upon his solitude, or the incommunicativeness of the extreme introvert who dreads revealing his mind to any but intimate, admiring friends, the result was the curious need of this most independently minded of all men for an impresario to get his work before the public.

That the *Principia* might not have been written now seems unimaginable. For more than two centuries natural science had been moving toward that climax. Like *De revolutionibus orbium coelestium* and the *Origin of Species*, *Philosophiae Naturalis Principia Mathematica* was an inevitable book. It was necessary, and there was no one but Newton to write it. Once he had given in to Halley's urging to develop his Cambridge lectures on motion into a cosmic system, he resolved to place it beyond controversy, first, of course, by rigour, but also by such abstruseness as 'to avoid being baited by little smatterers in mathematics'.[32] Admiration of the prodigious mathematics did not, however, entail compliance with the cosmology, as appeared in the first French review where Newton's geometry ('mechanics') was flattered as 'the most perfect that one could imagine', but his *System of the World* dismissed as being supported 'only by hypotheses that are, most of them, arbitrary', and his theory of universal gravitation as a 'supposition [that] is arbitrary as it has not been proved'.[33] If Newton expected the Continental heirs of Descartes to intone 'Q.E.D.' in unison with his British friends, then he had not reckoned with Leibniz who was a 'smatterer', neither in mathematics nor in natural philosophy. The mathematical

[31] Sir David Brewster, *Memoirs of the Life, Writings, and Discoveries of Sir Isaac Newton* (Constable, Edinburgh, 1855), i. 95, Letter of 9 Dec. 1675.

[32] More, op. cit. 301–2: 'He also told his friend, the Rev. Dr. Derham, that "to avoid being baited by little smatterers in mathematics, he designedly made his *Principia* abstruse; but yet so as to be understood by able mathematicians who, he imagined, by comprehending his demonstrations would concur with him in his theory".'

[33] Quoted in Koyré, *Newtonian Studies* 115, from *Journal des Sçavans*, 2 Aug. 1688, 153f.

demonstration of the inverse square law of attraction would not in itself compel assent to a theory of planetary motion which left unresolved questions about the nature of gravity. Gravitational force appeared in the system as a mysterious property of matter whose effects were demonstrated but whose cause and means of operating were unexplained. Gravity, in short, Leibniz complained, was an occult quality.

This criticism was particularly offensive, since in the very first sentence of the Preface to the *Principia* Newton had aligned himself with 'the moderns, rejecting substantial forms and occult qualities . . .'. To defend his fundamental concept by inventing some theoretically possible causal explanation of the force would be to expose himself to the equally odious charge of inserting an unverifiable hypothesis at the foundations of his system. Newton was in the awkward position of attempting to justify his inability to explain gravity mechanically while insisting that gravity was not an occult quality, not an innate or essential and thus irreducible property of matter. A firm stand on metaphysical principle was called for, and Newton took it on the ground that the universe is simply not altogether explicable in terms of mechanical causation. The 'fault', therefore, in this case, did lie in the stars and not in Newton's philosophy. After the dynamics of the system have been explained, questions about the First Cause, about the Act of Creation, about the continuing influence of Divine Providence and its Purposes will remain and admit of no mechanistic answers. Newton and God stood to benefit mutually from this solution; limits to the experimental method were set by the nature of things, not by Newton's faltering; and God regained control of the cosmic forces that on a Hobbesian view were inherent in the matter of a self-contained and self-perpetuating universe. Methodological and theological discussions run together on Newton's pages because he felt that he had, in Kant's phrase, 'to limit knowledge in order to make room for faith' and, conversely, that by preserving a domain of faith he could justify the limitations on knowledge attainable by his method. It is not always clear whether the promotion of the faith or the defence of his method is uppermost in Newton's mind. Certainly he anticipated the progressive narrowing of areas of uncertainty. Nothing is ever certified as unknowable, not even the cause of gravity, but only as 'not yet discovered'.

Although Newton's religious convictions were not reflected on the surface of the first edition of the *Principia*, within five years he was writing to Richard Bentley of his pleasure at finding that his scientific work confirmed religious belief, and confessing that he had hoped for this result even while writing the book. Bentley had been invited to deliver the first of the annual series of sermons endowed by Sir Robert Boyle to marshal the forces of natural science in defence of Christianity. After demolishing Hobbes and Spinoza, Bentley reached the pinnacle of his performance by demonstrating the existence of Divine Providence from the evidence of design in nature disclosed by Newton's discoveries. Before publishing *A Confutation of Atheism*,[34] as he entitled his set of eight lectures, he wrote to Newton for assurance that the *Principia* had been properly interpreted. Newton's four letters[35] suggest that it was his young admirer's questions which forced him to mark out in his own mind the limits of mechanistic explanations by distinguishing between celestial motions derivable from natural causes and others which 'required the divine Arm to impress them'. He had been naturally reluctant to publish his scientific research together with theological inferences which, however manifestly evident they appeared to him, could not be experimentally confirmed, and his second great work, the *Opticks*, was equally discreet in its first appearance. His agnostic silence about ultimate causes left the impression that he had posited gravity as an essential and inherent property of matter which neither needed nor permitted derivation from any more

[34] (London, 1693). The seventh and eighth sermons are reprinted in facsimile (in reversed order) in *Isaac Newton's Papers and Letters*, 313–94, with the original, separate pagination preserved.

[35] *Four Letters from Sir Isaac Newton to Doctor Bentley Containing Some Arguments in Proof of a Deity* (London, 1756), reprinted in facsimile in *Isaac Newton's Papers and Letters*, 279–312, with the original continuous pagination preserved. The letters and the extracts from the sermons are prefaced by a witty, sensitive essay by Perry Miller which probes at the hidden differences underlying Bentley's overbearing dogmatic tone and Newton's enigmatic subtleties.

fundamental source. In his second letter, he is most emphatic in correcting Bentley on this point, which many others, both advocates and opponents of the system, will misinterpret: 'You sometimes speak of Gravity as essential and inherent to Matter. Pray do not ascribe that Notion to me; for the Cause of Gravity is what I do not pretend to know, and therefore would take more time to consider of it.'[36] He returns to the same subject in his next letter, pointing out both the theoretical difficulties and the negative theological implications of assuming gravity to be innate.[37] Newton adhered to this policy of reserving his religious thoughts for private meditation and correspondence until the second edition of the *Principia* was in preparation. Then he was persuaded by Bentley and his able and devoted editor, Roger Cotes, to append a defence of his philosophy of religion and science.

Although roughly four of every five pages of the *Principia* were altered for the second edition, the philosophically interesting features of the revision are, in addition to Cotes's helpful Preface, the 'Rules of Reasoning in Philosophy', which head the third and final Book and the famous 'General Scholium' which concludes it. In these *Regulae philosophandi* Newton compressed his methodological principles into four rules, as had Descartes his very different ones in the *Discourse on Method*. Alexandre Koyré has reviewed

[36] Letter of 17 Jan. 1692/3, 20.

[37] Letter of 25 Feb. 1692/3, 25–6: 'It is inconceivable, that inanimate brute Matter should, without the Mediation of something else, which is not material, operate upon, and affect other Matter without mutual Contact, as it must be, if Gravitation in the Sense of *Epicurus*, be essential and inherent in it. And this is one Reason why I desired you would not ascribe innate Gravity to me. That Gravity should be innate, inherent and essential to Matter, so that one Body may act upon another at a Distance thro' a *Vacuum*, without the Mediation of any thing else, by and through which their Action and Force may be conveyed from one to another, is to me so great an Absurdity, that I believe no Man who has in philosophical Matters a competent Faculty of thinking, can ever fall into it. Gravity must be caused by an Agent acting constantly according to certain Laws; but whether this Agent be material or immaterial, I have left to the Consideration of my Readers.' Miller, op. cit., 276, takes the last sentence as hinting darkly at heterodoxy: 'This hardly seems the tone of one who has joined a crusade against materialistic atheism!' However, the 'Readers' to whom Newton here refers are, of course, the readers of the first edition of the *Principia* which does not explicitly raise such undecidable questions.

the painful stages of revision and excision through which
Newton's 'Rules of Reasoning in Philosophy' passed after their
partial appearance in the first edition, accompanied by physical
and astronomical doctrines, and all, significantly, labelled
'Hypotheses'.[38] Newton's first rule states the principle of parsimony; the second prescribes economy in the assignment of causes
to similar effects. The third rule formulates the principle of the
uniformity of nature, and the fourth prescribes observation and
empirical confirmation as a defence against speculatively based
criticism. The 'Regulae' are as follows, with the fairly lengthy
explanation of the third omitted:

### RULE I

*We are to admit no more causes of natural things than such as are both
true and sufficient to explain their appearances.*

To this purpose the philosophers say that Nature does nothing
in vain, and more is in vain when less will serve; for Nature is
pleased with simplicity, and affects not the pomp of superfluous
causes.

### RULE II

*Therefore to the same natural effects we must, as far as possible, assign
the same causes.*

As to respiration in a man and in a beast; the descent of stones
in *Europe* and in *America*; the light of our culinary fire and of the
sun; the reflection of light in the earth, and in the planets.

### RULE III

*The qualities of bodies, which admit neither intensification nor remission
of degrees, and which are found to belong to all bodies within the reach
of our experiments, are to be esteemed the universal qualities of all
bodies whatsoever.*

### RULE IV

*In experimental philosophy we are to look upon propositions inferred by
general induction from phenomena as accurately or very nearly true,
notwithstanding any contrary hypotheses that may be imagined, till such*

[38] *Newtonian Studies*, ch. vi.

*time as other phenomena occur, by which they may either be made more
accurate, or liable to exceptions.*

This rule we must follow, that the argument of induction may
not be evaded by hypotheses.

In the third rule, Newton is of course referring to primary
qualities, and in his empiricist explanation of the rule he contends,
presumably against Descartes, that all such qualities as 'extension,
hardness, impenetrability, mobility, and inertia' are revealed to
us in sense experience, and that when the experience is invariable,
as it is in the case of gravity, we are justified in inferring that the
quality belongs to all bodies. As Cotes argues in the Preface,
generalization would be impossible unless this Rule which is
presupposed in all analogical reasoning were accepted. The
inference of a law of universal gravitation from the gravity of
terrestrial objects rests upon an

... axiom which is received by all philosophers, namely, that effects of
the same kind, whose known properties are the same, take their rise
from the same causes and have the same unknown properties also. ...
All philosophy is founded on this rule; for if that be taken away, we
can affirm nothing as a general truth. The constitution of particular
things is known by observation and experiments; and when that is
done, no general conclusion of the nature of things can thence be
drawn, except by this rule.[39]

In the fourth rule, added in the third edition, 'hypotheses' is
used in the pejorative sense suited to the speculations of Newton's
adversaries. It is interesting that Newton originally conceived of
his Rules as Hypotheses in the sense of unproved axioms or
postulates, and that he relies upon them in subsequent demonstrations as principles of inference. Although justified as methodological necessities, Newton's rules are metaphysically embarrassing.
They are exceptions to Cotes's patriotic echo of Newton's claim
to 'assume nothing as a principle, that is not proven by phenomena'. The experimental philosophers, Cotes continues, 'frame no
hypotheses, nor receive them into philosophy otherwise than as
questions whose truth may be disputed'.[40] Whether the methodo-

[39] p. xxvi.                    [40] p. xx.

logical axioms are called 'Hypotheses' or 'Rules', they remain principles which are assumed and not proven by phenomena. They express decisions, wise ones no doubt, whose justification, if it is forthcoming at all, must derive from somewhere beyond the limits of experimental philosophy.

Shortly before the revision of the *Principia* was completed, Cotes called Newton's attention to a 'very extraordinary Letter', one of three written by Leibniz to Hartsoecker, a Dutch physician, translated and published on 5 May 1712, in 'a Weekly Paper called *Memoires of Literature* and sold by Ann Baldwin in Warwick-Lane'.[41] Leibniz, foremost amongst a solid bloc of Continental scientists who defended one or another version of Descartes's theory of vortices against universal gravitation, condemned Newton (by implication, without actually mentioning his name) for founding his system upon an occult quality, the *vis gravitas*, thus abandoning his mechanical principles and resorting to a miracle as the ultimate explanation of celestial phenomena. Leaving the main burden of polemics to be borne by the enthusiastic Roger Cotes in the Preface, Newton opens his General Scholium with a terse paragraph in which the entailments of the 'hypothesis of vortices' are disconfirmed by the observed motions of planets and comets. Next, after affirming the capacity of the laws of gravity to explain the regularity and continuance of celestial bodies in their orbits, he concedes, or rather insists, that these same laws cannot account for the initial arrangement of the system of orbits. In other words, mechanical principles are adequate for explaining the observed motions of celestial and terrestrial bodies, but they are insufficient for 'deriving the frame of the world', to borrow a phrase from his fourth letter to Bentley. 'This most beautiful system of the sun, planets, and comets', he writes in the General Scholium, 'could only proceed from the counsel and dominion of an intelligent and powerful Being.'[42]

Dissassociating himself from pantheism and from Henry More's

---

[41] J. Edleston, *Correspondence of Sir Isaac Newton and Professor Cotes* (London, 1850), 153. See Cajori, n. 52, pp. 668–70; Koyré, *Newtonian Studies*, 140–3.

[42] p. 544.

identification of God with space, he then propounds the Argument from Design, alternating in time-honoured fashion between proclaiming God beyond all human comprehension and assigning to him the stock attributes. In view of the limits of experimental philosophy which he proceeds to draw in the next paragraph, the most interesting statement in this theological section is the last one: 'And thus much concerning God; to discourse of whom from the appearances of things, does certainly belong to Natural Philosophy', or, in the more faithful rendering suggested by Cohen, 'And thus much concerning God; to discourse of whom from *phenomena*, belongs to *experimental philosophy*.'[43]

Presumably in answer to Leibniz and the Cartesians, Newton admits that he has not assigned the cause of gravity, for the very good reason that he has not been able to discover it:

But hitherto I have not been able to discover the cause of those properties of gravity from phenomena, and I frame no hypotheses; for whatever is not deduced from the phenomena is to be called an hypothesis; and hypotheses, whether metaphysical or physical, whether of occult qualities or mechanical, have no place in experimental philosophy.[44]

In the following paragraph, which concludes the General Scholium and hence the entire *Principia*, he does formulate a hypothesis about a most subtle, electric, elastic spirit, inhering in all bodies, which might account for attraction, phenomena of light and heat, sensation, and the motor responses of animals as well. Having made the point that he could speculate as freely as any other, he immediately withdraws this hypothesis because of the insufficiency 'of experiments which is required to an accurate determination and demonstration of the laws by which this electric and elastic spirit operates'. Why, then, did he feel no reticence about his theological hypothesis? It is certainly curious that the stipulated factor in the way of advancing the hypothesis of a subtle spirit, the inability to determine accurately how it works, is acknowledged to operate against the hypothesis of a

---

[43] *Franklin and Newton*, 142. The Latin reads, 'Et haec de Deo: de quo utiq: e phaenominis dissere, ad philosophiam experimentalem pertinet.'
[44] p. 547.

God who, among many other things, is all power to act, 'but in a manner not at all human, in a manner not at all corporeal, in a manner utterly unknown to us'.[45]

It has been said by Newton's biographer, More,[46] and more recently by Hurlbutt,[47] that Newton wrote the General Scholium mainly to thwart Leibniz's insinuations of atheism. The same view

[45] p. 545.

[46] Op. cit. 555: 'But this apologia [the General Scholium] did not fully satisfy Bentley and Cotes. It did not sufficiently crush the Cartesians or manifest the glory of the *Principia*; it softened the denial that occult qualities had been introduced; it was silent as to Leibniz and the invention of the calculus. *Most important of all* it did not hurl back with scorn the charge of the materialism of his philosophy, and the irreligion of its author, which Leibniz had insinuated in the ear of that royal blue stocking, the Princess of Wales, who had just come to England from Hanover and the teaching of Leibniz.' (My italics.) More does not disclose his source of information about warnings 'insinuated in the ear of' Princess Caroline. It is true that when Leibniz decided to renew the attack upon Newton's claim to priority in the discovery of the infinitesimal calculus, he opened with a letter to the Princess in England cautioning her about Newton's 'very odd Opinion concerning the Work of God'. She showed the letter to Samuel Clarke, with whom she had weekly philosophical discussions and thus initiated the famous Leibniz–Clarke correspondence. (G. H. Alexander's *The Leibniz–Clarke Correspondence* (Manchester U.P., 1956) is the standard modern edition of *A Collection of Papers, which passed between the late learned Mr. Leibniz and Dr. Clarke. In the years 1715 and 1716. Relating to the Principles of Natural Philosophy and Religion* (London, 1717)). But this letter is dated November 1715, two and a half years after Newton had mailed his manuscript of the General Scholium to Cotes. Indeed, Alexandre Koyré interprets the Leibniz–Caroline letter as a reply to the General Scholium and Cotes's Preface to the second edition of the *Principia*. (See *From the Closed World to the Infinite Universe* (Harper Torchbook, New York, 1958), 235.) Koyré's view would surely represent an over-correction, for the correspondence between Leibniz and Bernoulli at the time makes it clear that Leibniz was responding in self-defence to a paper written by John Keill in defence of Newton and published in *Journal Litteraire*, July–August, 1714. (See *Commercium Philosophicum*, 'Bernoulli et Leibniz', and More, op. cit., ch. xv.)

[47] Robert H. Hurlbutt III, *Hume, Newton, and the Design Argument* (Univ. of Nebraska Press, Lincoln, 1965), 5: 'It can be speculated . . . that Newton would rather have kept his science and his theology separate. Such a wish, however, would have been dashed for the simple reason that his opponents did not wish to do so, and as a consequence they attacked him on theological grounds. Leibniz called the *Principia* a Godless book, and Berkeley criticized Newton's conceptions of absolute space and absolute time as being atheistical notions. Newton's response was to add to the second edition of the *Principia*, produced in 1713, the famous *General Scholium* to Book III, an addition in which he presented some of his basic ideas in theology.' The reader is referred to Berkeley's *Principles of Human Knowledge*; the reference to Leibniz is not documented.

is suggested by Cajori, who presents Leibniz together with
Berkeley as attacking Newton's system on theological grounds
and sums up the relevant arguments of *Principles of Human
Knowledge* by saying, 'Thus the absolute space, time, and motion
of Newton was attacked as an atheistic conception.'[48] However,
the letter in which Cotes solicited the General Scholium makes no
mention of Berkeley, nor of atheism when specifying Leibniz's
objections to 'your Book . . . that it deserts Mechanical causes, is
built upon Miracles, and recurrs to Occult qualities'.[49] Nor do
Leibniz's letters to Hartsoeker imply a charge of atheism at all;
quite the reverse. He complains that by declining a mechanical
explanation of gravity, proponents of attraction desert natural
causes for miracles; their fault is not to have excluded God, but
to have relied upon his continuous intervention to preserve
regular motion within the system:

> Such is the method of those who say, after M. de Roberval's
> *Aristarchus*, that all bodies attract one another by a law of nature, which
> God made in the beginning of things. For alleging nothing else to
> obtain such an effect and admitting nothing that was made, whereby
> it may appear how he attains to that end, they have recourse to a
> miracle, that is, to a supernatural thing, which continues for ever, when
> the question is to find out a natural cause. . . .[50]

It appears to me that Newton's Argument from Design was
not presented in order to counter a charge of atheism, but rather
to back up a methodological presupposition of his system, viz.
that the natural order is not wholly explicable in terms of mechanical causation. Charged by Leibniz and the Cartesians with
deserting mechanical causes, he replies in effect that he had never
contracted to give causal explanations of those fundamental forces
of nature from which mechanistic explanations of observable
phenomena are mathematically derived. It is enough that the
detection of these forces has yielded laws to explain celestial and
tidal motions. It is unreasonable to demand that gravity and the

---

[48] Op. cit. 668.                              [49] J. Edelston, op. cit. 153.
[50] Quoted in Alexandre Koyré, *Newtonian Studies* 141, from *Die philosophischen
Schriften von G. W. Leibniz*, ed. G. J. Gerhardt (Berlin, 1875–90), 517 f., the first
of the three letters to which Cotes referred.

rest be explained in the same way, i.e. be derived in accordance with mechanical principles from yet more fundamental sources, before being permitted to exercise their explanatory power in a system of rational mechanics. If it is agreed that the First Cause is a supremely intelligent Designer whose nature and ways surpass human understanding, then it must be accepted that natural scientists may have to stop short of fully explaining 'the Laws of the Actions of the Spirit or Agent by which this Attraction is performed', as Newton remarked several years later in an anonymous review of the *Commercium Epistolicum*.[51] Continuing to speak of himself in the third person, he adds, 'And for the same Reason he is silent about the Cause of Gravity, there occurring no Experiments or Phenomena by which he might prove what was the Cause thereof.' It now emerges that Newton's affirmation of a cosmic Designer of infinite intelligence and power is compatible with his withdrawal of the subtle spirit hypothesis. The two gestures, the affirmation and the retraction, together demarcate the realms of Divine wisdom and human knowledge. The helplessness of the experimental philosopher when confronted with the ultimate question of how God impressed his design upon the *materia prima* signals the limits of mechanical explanations. Newton does not take present limits to be permanently fixed. In expectation of lighting the margin of darkness, Newton will return to his hypothesis of the aether in other contexts where speculation is appropriate.

Newton could be confident that Leibniz would not challenge his Argument from Design, and was himself so far from having reservations about the validity of the inference that he included

51 'An account of the Book entitled *Commercium Epistolicum*', *Philosophical Transactions of the Royal Society*, 1715. The *Commercium Epistolicum* was the official report of a Royal Society committee appointed to investigate Leibniz's complaint that he had been unjustly accused by John Keill of plagiarizing Newton's invention of the arithmetic of fluxions or differential calculus. The impartiality of the report may be surmised from the facts that Newton was then President of the Royal Society, that the committee, before which Leibniz was never called to testify, was heavily laden with Newton's intimate friends, that Newton oversaw the preparation of both the original, privately circulated report of 1713 and the revised misdated edition of 1722, which he further altered without notice and annotated and prefaced with his own anonymous review.

such 'discourse' as part of Natural or Experimental Philosophy. The evidence of Design, which was apparent to any attentive observer of nature, became compelling as the mathematical simplicity and coherence of the laws governing the universe were disclosed. The inference from Design to a cause 'very well skilled in mechanicks and geometry' was automatic and, if challenged, could be defended by argument by analogy with constructions proceeding from human intelligence. Thus natural science supplied an evidential basis for the cardinal doctrine of natural theology, and Newton in fact described himself as one who 'teaches that Philosophers are to argue from Phaenomena and Experiments in the Causes thereof, and thence to the Causes of those Causes, and so on till we come to the first Cause . . .'.[52]

How did Newton reconcile his hypothesis of the Deity with his dictum '*hypotheses non fingo*'? The answer is clear that for Newton the existence of God was no hypothesis but a certain truth manifested by the evidence of intelligence and choice in the design of the world. This certitude is unshaken by his present inability to offer any verifiable account of the means through which the Designer has arranged for such forces as attraction to operate. The 'Frame of the World' is plain enough in outline, and much of its structure is displayed in the Newtonian model. Of the remainder, what is attributable to mechanical principles will eventually be explained by Experimental Philosophy. Whatever is inexplicable by that method are divine mysteries which surpass all understanding.

## Section 4. *Methodology and Theology*

The deductive form of the *Principia* demanded and facilitated speculative austerity. It was conceived as a synthesis of discoveries by Newton's great predecessors, and aimed to demonstrate old truths rather than to reveal new ones. Its beauty was the creation of the logical intellect at work in ordering, integrating, unifying, deriving the movements of the spheres from three simple laws.

---

[52] 'An account of the Book entitled *Commercium Epistolicum*', *Philosophical Transactions of the Royal Society*, 1715.

The usual discipline imposed by mathematical rules was reinforced by the accumulation of astronomical observations to which Newton's conclusions had to conform. He took no risks with the empirically non-committal mathematical theorems, and those which were found to fit the facts were no longer 'hypotheses' but 'general conclusions deduced from phenomena'. The restraints imposed upon his speculative tendencies by the purpose and form of the *Principia* were relaxed in the inquisitive atmosphere of his second great work, the *Opticks*. The *Principia* had realized the potentialities of generations of scientific research; it was the crowning achievement of the scientific revolution. The *Opticks* was a work of exploration, enterprising rather than retrospective. In this field there were no inventories of relevant observations comparable to those available in astronomy. The inner structures of common objects handled daily by men were less accessible to observation than remote planets and stars. The reader of the *Opticks* follows Newton in the exploration of unknown regions beneath the surfaces of familiar things. The *Principia* presents him with a closed system which renders the cosmos intelligible in sophisticated, forbiddingly technical, abstruse language readable by few. The *Principia* was intended for 'readers of good mathematical learning',[53] the *Opticks* was addressed 'to Readers of quick Wit and good Understanding not yet versed in Opticks'.[54] In place of the geometrical projections and demonstrations of the *Principia*, one finds in the first Book of the *Opticks* 'The Proof by Experiments' and diagrams to illustrate experimental apparatus, and in the second Book 'Observations' and illustrations of them.

The aim of Book I of the *Opticks*, to establish the properties of light, is realized through experimental procedures and there is nothing speculative in it. The second Book is concerned with the properties of matter that would account for the coloration of physical objects ('natural bodies'). It begins with twenty-four sets of observations of a familiar but puzzling type of phenomenon, of clear transparent substances displaying colours when thinned out into films ('plates'), as water in bubbles. With the aid of conclusions established in the first Book, Newton is able to explain the

---

[53] p. 397 (Preface to Book III).     [54] p. 20 (following the Axioms).

phenomenon by the hypothesis that light rays striking such a surface are subject to alternate 'Fits of easy Reflexion and . . . Fits of easy Transmission'.[55]

Newton's investigation '*Of the permanent Colours of natural Bodies, and the Analogy between them and the Colours of thin transparent Plates*',[56] in Part iii of Book II is intended for 'compleating the Theory of Light, especially as to the constitution of the parts of natural Bodies, on which their Colours or Transparency depend'.[57] What Newton is setting out to discover is nothing less than the structure of matter. Obviously he could not move about in the realm of molecular physics undirected by hypotheses. Lacking a microscope of sufficient magnification, he could not observe even 'some of the greatest of those corpuscles'.[58] And even if he had had 'one that would magnify three or four thousand times', the objects of his speculation, the ultimate constituents of matter, would still have remained beyond his view. 'For it seems impossible to see the more secret and noble works of Nature within the corpuscles by reason of their transparency.'[59] Given these practical and theoretical limits to observation Newton had to content himself with indirectly confirming his hypotheses by testing their consequences against phenomena—had to content himself, that is to say, with the classic method of empirical science which he was doing so much to consolidate.

According to the 'Advertisement To First Edition' of the *Opticks* (1704) Newton had not been active in experimental optics for about seventeen years before 'the importunity of friends' (and the death of enemies)[60] decided him to publish. He was left with a rich inventory of observations and a set of untested hypotheses for interpreting them. Since he could not 'now think

---

[55] Book II, Part iii, p. 281: 'DEFINITION. *The returns of the disposition of any Ray to be reflected I will call its* Fits of easy Reflexion, *and those of its disposition to be transmitted its* Fits of easy Transmission, *and the space it passes between every return and the next return, the* Interval of its Fits.' 278: 'Prop. XII. *Every Ray of Light in its passage through any refracting Surface is put into a certain transient Constitution or State, which in the progress of the Ray returns at equal Intervals, and disposes the Ray at every return to be easily transmitted through the next refracting Surface, and between the Returns to be easily reflected by it.*'

[56] p. 245.          [57] pp. 193–4.          [58] p. 261.          [59] p. 262.

[60] Robert Hooke, his chief antagonist, had died the year before.

of taking these things into further Consideration',[61] he needed a way to accommodate his imaginative anticipations of theoretical truths to his principle of affirming only experimentally verified conclusions, and he found it in the simple device of asking questions. The purely rhetorical character of the questions is betrayed by their negative form, as Cohen observes.[62] To ask, as he does in Query 27, 'Are not all Hypotheses erroneous which have hitherto been invented for explaining the Phaenomena of Light, by new Modifications of the Rays?' is surely to imply that they are. Newton's queries, then, imply Newton's answers plainly enough, and so do the discussions which become increasingly lengthy as the questions become progressively more difficult.

To the sixteen Queries of the first edition, seven (two of them, 20 and 23, partly theological in content) were added to Samuel Clarke's Latin translation of 1706. In the second English edition of 1717 (reprinted the following year) eight new Queries were inserted after number 17, those of particular theological interest being renumbered 28 and 31. Newton's questions about the propagation of light, the interaction of light and matter, about heat and combustion, about electrical, magnetic, and chemical phenomena, about the physiology of sight and motor behaviour, and about the cause of universal gravitation, represented the quintessence of nearly half a century of profound meditation and no further queries were added to the second Latin edition in 1719 nor to the third and fourth English editions of 1721 and 1730. Historians of philosophical thought have paid particular attention to Queries 28 and 31, for these are prime sources of information about his religious opinions and his conception of scientific method.

In Query 28 Newton calls into question a group of hypotheses that would explain light as the propagation of pressure or motion through a fluid medium. Christiaan Huygens's wave hypothesis was the most distinguished example of this type. Such hypotheses rest upon an analogy between the transmission of light and the flow of water. This plausible analogy breaks down when its

---

[61] p. 338.
[62] *Franklin and Newton*, 164; as does Koyré, *Newtonian Studies* 50.

implications are carefully examined. Consider a cataract exerting pressure in the pool below, moving the water down the river-bed —the path of least resistance. If the stream meets an obstacle, a partly submerged rock, say, the water flows around it, spreading out on both sides and bending back toward the quiescent area on the downstream side of the rock. If light moved in an analogous way, it too would bend around obstructions, illuminating their shadows, and twist and turn through crooked passages like water. Newton turned up other difficulties, such as the inability of the planets to sustain their motions against the calculated resistance of such a fluid medium. He then used his falsification of this hypo-thesis as a warrant for dismissing all hypotheses feigned 'for explaining all things mechanically'. But since it is so clear that the fluid-medium hypothesis has been eliminated in order to make room for the hypothetical aether, his familiar stricture against hypotheses at this point is bewildering:

And for rejecting such a Medium, we have the Authority of those the oldest and most celebrated Philosophers of *Greece* and *Phoenicia*, who made a *Vacuum*, and *Atoms*, and the Gravity of Atoms, the first Principles of their Philosophy; tacitly attributing Gravity to some other Cause than dense Matter. Later Philosophers banish the Consideration of such a Cause out of natural Philosophy, feigning Hypotheses for explaining all things mechanically, and referring other Causes to Metaphysicks: Whereas the main Business of natural Philosophy is to argue from Phaenomena without feigning Hypotheses, and to deduce Causes from Effects, till we come to the very first Cause, which certainly is not mechanical . . .[63]

Of the 'Later Philosophers' the chief representative is Descartes. The 'Cause' which has been excluded from the consideration of natural philosophy is the First Cause, God. The feigned 'Hypo-theses' are such fictions as the plenum, the conservation of momentum, and the vortices out of which Descartes built his imaginary world in *Le Monde*. The chief objection to using such hypotheses, apart from their empirical falsity, is the illusory (and blasphemous) hope they foster of completely explaining the universe in terms of mechanical causation. Despite Descartes's

[63] p. 369.

placating gesture of casting God in the dual role of guarantor of the mathematical physicists' clear and distinct ideas and of the preserver of the cosmos, the Cartesian system of the world appeared to Newton as a self-regulating machine purportedly explicable in terms of mechanistic materialism. The order of investigation prescribed by Newton here as elsewhere—'from Phaenomena . . . to deduce Causes from Effects, till we come to the very first Cause'—is the reverse of Descartes's high *a priori* method.[64] Descartes resolves the metaphysical question of God's existence as a prolegomenon to physics or natural philosophy. Neither of Descartes's arguments for the existence of God owes anything to observation of nature; nor could they, since their role is to vindicate belief in the reality of the external world. What Descartes calls his 'principal argument' is a modified cosmological argument in which ideas appearing in his own consciousness are substituted for the palpable universe. His ontological argument proceeds formally in the traditional way from the analysis of the concept of a Perfect Being. Not only did Descartes's method seem to Newton backwards and subjective, but remiss in

[64] See the comparison of Newton and Descartes in the first biographical study of Newton, Fontenelle's *The Elogium of Sir Isaac Newton*, Tonson ed. (London, 1728), 15–16, reprinted in facsimile in *Isaac Newton's Papers and Letters*, 457–8: 'These two great men, whose Systems are so opposite, resembled each other in several respects, they were both Genius's of the first rank, both born with superior understandings, and fitted for the founding of Empires in Knowledge. Being excellent Geometricians, they both saw the necessity of introducing Geometry into Physicks; For both founded their Physicks upon discoveries in Geometry, which may almost be said of none but themselves. But one of them taking a bold flight, thought at once to reach the Fountain of All Things and by clear and fundamental ideas to make himself master of the first principles; that he might have nothing more left to do, but to descend to phenomena of Natures as to necessary consequences; the other more cautious, or rather more modest, began by taking hold of the known phenomena to climb to unknown principles; resolved to admit them only in such manner as they could be produced by a chain of consequences. The former sets out from what he clearly understands, to find out the causes of what he sees; the latter sets out from what he sees, in order to find out the cause, whether it be clear or obscure. The self-evident principles of the one do not always lead him to the causes of phenomena as they are; and the phenomena do not always lead the other to principles sufficiently evident. The boundaries which stop'd two such men in their pursuits through different roads, were not the boundaries of Their Understanding, but of Human understanding it self.'

ignoring the evidence of God's presence in Nature, and arbitrary in excluding final causes from consideration. Or so it seems, for the passage quoted above continues without a break from those statements about method to questions about mechanically inexplicable phenomena, to teleological questions, to questions about 'a Being incorporeal, living, intelligent, omnipresent . . .'.[65]

Query 28 is only one of a number of places in Newton's writing where the close connection in his mind between methodological and theological questions is displayed. It appears in a very early paper on Descartes only recently discovered,[66] in a polemical and anonymous defence of his gravitational theory against Leibniz,[67] in the General Scholium to the *Principia*, and in Query 31. This pairing of audacious theological speculation with the firm rejection of hypotheses cannot be accepted on the grounds that Newton's hypotheses are not really hypotheses because they are 'not further insisted upon', not categorically affirmed but only suggested by rhetorical questions. Everyone's hypotheses are tentative. Descartes's cosmological hypotheses are presented in *Le Monde* as pure possibilities of the imagination which are found by a happy chance to entail a world very like the one we see around us. The crucial difference between illicit, feigned hypotheses and legitimate, explanatory ones is presented as being largely a matter of the position each holds in the order of investigation. The illicit hypotheses are introduced by speculative *a priori* thinkers at the first stage of inventing some very general, largely imaginative system. A fairly casual acquaintance with natural phenomena provides the imagination with sufficient material to work upon. Dissident facts can be either ignored or accommodated by subsidiary *ad hoc* hypotheses. Legitimate hypotheses—best called by some other name, such as 'Queries', to avoid the appearance of guilt by association—show up not at the beginning of an investigation but near the end, when the bounds of observation and

---

[65] p. 370.

[66] 'De gravitatione et aequipondo fluidorum', in A. Rupert Hall and Marie Boas Hall, *Unpublished Scientific Papers of Isaac Newton* (Cambridge U.P., 1962), 82 f.

[67] 'An account of the Book entitled *Commercium Epistolicum*', *Philosophical Transactions of the Royal Society*, 1715.

experiment have been reached, at least temporarily. In the beginning is the observation of phenomena; then whatever experimental manipulation is possible and necessary to elicit the causes; then the formulation of general laws to whose operation invariable experience attests. At this point, hypotheses are permissible, even desirable if they suggest further lines of empirical research. Their function is not to anticipate the outcome of experiments, but to suggest explanations of established results: e.g. that gravitational force may be transmitted through an exceedingly rare, elastic aether.

Query 31 illustrates the approved procedure, with the obvious qualification that the question itself clearly implies the working hypothesis of a force acting between the particles of physical objects: 'Quest. 31. Have not the small Particles of Bodies certain Powers, Virtues, or Forces, by which they act at a distance . . . upon one another for producing a great Part of the Phaenomena of Nature?'[68] Reasoning by analogy with the forces of gravity, magnetism, and electricity known to act between gross bodies, it seems 'not improbable' that the cohesive force binding the particles is also one of attraction:

For Nature is very consonant and conformable to herself. How these Attractions may be perform'd, I do not here consider. What I call Attraction may be perform'd by impulse, or by some other means unknown to me. I use that Word here to signify only in general any Force by which Bodies tend towards one another, whatsoever be the Cause. For we must learn from the Phaenomena of Nature what Bodies attract one another, and what are the Laws and Properties of the Attraction, before we enquire the Cause by which the Attraction is perform'd.[69]

Newton begins with a densely packed catalogue of chemical reactions, asking if each one of these phenomena does not manifest the operation of forces of attraction or repulsion between particles. For example, 'When therefore Spirit of Salt precipitates Silver out of *Aqua fortis*, is it not done by attracting and mixing with the *Aqua fortis*, and not attracting, or perhaps repelling Silver?'[70] An example of 'Properties of the Attraction' is the even

[68] pp. 375–6.    [69] p. 376.    [70] p. 383.

distribution of salt particles in solution which implies a repulsive force separating them at the maximum possible distance. An example of 'the Laws . . . of Attraction' is the reciprocal relation between the distance water (even *in vacuo*) will ascend between two partly submerged parallel polished mirrors and the space separating them.

If, as it appears, the cohesiveness of solid, homogeneal bodies is the result of the short-range attracting force of their particles, it also 'seems probable' that the particles themselves are 'solid, massy, hard, impenetrable, moveable'.[71] For even liquids display their solid constituents in process of freezing, distillation, or sublimation. Since some compounds are hard despite the relatively great spaces between their solid particles, clearly every one of the individual particles must be 'incomparably harder than any porous Bodies compounded of them'.[72] Indeed these particles must be indestructible if the universe is not to wear out, decompose, disintegrate, or undergo such a metamorphosis that nothing recognizable remains. Given these irreducible atoms as the ultimate constituents of matter, 'the Changes of corporeal Things', as the Greek atomists had said, must be the results of 'the various Separations and new Associations and Motions of these permanent Particles'.[73]

And thus Nature will be very conformable to her self and very simple, performing all the great Motions of the heavenly Bodies by the Attraction of Gravity which intercedes those Bodies, and almost all the small ones of their Particles by some other attractive and repelling Powers which intercede the Particles.[74]

The deeper Newton probes the unlit recesses of matter, the fainter becomes the questioning tone. It was, apparently, a matter of discretion and caution to pose as a question the attractive force which binds the particles of physical objects. It seems to Newton 'that these Particles . . . are moved by certain active Principles such as is that of Gravity . . . These Principles I consider . . . general Laws of Nature . . . their Truth appearing to us by Phaenomena . . . For these are manifest Qualities . . .'.[75] What need is there to

[71] p. 400.                [72] Ibid.                [73] Ibid.
[74] p. 397.                                        [75] p. 401.

question laws whose truth appears 'to us by Phaenomena'? Or qualities which are 'manifest'? The electro-magnetic properties of Newtonian particles are not really hypothetical, because they truly explain the observable properties and actions of physical objects—the expansion of heated vapours, for example. Boyle's coiled and springy air particles are fictions, because 'vast Contraction and Expansion seems unintelligible'[76] on that hypothesis. The Cartesian 'law' of the conservation of momentum is a hypothesis which is disconfirmed by experiments demonstrating losses of motion to exceed gains and which is, furthermore, incompatible with the vortex theory to which it is joined. The Newtonian law of gravitational attraction is not a hypothesis for it is sufficient and necessary to account for the preservation of motion in a universe subject to the *Vis inertiae*. Newton's usage, it seems, implies a normative, polemical sense of 'hypothesis' in addition to the senses recognized by Cohen. The principles of others are not really principles because they are false; they are hypotheses. Newton's hypotheses are not really hypotheses because they are true; they are principles.

The superior standing of Newton's principles derives from his method of which he gives a summary account in the last paragraph but one of the *Opticks*:

As in Mathematicks, so in Natural Philosophy, the Investigation of difficult Things by the Method of Analysis, ought ever to precede the Method of Composition. This Analysis consists in making Experiments and Observations, and in drawing general Conclusions from them by Induction, and admitting of no Objections against the Conclusions, but such as are taken from Experiments, or other certain Truths. For Hypotheses are not to be regarded in experimental Philosophy. And although the arguing from Experiments and Observations by Induction be no Demonstration of general Conclusions; yet it is the best way of arguing which the Nature of Things admits of, and may be looked upon as so much the stronger, by how much the Induction is more general. And if no Exception occur from Phaenomena, the Conclusion may be pronounced generally. But if at any time afterwards any Exception shall occur from Experiments, it may then begin to be pronounced with such Exceptions as occur. By this way of Analysis we

[76] p. 396.

may proceed from Compounds to Ingredients, and from Motions to the Forces producing them; and in general, from Effects to their Causes, and from particular Causes to more general ones, till the Argument end in the most general. This is the Method of Analysis: And the Synthesis consists in assuming the Causes discover'd, and establish'd as Principles, and by them explaining the Phaenomena proceeding from them, and proving the Explanations.[77]

The 'Hypotheses', which, he says, 'are not to be regarded in experimental Philosophy', are empirically groundless theoretical possibilities advanced against experimentally confirmed general conclusions. Even if Newton's 'general Conclusions' appear to be hypotheses by another name, especially when used in the synthetic or compositive phase of the proceedings, they differ in kind from the purely speculative hypotheses which he, as an empirical scientist, rightly decides to ignore. (The hypotheses of Hooke, Boyle, Huygens, and others, even of Descartes, are not ignored, but carefully examined by deductive elaboration and testing against phenomena.) Not only are Newton's principles assumed in explanations which 'tell us how the Properties and Actions of all Corporeal Things follow from those manifest Principles',[78] but these same principles serve as points of departure for further analysis or resolution. They point to the discovery of ever more general causes and ultimately to the first Cause—'so far as we can know by natural Philosophy what is the first Cause'.[79] But now Newton is well beyond the limits of empirical verification and must content himself with 'leaving the Hints to be examin'd and improv'd by the farther Experiments and Observations of such as are inquisitive'.[80]

'Inquisitive' thinkers, both scientific and religious, responded in sufficient number to confer the name of Newton upon the main stream of eighteenth-century English thought. Natural philosophers such as Edmund Halley, Joseph Black, Benjamin Franklin, Joseph Priestly, and Henry Cavendish, who took Newton's suggestions for empirical research, belong to the history of natural science. The philosophically provocative writers were those who undertook the riskier venture of working out the moral and

---

[77] pp. 404–5.　　　　[78] p. 401.　　　　[79] p. 405.　　　　[80] Ibid.

theological implications of Newtonian science. Their programme was already well advanced, Bentley having inaugurated it in the 1660s by his series of Boyle Lectures. The *Confutation of Atheism* was cut to the pattern to which a train of zealous authors would tailor their efforts to exploit Newton's science for the glory of God and the moral improvement of mankind. In the very year that the *Opticks* was first published, 1704, its Latin translator, Samuel Clarke, began his first set of Boyle Lectures, *Demonstration of the Being and Attributes of God*, followed the next year by *Discourse Concerning the Unchangeable Obligations of Natural Religion*. Although Clarke considered himself a Newtonian theologian and moralist, his mental habits had taken shape under the mathematical influence of Descartes. Accordingly, his *a priori* treatment of religious and ethical questions (which run together in natural religion) is more akin to the deductive form of the *Principia*, the predominantly synthetic work, than to the mainly inductive analyses of the *Opticks*. Clarke was joined in his misbegotten effort to rationalize (which usually meant to mathematicize) natural religion by William Whiston and William Wollaston, John Balguy and Richard Price, who with many another ponderous reasoner formed the Intellectual School. Even theologians and moralists who found Clarke's pseudo-mathematical apparatus embarrassingly artificial shared his dream of reflecting the glory of the Newtonian synthesis in a system of natural religion. Titles alone sometimes herald Newton's influence upon the books of the day: *Astronomical Principles of Religion* by William Whiston, Newton's much abused friend and his successor in the Lucasian Chair of Mathematics at Cambridge, *Philosophical Principles of Natural Religion* by Dr. George Cheyne, Hume's physician, Francis Hutcheson's *Philosophiae Moralis Institutio Compendiaria*, of which Hume's criticisms were invited by the author, and John Craig's *Theologiae Christianae Principia Mathematica*, to which Hume was supposed by his editors, Green and Grose, to be referring in his discussion of historical evidence in the *Treatise* (T 145).

The urge to put religious and ethical doctrines upon equal footing with the theories of physical science is understandable.

The magnitude of the epistemological difficulties lurking beneath the surface remained unsuspected until Hume sounded the foundations of human knowledge. Consequently, the dangerous lean of the religious edifice was not at first detected by pious workers busily decorating it with the trappings of scientific thought. What had begun as an attempt to show how much of what was essential to Christianity could be established by reason ended by claiming that only what could be rationally defended was essential. Although the deist movement has been traced back to Lord Herbert of Cherbury's *De Religione Laici*, its gathering momentum can be measured between John Locke's *Reasonableness of Christianity* of 1695 and Anthony Collins's *Discourse on Free-thinking* of 1713. By then it had become clear that the net result of the scientific spirit which animated such deists as Mathew Tindal and John Toland, Thomas Woolston and Anthony Collins, would be to purify religion of all mysterious and supernatural ingredients and to superannuate the clergy. Scriptural authority was undermined, dogmatics subverted, prophecy disparaged, miracles discredited, and God as Saviour supplanted by a vague, remote, indifferent Being preoccupied with the mechanical efficiency of his cosmic clockwork. Thinkers who tried both to move with the times and to cling to the mainstays of Christian belief took upon themselves the heavy burden of reconciling faith and reason; they were required to show that the God of Revelation was the historical incarnation of the Deity whose being and attributes were exhibited by natural religion. Life was simpler for orthodox reasoners like Richard Bentley, William Warburton, and Dean Swift, who took a firm stand upon traditional ground to thunder (not always in unison) against the infidel, imbecile deists. However venomous the deist controversy, malicious and savage its attacks, contemptuous and unyielding its defences, a single intellectual conviction cut across the deep theological divisions separating the parties concerned. Unshakeable confidence in the Argument from Design provided the necessary margin of theological agreement upon which their vituperative wrangling could take place.

What Newton had contributed to this venerable proof—the

one of Aquinas's Five Ways anticipated as far back as Anaxagoras
—was the strengthening of the major premiss. Evidence of design
must have impressed the earliest disinterested observer of the
natural order. Certainly, the first article of faith sustaining the
scientific revolution was that beneath the dizzying complexities
and unceasing changes of the empirical world certain simple,
permanent principles explaining natural processes would be found.
The *Principia* had vindicated that faith by displaying those
principles in the elegant form which only rigorous mathematical
thinking could impose upon them. One was no longer required
to accept the intelligibility of the universe on trust, for now it had
been demonstrated. Granted that the universe was an intelligible
design, did it not follow that it had been intelligently designed?
This momentous inference was licensed by the same principle
of analogical reasoning, laid down in Newton's first three Rules of
Reasoning in Philosophy, that allowed the universal ascription of
gravity to celestial bodies on the grounds of its manifest presence
in terrestrial bodies. Newton's assurance that discourse of God
belonged to experimental philosophy presumably rested on his
confidence that the strength of analogical arguments would be
unimpaired by extension into the religious domain. His admirers
—and who was not an admirer of Newton?—shared his theological optimism. Christians, Deists, and those who tried to be both
alike rested secure in the belief that the Newtonian system supplied
the premiss and that the Newtonian method authorized the
principle of inference of the Argument from Design. Hume
accepts the premiss, but questions the inference. Does he, then,
merit his reputation as a Newtonian methodologist?

# PART III

## Principles of Method, Newton's and Hume's

### Section 1. *Hume's Acquaintance with Newton*

I т is odd that Newton is nowhere mentioned in the *Treatise* upon which he is said to have had such a great influence.[1] There is a single explicit reference to the Newtonian philosophy on the very last page, in the final paragraph of the Appendix. Here Hume is amplifying the argument of Book I, Part ii, Section 5, that the idea of a vacuum is inconceivable and that the dispute between proponents of the vacuum and of the plenum must therefore at one level be merely verbal, and at another, ontological, level 'exceed all human capacity'. It is quite uncertain whether the expression, 'the Newtonian philosophy', refers to Newton's own work or to that of such followers as Samuel Clarke,[2] William Whiston,[3] George Cheyne,[4] and Colin Maclaurin,[5] who exploited

[1] In support of his claim 'that Newton, rather than Bacon, was Hume's master', John Passmore states that 'He refers to Bacon twice in the *Enquiries* (129, 219) but not at all in the *Treatise*' (*Hume's Intentions*, 43, n. 2). Hume does in fact mention Bacon in the Introduction to the *Treatise* (T xxi), but, as I have said, he does not mention Newton in that work.

[2] *A Discourse Concerning the Being and Attributes of God* (Boyle Lectures, 1704–5). Hume rebuts Clarke's defence of the Law of Universal Causation in Bk. I, Pt. iii, S. 3 of the *Treatise* (pp. 80–1).

[3] *A New Theory of the Earth* (London, 1696).

[4] *Philosophical Principles of Religion: Natural and Revealed* (London, 1715). Hume's early letter to a physician, written in the spring of 1734, in which his health and progress in studies are described at length, is thought to have been intended for Dr. George Cheyne. See J. Y. T. Greig, *The Letters of David Hume*, i. 12 n., and Norman Kemp Smith, *The Philosophy of David Hume* 14–16.

[5] *An Account of Sir Isaac Newton's Philosophical Discoveries* (London, 1748; reprinted in facsimile by Johnson Reprint Corporation, New York and London, 1968). Maclaurin was appointed Professor of Mathematics at the University of Edinburgh, on Newton's recommendation, in 1725, when Hume was still a student there. I have cited this posthumous work of later date than the *Treatise*

Newton's science in the interests of theology. I doubt that Hume
had mathematics enough to read the *Principia*, if 'reading' includes
following the geometrical demonstrations. In order to restrict his
audience and diminish the opportunities for controversy, Newton
changed his mind about presenting the 'System of the World' in
'a popular method' and proceeded 'in the mathematical way'. He
warns even 'readers of good mathematical learning' against the
time-consuming effort of mastering all the propositions of the
preceding two books and specifies the sections which contain
indispensable principles. Locke found the geometry unmanageable
but accepted the derivative physics as a revelation of the universe.
Diderot objected to the abstruse mathematics as a veil placed
between the people and nature and directed students away from
the *Principia* to the *Opticks* which was, as I. B. Cohen has shown,
by far the more comprehensible and influential work in the
eighteenth century. Outside 'that small company of able mathematicians who', as Cohen has said, 'needed no intermediary
between themselves and Newton', intellectuals in Hume's day
learned Newtonian mechanics from such popularizers as Henry
Pemberton and Voltaire.

Kemp Smith's illuminating comparison of the discussion of
space and time in the *Treatise* with Pierre Bayle's *Dictionary*
article on Zeno of Elea[6] shows—although I do not think that this
was the intention—that Hume could have dealt with the controversy about the vacuum in the way that he did without ever
having read Newton or, for that matter, any of his followers.

Having shown that the Cartesian theory of motion in a plenum
was untenable, Newton faced a dilemma, since he also regarded
the supposition 'that one body may act upon another at a distance
through a vacuum without the mediation of anything else'[7] as
absurd. He could not escape with Zeno by concluding that motion

(of the year the first *Enquiry* was published, in fact) on the assumption that Hume
may have taken the opportunity of attending lectures delivered by the brilliant
mathematician and apparently popular exponent of Newton's natural philosophy.

[6] *The Philosophy of David Hume*, ch. xiv and apps. A and C, esp. app. A, S. 5,
pp. 307–17 and app. C, pp. 325–38.

[7] From the third of *Four Letters from Sir Isaac Newton to Doctor Bentley Containing
Some Arguments in Proof of a Deity* (London, 1756), pp. 25–6.

was impossible without demolishing the foundation of his mechanics. Nor was he prepared to evade the threat by the acataleptic move later proposed by Bayle of declaring motion to be incomprehensible. He therefore resolved his problem of accounting for action at a distance by the professedly speculative hypothesis of an ethereal medium. When Hume refers to this concept, and to the *vis inertiae* in a first *Enquiry* footnote[8]—his only mention of Newton in that book—he clearly and contentiously distinguishes between 'Sir Isaac Newton' and 'some of his followers'. Presumably his objection to the Newtonians, so briefly and elliptically expressed here, is that they exceeded the authority of their founder and the limits of sound empiricism by positing the Deity as the continuously operative efficient cause of motion. Although Hume may have been correct in the methodological point concerning experimental verification, he seems to have underestimated at this moment the distance that Newton

---

[8] To p. 73 (VII i): 'I need not examine at length the *vis inertiae* which is so much talked of in the new philosophy, and which is ascribed to matter. We find by experience, that a body at rest or in motion continues for ever in its present state, till put from it by some new cause; and that a body impelled takes as much motion from the impelling body as it acquires itself. These are facts. When we call this *vis inertiae*, we only mark these facts, without pretending to have any idea of the inert power; in the same manner as, when we talk of gravity, we mean certain effects, without comprehending that active power. It was never the meaning of Sir Isaac Newton to rob second causes of all force or energy; though some of his followers have endeavoured to establish that theory upon his authority. On the contrary, that great philosopher had recourse to an ethereal active fluid to explain his universal attraction; though he was so cautious and modest as to allow that it was a mere hypothesis, not to be insisted on, without more experiments. I must confess, that there is something in the fate of opinions a little extraordinary. Des Cartes insinuated that doctrine of the universal and sole efficacy of the Deity, without insisting on it. Malebranche and other Cartesians made it the foundation of all their philosophy. It had, however, no authority in England. Locke, Clarke, and Cudworth, never so much as take notice of it, but suppose all along, that matter has a real, though subordinate and derived power. By what means has it become so prevalent among our modern metaphysicians?'

The opening Section of the first *Enquiry* also contains a passage which clearly refers to Newton, although it does not name him: 'Astronomers had long contented themselves with proving, from the phaenomena, the true motions, order and magnitude of the heavenly bodies: Till a philosopher, at last, arose, who seems, from the happiest reasoning, to have also determined the laws and forces, by which the revolutions of the planets are governed and directed' ($E_1$ 14).

himself would depart from the canons of empirical science when impelled by the force of a theological notion.

There is also one mention of Newton in the second *Enquiry*, in the last line of Section III, Part iii. To warrant extending the utility principle from the artificial to the natural virtues, Hume appeals to the methodological principle of parsimony, which he had also adduced in the *Treatise*: 'It is entirely agreeable to the rules of philosophy, and even of common reason; where any principle has been found to have a great force and energy in one instance, to ascribe to it a like energy in all similar instances.' Then he adds, in his only published reference to Newton's text, 'This indeed is Newton's chief rule of philosophizing', and cites 'Principia, Lib. III' (E$_2$ 204; cf. T 282, 240).

I know of only three other direct references to Newton in the whole of Hume's published writing. The first occurs in an essay, 'Of the Rise and Progress of the Arts and Sciences', where the influence of political circumstances upon cultural achievement is discussed. To illustrate his thesis that a group of politically independent states provide a more salutary intellectual climate than a vast, centrally controlled empire such as the Roman, Hume asks, 'What checked the progress of the Cartesian philosophy, to which the French nation shewed such a strong propensity towards the end of the last century, but the opposition made to it by the other nations of Europe, who soon discovered the weak sides of that philosophy?' (G & G III 183). He then adds the exasperatingly non-committal observation: 'The severest scrutiny, which Newton's theory has undergone, proceeded not from his own countrymen, but from foreigners; and if it can overcome the obstacles, which it meets with at present in all parts of Europe, it will probably go down triumphant to the latest posterity.'

Hume's next comment on Newton is found toward the end of the concluding chapter of the final volume of *The History of England*. This is the passage which is so frequently cited as testimony to Hume's admiration for Newton and thus as indirect evidence of the scientist's positive influence upon Hume's philosophy:

In Newton this island may boast of having produced the greatest and rarest genius that ever rose for the ornament and instruction of the

species. Cautious in admitting no principles but such as were founded
in experiment; but resolute to adopt every such principle, however new
or unusual: from modesty, ignorant of his superiority above the rest
of mankind; and thence less careful to accommodate his reasonings to
common apprehensions: more anxious to merit than acquire fame: he
was, from these causes, long unknown to the world; but his reputation
at last broke out with a lustre which scarcely any writer, during his
own lifetime, had ever before attained. While Newton seemed to draw
off the veil from some of the mysteries of nature, he showed at the same
time the imperfections of the mechanical philosophy; and thereby
restored her ultimate secrets to that obscurity in which they ever did
and ever will remain. He died in 1727, aged 85. (H lxxi)

Undeniably, this is superlative praise, even from Hume, who was
often generous in bestowing compliments. But the philosophically
interesting sentence is the third one, and it seems to me enigmatic.
Why did Hume say that 'Newton *seemed* to draw off the veil from
*some* of the mysteries of nature . . .'? And did he wish to suggest
that Newton's showing of 'the imperfections of the mechanical
philosophy' was inadvertent or that it was planned? Certainly,
Newton was aware of the *limitations* of the mechanical philosophy
and eager to insist upon them in order to preserve a region for the
free ranging of theological speculation. The failure of mechanical
principles to explain certain natural phenomena left a residue of
problems to be resolved by natural religion. Newton did not
conclude, as did Hume in the first *Enquiry*, that questions 'concerning the origin of worlds . . . lie entirely beyond the reach of
human capacity' ($E_1$ 81),[9] but that the celestial harmony 'argues'
the first cause 'to be not blind and fortuitous' but intelligent,
indeed one 'very well skilled in mechanics and geometry'.[10] It is
always stressed that when Newton reached the limits of experimental verification in his scientific work, he admitted it. But no
one, I think, allows that he was as content as Hume with restoring
the ultimate secrets of nature to perpetual obscurity. His words
do not have the ring of one acquiescing in Hume's verdict that

---

[9] Cf. $E_1$ IV i, esp. pp. 30–1; VII i, esp. pp. 72–3; XII iii, esp. p. 162.
[10] First of *Four Letters from Sir Isaac Newton to Doctor Bentley* . . ., p. 8.

'These ultimate springs and principles are totally shut up from human curiosity and inquiry' ($E_1$ 30). On the contrary, it is his habit to admit only that the 'Causes' of principles recognized as ultimate by Hume ('Elasticity, gravity, cohesion of parts, communication of motion by impulse' ($E_1$ 30)) 'are not yet discover'd . . . and leave their Causes to be found out'.[11]

Regarding answers to ultimate questions, John Passmore remarks, 'Newton put such hypotheses aside regretfully, as not yet "deducible from the phenomena"; Hume rejects them outright.'[12] But Newton did not always leave them aside, as Passmore, of course, realized.[13] He pursued them in letters, in the Queries, and in the *General Scholium* to Book III of *Principia*, freely speculating on first and final causes. Allowing for the moment that Newton distinguished rigorously, even puritanically, between empirical and speculative doctrines, the question remains of how Hume assessed these theological performances against his own dictum that 'no philosopher who is rational and modest, has ever pretended to assign the ultimate cause of any natural operation' ($E_1$ 30). Regrettably, he has not told us in so many words. The paragraph on Newton in his *History* follows one on Robert Boyle, who, surprisingly, he exonerates 'from that boldnesss and temerity which had led astray so many philosophers' (H lxxi). Although Hume had just complimented Boyle and Newton as 'men who trod with cautious and therefore the more secure steps, the only road which leads to true philosophy', he speaks ironically, in fact contemptuously, 'of the mechanical philosophy; a theory which, by discovering some of the secrets of nature, and allowing us to imagine the rest, is so agreeable to the natural vanity and curiosity of men' (H lxxi).

The last mention of Newton in Hume's work is made by Cleanthes in Part I of *Dialogues Concerning Natural Religion*. He is answering Philo's objection that theological speculations are not to be trusted since they are 'very subtile and refined', going 'quite

---

[11] *Opticks*, 402.  [12] *Hume's Intentions*, 51.
[13] Ibid. 49–50: 'Newton never questions that there is an ultimately intelligible scheme of things, in the sense that if we only knew enough we should see why everything must be as i ι.s. That is why he never doubts that there is a "cause" of gravity.'

beyond the reach of our faculties', beyond 'common sense and experience'. He argues that Philo, like other sceptics, does not consistently enforce comparable restrictions upon natural science: 'In reality, would not a man be ridiculous, who pretended to reject NEWTON's explication of the wonderful phenomenon of the rainbow, because that explication gives a minute anatomy of the rays of light; a subject, forsooth, too refined for human comprehension?' (D 136). This question points candidly at the tight-rope which Hume had to walk in order to deliver the credentials for 'experimental reasoning' without supporting himself by any principle which might accredit 'theological reasonings'.

Hume's letters are even less helpful than his published work in estimating the extent and direction of Newtonian influence upon his philosophical development. In the 675 letters which have survived, amounting to almost 1,100 printed pages, Newton's name is mentioned only once. And that reference is casual, incidental, philosophically insignificant: commenting on his brother's marriage, he observes that women are the only heavenly bodies whose courses Newton was unable to predict (L I 159). During his sojourn in Paris in the sixties as Secretary to Lord Hertford, Ambassador to France, Hume often met d'Alembert, Buffon, and Diderot amongst others, and wrote home enthusiastically about them. Apart from mentioning the purchase of Buffon's *Histoire naturelle* (L II 82), his letters give no indication that he concerned himself with their scientific ideas. He refers to them as 'Men of Letters' and expresses his admiration of their manners, morals and conversation (e.g. L I 418). It does appear from a letter of 10 May 1762 to Benjamin Franklin (L I 357) that he presented a paper of Franklin's on 'preserving houses from thunder' to the Philosophical Society of Edinburgh, of which he was joint secretary. To the best of my knowledge, this was Hume's only personal involvement, tenuous though it was, in scientific research. And his interest in the experimentations of others seems to have been somewhat less than absorbing. In a letter of 1756 to John Clephane he wrote, 'I have seen (but, I thank God, was not bound to read) Dr. Birch's "History of the Royal Society"' (L I 231). Two years later, writing to his publisher, Andrew Millar, to ask for an introduction to Thomas Birch, Hume remarks, 'I have a great Esteem for his Character; have heard that he is very communicative, and is very willing, and even desirous, to give information to any Body that applies to him. Such an Acquaintance would be very useful and agreeable to me' (L I 273). It is plain from the context that the sort of information Hume was looking for was relevant to a new volume of his *History*, then in progress.[14] In his last illness, Hume was treated by Joseph Black, Professor of Medicine and of Chemistry at the University of Edinburgh. Despite his brilliant achievements as a scientist, favourably compared with Newton's in the *Opticks*,[15] he is mentioned by Hume only in the role of attending physician.

The failure to find in Hume's correspondence any evidence of a genuine, active interest in the work of 'experimental philosophers' is not, of course, compelling evidence for his indifference to natural science. For that matter, he never mentions Bacon nor Berkeley in his letters, nor Descartes nor Spinoza, nor Malebranche nor Leibniz, nor even John Gay nor David Hartley. But it would be rash to conclude that he took no interest in their work. None the less, a reading of Hume's letters does something to fix his interests in perspective. It suggests to me that after his early, reclusive, system-building period, history, politics, and religion gained priority, literature a secure but secondary place, that moral considerations coloured all his interests, and that natural philosophy shifted quickly to the periphery.[16]

[14] See Letter 145 to Andrew Millar, 4 Mar. 1758 (L I 272).

[15] In 'Joseph Black and Fixed Air', *Isis*, 48, 1957, 125, Henry Guerlac refers to Black's *Experiments upon Magnesia Alba, Quicklime and some other Alcaline Substances* as this 'brilliant model, perhaps the first successful model, of quantitative chemical investigation . . . a classic exemplar of experimental science worthy of comparison with Newton's *Opticks*'. (Quoted in D. L. Hurd and J. J. Kipling, *The Origins and Growth of Physical Science* (Penguin, Harmondsworth, 1964), Vol. 1, p. 264.)

[16] It is true that in June 1755 Hume offered his publisher *Some Considerations previous to Geometry and Natural Philosophy* along with three other 'short Dissertations'. (See Letter 111 to Andrew Millar, 12 June 1755 (L I 222).) Shortly afterward he was persuaded by his friend, Lord Stanhope, that his treatment of the metaphysical principles of Geometry was unsatisfactory and he withdrew the work. (See Letter 465 to William Strahan, 25 Jan. 1772, L II 252, where Hume recalls the decision but forgets whether Philip Stanhope objected to 'some

The claim that Hume's philosophical development was profoundly affected by the Newtonian method is as probable as any assertion of an unacknowledged influence can be. Whether the influence came directly from a first-hand study of Newton's work, or indirectly from Maclaurin's lectures at Edinburgh, or through the writings of other disciples of Newton, its presence is unmistakable. It could hardly have been otherwise; for Hume began to write when Newtonian science was being celebrated as the greatest intellectual achievement of modern times. Inevitably, certain methodological differences between the natural and the moral philosopher appeared when the method of physical science was adapted to mental, moral, and social phenomena. But the 'experimental method of reasoning' which Hume aimed to introduce into moral subjects was essentially the Newtonian method. It has often been remarked that the attraction of the Newtonian method was a force determining Hume's course from the start. But there was also a counter-force whose effects have been much less carefully observed until recently.

Newtonianism, as we have seen, was not limited to a set of verifiable theories about physical phenomena. The mechanical philosophy was esteemed by Newton himself as well as by his followers as much—or even more, it seems at times—for its theological implications as for its intrinsic scientific value. Despite Newton's distinction between experimentally confirmed laws and speculative hypotheses, he sometimes phrased his metaphysical conjectures as logically coercive because they had been deduced from the phenomena. His pride in his work and the admiration of his followers were immensely deepened by the conviction that his scientific discoveries strengthened the rational foundations of religious belief. The undermining of these foundations is the principal effect of Hume's sceptical examination of the pretensions of metaphysics. If any facet of Hume's philosophy is as plain to see as the positive influence of Newtonian method, it is the condemnation of such theological speculation as the Newtonians

Defect in the Argument or in its perspicuity'.) So far as I have been able to determine, this unpublished paper has been lost, and Hume never returned to the philosophical problems inherent in mathematics and natural science.

indulged in. Hume never, of course, counters a dogma by dogmatic contradiction. He always argues that reaching the desired conclusion requires violating a principle of method vital to the very science from which the theologian borrows prestige. Thus Hume's relations with Newtonianism were too complex and equivocal to be adequately expressed by calling him the Newton of the moral sciences. That formula states a half-truth which needs to be supplemented by stressing his extreme aversion to the theological developments of the Newtonian synthesis which were so fashionable in his day.

The positive influence of Newtonianism is most apparent in the *Treatise*. Even in that first work, particularly in the final Part of Book I, conclusions antithetical to the natural religion sponsored by the Newtonians are forcefully drawn. Other sceptical indiscretions were removed in order to avoid offending Bishop Butler, whose opinion of the manuscript Hume hoped to solicit before publication.[17] None the less, Hume's confidence in the methods of empirical science, and his ambition to discover a set of principles to explain the inner world comparable to Newton's system of the external world, are revealed in the early pages. As we have seen, Hume's youthful ambition faded; even in the *Treatise* his constructive designs were constantly threatened by his critical impulses, and later the system was set aside, disowned, in fact, when Hume's analytical tendencies became independent. It seems to me unlikely that this strengthening of the destructive side of Hume's intellectual character was unrelated to his awareness of the theological constructions being raised on the foundations of the mechanical philosophy. I would conjecture that after Hume had written his first book—indeed, even before he had finished it—he became increasingly concerned with checking the speculative excesses of the Newtonians. It is no conjecture, but a fact that confronts anyone who reviews his philosophical books in

[17] Hume called on Joseph Butler with a letter of introduction from Henry Home (Lord Kames), but found that he was staying in the country. Shortly afterward, Butler was made Bishop of Bristol, and Hume, feeling diffident about presenting himself to one who 'had arrived at that dignity', contented himself with sending the first volume (Books I and II) as soon as it was printed. (See Letters 7 and 8 to Henry Home, 4 Mar. 1737/8 and 13 Feb. 1739 (L I 25–7).)

order, that Hume became increasingly hostile toward religion, ever more determined to show that the doctrines of natural religion most cherished by the Newtonians are located beyond the limits of attainable knowledge: 'But here experience is, and must be entirely silent' ($E_1$ 153).

The mature Hume was not, I think, the sort of man to become obsessed with ideas or intellectual problems. But *The History of Natural Religion* and two essays which were suppressed, under threats of prosecution by Warburton,[18] 'On Suicide' and 'On the Immortality of the Soul', testify to his increasing preoccupation with religious questions. A full quarter of his first *Enquiry* is exclusively concerned with them, in addition to incidental sallies against the Occasionalists and the followers of Newton ('our modern metaphysicians') for positing the Supreme Being as the ultimate source of power or energy. The depth and persistence of Hume's interest in the Argument from Design, which Newton's scientific discoveries were appropriated to support, can be measured by his *Dialogues Concerning Natural Religion*, which were given their final revision in the year of his death, a quarter of a century after he first composed them. The Argument from Design was the logical nerve-centre of the natural religion flourishing in Hume's day. If the inference upon which it was based was valid, and the implications drawn from it warranted, then Hume would have to admit to being very short-sighted in drawing the limits of human knowledge where he did. Since he had fixed these limits as entailments of empiricism, he had either to show that the theological adventures of the Newtonians violated the methodological principles so puritanically insisted upon within Newtonian science or withdraw from his basic philosophical position. Thus an appreciation of Hume's response to the religious aspect of the Newtonian movement is as important for understanding his mature philosophy as recognizing the

---

[18] See E. C. Mossner, 'Hume's *Four Dissertations*: An Essay in Biography and Bibliography', *Modern Philology* 47 (1950), 37–57, and Richard Wollheim, ed., *Hume on Religion* (Fontana, Collins, London and Glasgow, 1963, which includes these two essays), esp. Introduction, 11–12, and T. H. Grose, 'History of the Editions', *David Hume The Philosophical Works*, edd. T. H. Green and T. H. Grose (London, 1882), iii. 67–72.

impact of the Newtonian method for understanding his first work. Robert Hurlbutt has recently examined that response in his book, *Hume, Newton, And The Design Argument*.[19] Coming after A. E. Taylor's distorted version of Hume's attitude toward Newton, science, and the Royal Society,[20] and after John Randall's unscrupulous and irresponsible fabrication about it,[21] Hurlbutt's sensible treatment of this moment of intellectual history is welcome.

I suspect that Hurlbutt began with a bolder and simpler thesis than he found himself able to sustain as his research progressed. Without wishing to imply any criticism, I would conjecture that he had hoped to show that Hume's sniping at natural religion, particularly at the Design Argument, was aimed directly at Isaac Newton. Hume's preference for dealing with positions in a general way, rather than with the arguments of individuals, created a difficulty which was aggravated by his evident intention

[19] University of Nebraska Press, Lincoln, 1965.

[20] *Philosophical Studies* (Macmillan, London, 1934), ch. ix, 'David Hume and the Miraculous': 'We miss half of Hume's irony unless we understand that it is meant to hit not only "dangerous friends or disguised enemies to the Christian religion", but also "dangerous friends or disguised enemies" to Newtonian science. I trust that I need not say that I do not myself regard amused detached contemplation of either Christianity or natural science as a right attitude in a rational man. But it is an attitude very characteristic of the century of so-called "good sense", and none the less likely to be the secret attitude of David Hume...' (p. 333). For Antony Flew's reply to Taylor's criticism of Hume's essay 'Of Miracles' ($E_1$ X), see 'Hume's Check', *Philosophical Quarterly* 9, no. 34 (Jan. 1959), 1–18, and *Hume's Philosophy of Belief*, ch. viii.

[21] 'David Hume: Radical Empiricist and Pragmatist', in *Freedom and Experience*, edd. Sidney Hook and Milton R. Konvitz (Cornell University Press, Ithaca and New York, 1947), 293: 'Hume wrote for two purposes: to make money, and to gain a literary reputation. He acknowledged, "My ruling passion is the love of literary fame." As a youth he studied Locke and Berkeley, and Cicero and the ancient Academic skeptics; in their thought he saw the chance to reach startling conclusions and become a shocking success. Berkeley had attacked Newtonian science for serious reasons; he was a crusader, interested in a sound and consistent science. Hume subtly criticized it primarily to attract attention to the Scotsman David Hume. He hated Newton and Locke as Englishmen, besides; for next to priests Englishmen were his most cordial hatred.' Randall was well answered by E. C. Mossner in 'Philosophy and Biography: The Case of David Hume', *Philosophical Review* 59 (1950), reprinted in V. C. Chappell, ed. *Hume, Modern Studies in Philosophy* (Doubleday Anchor, New York, 1966).

on one occasion already noted to protect Newton against the excesses of enthusiastic followers. Hurlbutt's assessment of the importance of Newtonian theism as 'the first concerted attempt to square modern experimental science with Christianity'[22] is sound, and there is a sense in which his central thesis that Hume's 'attack was aimed primarily at the Newtonian attempt to bring about a rapprochement between science and religion'[23] is defensible. The term 'Newtonian' symbolizes the ambiguities which I imagine Hurlbutt running up against while reconstructing the intellectual scene viewed by Hume. As with Christianity and Marxism, it is a little difficult to say whether or not the founder of this movement should be considered a member and, what is more to the point, whether Hume regarded Newton as a Newtonian.

While insisting as a scientist upon limits to inquiry later endorsed by Hume, Newton not only condoned and apparently encouraged others in exceeding them, but was himself lured by 'sublime topics' into that fairyland which lies on the far side of human experience. Such aberrant performances must have dismayed Hume who valued the experimental method as much for the crippling restrictions that it imposed upon theologians as for the control and direction that it gave to scientists. He may have been reassured by Newton's official commitment (not always honoured) to distinguish sharply between the verifiable laws of empirical science and the speculative hypotheses and queries of natural religion. Perhaps for that reason he did not publish a single word to reprove Newton, but many to praise him, reserving his censure for 'some of his followers'. And when Hurlbutt looks for the originals of the theological doctrines reformulated and assailed by Hume, he finds them not in the pages of Newton but in those of the Newtonians, in Cheyne's, for example, and especially in Maclaurin's. Since 'On the whole, however,' as Hurlbutt says, 'Newton's followers adhered to his methodological and theological convictions', the question of whether Hume was mainly preoccupied with the leader's defections or with the followers' misappropriation of scientific credit is academic rather

---

[22] *Hume, Newton, And The Design Argument*, p. xii.          [23] Ibid.

than philosophical, more a matter of biography than of logic. The central issue which Hurlbutt has clarified is methodological, involving the right to use scientific discoveries as premisses in theological arguments and to extend the methods of natural science into the region of natural religion.

## Section 2. *Rules of Reasoning*

It will be remembered that Newton set out the 'Rules of Reasoning in Philosophy' at the head of his 'System of the World', the third Book of *Principia*. Hume lays down his 'Rules by which to judge of causes and effects' (T 173), just before beginning to treat 'Of the Sceptical and Other Systems of Philosophy'—the subject of Book I Part iv of the *Treatise*. It may seem surprising that the two sets of Rules are quite compatible, for their authors' interests in systems are totally different. Newton is concerned with the physical universe, with the world experienced by men who observe the heavens from the planet, Earth. The purpose of his system is to establish the principles by which celestial bodies move in harmony. Hume is not concerned with the world that is experienced but with the experience of the world and with philosophical systems devised to explain that experience. The purpose of his system is to show that the natural principles of the understanding are independent of the rational (or rationalizing) principles that would fortify them, and resistant to the sceptical principles that would destroy them. Newton's purpose is to construct a conceptual model of the physical universe, Hume's to undermine philosophical conceptions of the physical world. However, in Book II—'that most Newtonian section of the *Treatise*',[24] as Passmore calls it—Hume conducts an 'experimental' investigation 'Of the Passions'. And there the constructive side of Hume's philosophy is in ascendance, and his Rules are applied positively to the elaboration of psychological theory.

Both sets of Rules presuppose that the first object of science is to discover causal connections and the second to generalize about

[24] *Hume's Intentions*, 45.

such relations as appear to be universal. Newton explained certain
physical phenomena, notably planetary motion, as the effects of
universal gravitation; Hume explained certain mental phenomena,
notably belief, as the effects of association, gravity and association
being construed as analogous forms of attraction. Newton's first
two Rules are explicitly concerned with causation; Rule I formulates the principle of parsimony which is endorsed by Hume's
Rule 4. Hume states eight Rules, double the number on Newton's
list. The first three state the defining features of causal connection
elicited by Hume's previous analysis: spatial and temporal contiguity, the priority of the cause, constant conjunction. The
remainder, as John Passmore[25] has observed, anticipate John
Stuart Mill's 'Uniformity of Nature' and 'Canons of Induction'.
The fourth ('The same cause always produces the same effect, and
the same effect never arises but from the same cause'), characterized by Hume as 'Newton's chief rule of philosophizing', is
said to be derived from experience, and the others follow as
corollaries. The fifth Rule states that if different objects produce
the same effect, they must share a common quality which is the
causal agent;[26] the sixth that different effects produced by similar
objects must be attributed to some point of difference between the
causal objects; the seventh that from variations in the intensity of
an effect concomitant with similar variations in the cause, it may
be inferred that the composite effect is proportionate to the
number of causal factors operating; the eighth that if a given
object exists for a certain time without producing an effect, it
cannot be the sole cause of that effect. Hume concludes with some
remarks in the Newtonian spirit upon the difficulty and importance of devising experiments to exclude extraneous factors.

Newton formulated his Rules in a prescriptive manner, telling
us what we were to admit, to assign, to esteem, and how we were
to look upon empirical propositions. Certain ontological and
epistemological presuppositions lay behind his recommendations:
the simplicity and uniformity of nature and the reliability of

[25] *Hume's Intentions*, 52.
[26] Cf. *Treatise*, Bk. II, Pt. i, S. 3, pp. 281–2, where Hume amplifies his statement
of this Rule and applies it to his own psychological theory.

sensory evidence. An intensive examination of these presuppositions would have been out of place in a scientific treatise. In the
context of the *Principia*, it was quite proper to specify as Rules
the working methodological presuppositions of experimental
philosophy. They simply state the terms upon which the agreed
objectives of scientists can be achieved. As Cotes appropriately
argued in his Preface, if critics of the theory of universal gravitation reject the principle of analogical argument established by
Newton's first three Rules, then by implication they reject all
generalization and thereby all science. But in the first Book of the
*Treatise* Hume puts himself in quite a different and much more
precarious position by undertaking a critical analysis of the
metaphysical presuppositions of experimental philosophy.

'According to the precedent doctrine . . .', he begins by remind-
ing us, 'any thing may produce any thing' (T 173). Also, he has
concluded that the essence of causal necessity is 'that propensity,
which custom produces, to pass from an object to the idea of its
usual attendant' (T 165). Despite this unpromising background,
he hopes 'to fix some general rules' by which to determine actual
causal connections. Having stated the defining features of causation
in the first three Rules, in the fourth he affirms the principle of the
uniformity of nature, claiming to derive it from experience. But
he had shown earlier that this principle is neither demonstrable nor
the conclusion of a probable inference (T 89–90). It is a natural
principle of the understanding implicit in the habit of generalizing,
a psychological principle discernibly at work in mental operations
and explicable in terms of associative processes. Does it make
sense to present as a rule of causal inference what is no more than
a habit deeply engrained by the shuttling of the associative
mechanism? If there is merely empirical evidence that the
principle does in fact operate, but no rational justification for
trusting its tendencies, it is surely flattery to call it a Rule. Unless,
of course, Hume intends to elevate this descriptive, psychological
principle into a normative, logical rule. And certainly he does
hope to give his Rules the standing of rational precepts. By them
he hopes to regulate the judgement and so avoid the errors into
which the imagination blunders through its wayward habits of

association. In an earlier Section of Book I, Part iii (13), he advertised the present one by announcing that 'We shall afterwards take notice of some general rules, by which we ought to regulate our judgement concerning causes and effects; and these rules are form'd on the nature of our understanding, and on our experience of its operations in the judgements we form concerning objects' (T 149). How can Hume justify deriving this methodological 'ought' from a psychological 'is'?

From Hume's naturalistic viewpoint, scientific method represents a refinement of principles by which intelligence works in everyday life: 'philosophical decisions are nothing but the reflections of common life, methodized and corrected', as he says in the first *Enquiry* (E$_1$ 162). The natural principles of the understanding must serve as the norm by which to regulate experimental philosophy, for there could be no other which would not be perfectly arbitrary. Hume's conception of principles of causal inference being both natural and normative cannot be criticized as a faulty assumption—a factual error or a logical confusion; it is not an assumption at all, but a thesis, indeed the main thesis of his total philosophical programme. His formulation of a set of 'Rules by which to judge of causes and effects' which simply codify what is ordinarily meant by 'causality' and sanctify the principles of inference tacitly followed by cogent thinkers is the expected outcome of having founded all the sciences upon the science of human nature. Given this approach, such a piece of legislation needs no defence; 'and perhaps', he says, 'even this [Logic] was not very necessary, but might have been supply'd by the natural principles of our understanding' (T 175). It is the departures made from normal procedures that need defending, but which, in Hume's opinion, are not likely to get it.

Hume's position is obviously vulnerable. His Rules are drawn from the observed practice of the wise, whose judgements issue from 'the more general and authentic operations of the understanding' (T 150). How has Hume been able to distinguish the wise from the vulgar, whose mental habits are 'of an irregular nature, and destructive of all the most established principles of reasoning' (ibid.)? The wise are those who conscientiously follow general rules which are 'extensive and constant'; the thinking of the vulgar is 'capricious and uncertain'. Wisdom consists in fidelity to Hume's Rules, which are sanctioned by the authority of the wise. 'Clearly this is question-begging;' John Passmore insists, 'it assumes that we already know who "the wise" are, although it is precisely the point at issue whether there is such a thing as superior wisdom.'[27] To defend Hume against such a devastating objection is to risk being unfrocked for logical heresy. None the less, I shall venture an argument or two in his favour.

First, it seems to me that the tight circle in which Hume is said to revolve is an illusory one created by the false expectation that first principles can be given ultimate, rational justifications. It would have been inconsistent with Hume's professed reliance upon experience to attempt to establish principles *a priori*; consequently, he attends to his own mental acts and habits and dissects the procedures of natural science in order to observe the principles embedded there. Every methodologist must choose between laying down rules in a perfectly arbitrary way and attempting to elicit them from a study of methods in use. If he takes the first way, there will be no question at all of justifying his prescriptions. If he chooses the alternative, he must discriminate by common sense or intuition between good and bad practices. Independently of any theory, it would be common sense to discount the testimony of witnesses known to have a powerful motive to lie who report without corroborating evidence events which violate well-established laws of nature. And it would be common sense to denounce a purported method of prognostication which was rarely correct in its predictions. The methodologist would intuitively reject an explanation which cited an event as the efficient cause of a prior one. And he would intuit the error in affirming causal connections between events that were only occasionally conjoined. Although there is a prima facie correctness about such verdicts, there seems to be no way to prove the implicit principles upon which they are based. How could the principle, 'The cause must be prior to the effect', be *established*? It endorses a connotation of the word 'cause' as ordinarily used, and

27 *Hume's Intentions*, 60.

implies that judgements presupposing a contradictory sense represent some sort of mental confusion. I do not see how one could defend the proposition that an object existing for some time without producing an effect cannot be the sole cause of that effect, except by saying that a working conception of causality could not be retained if objects were admitted as the causes of effects they failed to produce.

What all this really amounts to saying is that methodologies are preceded by methods, theories by practice. To study methods in use, to distinguish those that accomplish a given purpose from those that defeat it, and then to state explicitly the rules or principles followed in the successful procedures seems to me a tenable approach for a methodologist to take. The approach would be viciously circular (or perfectly tautologous) if the only test for the success of a method were its adherence to the rules or principles which constituted it. For then every method would be equally sound basically, and practitioners would come to grief only through incidental violations of their adopted principles. But the realities of the situation are neither so convenient for the scientist nor so hopeless for the methodologist. For there are external tests, having to do with the verification, predictive value, and confirmation of the theories produced by a method, to which a given set of rules can be subjected.

Causality is both a natural and a philosophical relation. 'Thus tho' causation be a *philosophical* relation . . .', Hume explains, 'yet 'tis only so far as it is a *natural* relation, and produces a union among our ideas, that we are able to reason upon it, or draw any inference from it' (T 94). Paradoxically, habits of association which provide the natural basis for causal judgement also supply 'the principles, which are changeable, weak, and irregular . . . observed only to take place in weak minds' (T 225). Thus Hume admits 'that tho' custom be the foundation of all our judgements, yet sometimes it has an effect on the imagination in opposition to the judgement' (T 147–8). He has already explained that 'all kinds of reasoning from causes or effects are founded on two particulars, viz. the constant conjunction of any two objects in all past experience, and the resemblance of a present object to any one of them' (T 142). Just as a dog is conditioned to anticipate a blow upon observing a familiar threatening gesture, so a man observing one object or event expects another which has invariably followed it. It is an ultimately inexplicable fact of nature that ideas of successive, contiguous objects or events constantly conjoined in experience become associated in the imagination and a causal connection between them consequently presumed. In theoretical disciplines, analogous connections are traced between things which would not be associated in the imagination in the ordinary course of experience. The scientific or philosophical application of the causal principle requires tracing causal connections between events which are too remote in time or place to have become associated, and eliminating accidentally associated factors which are not essential to produce the effect. Habit and custom cease to be helpful here; in fact they become hindrances, impervious to causal sequences outside the run of everyday experience, little affected by negative instances, and influenced by irrelevant resemblances. They must be superseded by experimental investigations in which variables are controlled and inferences regulated by 'principles which are permanent, irresistible, and universal' (T 225).

Although the conflict between judgement and imagination is resolvable on Hume's doctrine, he cannot resist the rhetoric of paradox. The imagination, he tells us, is led astray by '*general rules*', by which he means such rash generalizations as 'An *Irishman* cannot have wit, and a *Frenchman* cannot have solidity' (T 146), and also that as a general rule the same effects will be expected of superficially similar causes. Such 'PREJUDICE' and groundless predictions can be corrected by invoking another sort of general rules, Hume's 'Rules by which to judge of causes and effects', in short. 'Thus our general rules are in a manner set in opposition to each other', he says, and foresees the sceptics' pleasure 'of observing a new and signal contradiction in our reason, and of seeing all philosophy ready to be subverted by a principle of human nature, and again sav'd by a new direction of the very same principle' (T 150). But the subverting and the saving principle are not 'the very same principle' at all; the former underlies the natural tendencies of an uncritical imagination, the latter a conscious effort to avoid the errors of unreflective associating. The distinction between the two might be expressed in Wittgenstein's terms as one between determined and rule-directed behaviour, and can be illustrated by the following example.

If a man observed (or at least heard about) the deterioration of numerous marriages of which one or both partners were addicted to alcohol, it would be natural for him to suppose that there was a causal connection between intemperance and domestic infelicity. Alcohol and domestic strife would become associated in his mind, and it would not be surprising if he took hard drinking to be the cause of bitter quarrelling. A scientific investigation of the subject, on the contrary, might reveal that in some cases alcoholism was the effect rather than the cause of domestic trauma. A sociologist would study case histories in order to determine priorities. He would also take into account cases of marital conflict between teetotallers and of marital bliss enjoyed by pairs of dipsomaniacs. The understanding of this social phenomenon which may emerge from his analysis of 'the complication of circumstances', to use Hume's phrase, will be expressed in a judgement of the cause–effect relationship between the use of alcohol and the character of marriages. Such a judgement is distinguished by the method it presupposes from a natural association in the imagination between causally experienced factors.

I think that this simple example expresses concretely what Hume intended by distinguishing between 'wise men' and 'the vulgar'. And I think that it also suggests the unfairness of John Passmore's verdict on Hume's inductive logic: 'In the end, then, psychology triumphs. Empirical reasoning fades away; it is found to be nothing more than the habitual procedure of those persons we choose to dignify as "the wise" or "the philosophical". The logical problem—how can empirical reasoning be justified?—vanishes as unanswerable.'[28] There is no doubt that psychology triumphs in the beginning, when Hume is investigating causality as a natural relation, as a principle of association on which the imagination habitually works. And certainly he claims that

[28] *Hume's Intentions*, 60.

causality as a philosophical relation, and therefore scientific method itself, presupposes the mutually attractive force of successive, contiguous, constantly conjoined ideas. However, re-flection on some of the conclusions reached through association shows the need of regulating the imagination's habits which tend to be 'irregular', 'capricious and uncertain'. Speaking of the imagination's susceptibility to 'superfluous circumstances', Hume says that 'We may correct this propensity by a reflection on the nature of those circumstances' (T 148).

The Rules evolved by such reflection are not arbitrary. They come of efforts to make principles of association self-consistent and conformable to their biological end of adapting expectation and response to past experience. It is natural to expect the kettle to boil after being put on the fire, but to err is human, and it is equally natural, apparently, to trust the rod to reform the child, however often this promise goes unfulfilled. In everyday life explanation and prediction tacitly assume that one event cannot be the cause of another which occurs in its absence, or which often fails to produce that effect. Until such assumptions have been articulated as principles they have no steady influence in disciplin-ing judgements. By stating his Rules, Hume does not answer merely the question imposed upon him by Passmore: 'What are the psychological peculiarities of the man who thinks scientific-ally—i.e. in the manner we choose to call scientific although such thinking has no formal peculiarities—as distinct from him we call superstitious?'[29] The formal peculiarities of scientific thinking are the features of natural processes of association reflected upon, corrected, and refined in order to avoid the slipshod conclusions of an undisciplined imagination.

Comparison of Hume's Rules with Newton's shows that they agree that the aim and method of science is the discovery of causes by experimental investigation. After exploring a little further, it becomes apparent that the two men differ implicitly about the grounds of that method. On Newton's view the method presupposes the simplicity and constancy of a natural world rationally designed by a Being 'well skilled in mechanicks and

[29] Ibid. 60-1.

geometry'. The universe is intrinsically rational and therefore potentially intelligible. On Hume's view, the method presupposes certain natural principles by which intelligence works to ensure adjustment to the environment. Although one may hope that the method is ratified by some 'kind of preestablished harmony between the course of nature and the succession of our ideas', there never can be any guarantee of that, since 'the powers and forces, by which the former [nature] is governed, be wholly unknown to us' (E₁ 44).

Such differing metaphysical opinions have no bearing on scientific practice. However, they do fix the prospective limits of human knowledge at different points. Perfect comprehension of a supremely intelligent creator's world is not envisioned even in Newton's optimistic view. But no definite limits are in sight, and Newton did encourage advancing 'from Phaenomena and Experiments in the Causes thereof, and hence to the Causes of those Causes, and so on till we come to the first Cause . . .'. On Hume's more penetrating view, the limits set by the very principles which make knowledge possible are plainly marked:

> It is confessed, that the utmost effort of human reason is to reduce the principles, productive of natural phenomena, to a greater simplicity, and to resolve the many particular effects into a few general causes, by means of reasonings from analogy, experience, and observation. But as to the causes of these general causes, we should in vain attempt their discovery. . . . These ultimate springs and principles are totally shut up from human curiosity and enquiry. (E₁ 26)

## Section 3. *Hypotheses*

Hume endorses Newton's strictures upon hypotheses. In the *Abstract*, he describes himself as one who 'talks' in the *Treatise* 'with contempt of hypotheses' (A 6). Like the other modern moral philosophers whom he admires, he proscribed hypotheses upon realizing that they are irreconcilable with an empirical science of human nature. He emulates even Newton's inconsistency by advancing hypotheses in the very book from which they are said to have been banished. He refers to his 'general position, that an opinion or belief is *nothing but a strong and lively idea deriv'd from a present impression related to it*' (T 105) as a 'new hypothesis' (T 107). He reiterates 'that all belief arises from the association of ideas, according to my hypothesis' (T 112) and shortly after explains how 'The present hypothesis will receive additional confirmation . . .' (T 115). Finally, he specifies the terms upon which he would admit that an alternative 'hypothesis' explained belief (T 178). His analogous explanation of pride and humility in terms of association is also frankly presented as a 'hypothesis' (T 289–90). His explanation of the love of fame on the basis of the sympathy principle is acknowledged to be a 'hypothesis' (T 324). And so is his claim for the egocentric and hedonistic basis of pride and humility and other passions (T 324, 325, 328). Numerous other examples can be found on the pages of the *Treatise* where the reader will meet the expression, 'according to my hypothesis', again and again (e.g. T 362, 387).

The discrepancy between a proclamation against hypotheses and a plentiful use of them is to be explained in Hume's case as it was in Newton's. Hume, like Newton, neglects to distinguish in so many words between groundless speculative hypotheses and verifiable working hypotheses. The distinction is, however, implicit in his usage. The 'most extravagant hypothesis' (T xvii) which has only the eloquence of its presentation to recommend it, 'any hypothesis, that pretends to discover the ultimate original qualities of human nature' are instances of unacceptable hypotheses mentioned in the Introduction to the *Treatise* as those which 'ought at first to be rejected as presumptuous and chimerical' (T xxi). When thus used pejoratively, 'hypotheses' is synonymous with 'conjectures' (T xxii) and in the first *Enquiry* with 'mere conjecture' ($E_1$ 145). When Hume later makes use of hypotheses in an acceptable form, 'hypothesis' is used interchangeably with 'principle' or 'general principle', 'doctrine', and, occasionally, a group of them with 'system'. Such hypotheses are distinguished from the discreditable type by their potential verifiability. In the fifth of Hume's set of 'Experiments to confirm this system' (T 337–8), for example, Hume considers what emotions will be

felt by a man who is shown a close relative or an intimate friend in
either a flattering or an unfavourable light. 'Before we consider
what they are in fact,' he proposes, 'let us determine what they
ought to be, conformable to my hypothesis' (T 337). Deducing
from his hypothesis that either pride or humility should result, he
then consults experience with gratifying results: 'This exact conformity of experience to our reasoning is a convincing proof of
the solidity of that hypothesis, upon which we reason' (T 338).

Whatever one may think of Hume's performance as an experimenter after comparing his *thought* 'Experiments' in Book II of
the *Treatise* with, say, Newton's first reported experiments on
light and colours, one must recognize that the two men agreed in
principle that admissible hypotheses ('principles', 'general conclusions', 'propositions collected by general induction from
phaenomena', or whatever else they may be called from time to
time) must be empirically testable—confirmed by observation,
facilitated, if necessary, by experiment. The fatal flaw in 'all
*hypothetical* arguments', Hume says of the inadmissible sort, is that
they lack 'the authority either of the memory or senses' and so are
'without foundation'. At some point, causal inferences must be
tied to 'some object, which we see or remember' (T 83).

Both Newton and Hume stress the distinction between empirically confirmed principles and theoretical explanations of them
which take the form of hypotheses in the conjectural sense. It will
be remembered that Newton insisted that his experimentally
established conclusions about the composition of white light were
independent of any hypothesis suggested to explain those properties. Similarly, he presented his theory of universal attraction
as empirically established; mathematically deduced gravitational
effects were observed to be manifestly present in phenomena. His
speculations about the cause of gravity, on the other hand, were
professedly hypothetical and 'not to be further insisted upon' until
experiments were forthcoming to determine the laws by which it
operates. Hume practised the same doctrine and preached an even
purer one:

Here [in the association of ideas] is a kind of ATTRACTION, which in
the mental world will be found to have as extraordinary effects as in

the natural. . . . Its effects are every where conspicuous; but as to its causes, they are mostly unknown, and must be resolv'd into *original* qualities of human nature, which I pretend not to explain. Nothing is more requisite for a true philosopher, than to restrain the intemperate desire of searching into causes, and having establish'd any doctrine upon a sufficient number of experiments, rest contented with that, when he sees a farther examination would lead him into obscure and uncertain speculations. In that case his enquiry wou'd be much better employ'd in examining the effects than the causes of his principle. (T12–13)

Although Hume did not always show such perfect restraint, he did uphold the Newtonian precept that confidence in empirically grounded results should not be shaken by doubts about hypotheses suggested to explain them. The observations which, for example, 'establish it as a general maxim in this science of human nature, that wherever there is a close relation betwixt two ideas, the mind is very apt to mistake them, and in all its discourses and reasonings to use the one for the other' are coercive despite any failings to explain this fact causally:

The phaenomenon may be real, tho' my explication be chimerical. The falshood of the one is no consequence of that of the other; tho' at the same time we may observe, that 'tis very natural for us to draw such a consequence; which is an evident instance of that very principle, which I endeavour to explain. (T 60)

Accordingly, in another place he insists that whether or not his explanation of the mind's 'much stronger propensity to pride than to humility' is accepted, 'the phaenomenon is undisputed' (T 390). And after he had lost confidence in the psychological theory by which he had explained sympathy in the *Treatise*, he continued to insist upon the manifest reality of sympathy and its validity as a principle—by then an 'ultimate' or 'original' principle—by which to explain moral phenomena:

It is needless to push our researches so far as to ask, why we have humanity or a fellow-feeling with others. It is sufficient, that this is experienced to be a principle in human nature. We must stop somewhere in our examination of causes; and there are, in every science, some general principles, beyond which we cannot hope to find any principle more general . . . and we may here safely consider these principles as original: happy, if we can render all the consequences sufficiently plain and perspicuous. ($E_2$ 219 n)[30]

If this comparison of positions on the central issue of hypotheses does not yield overwhelming evidence of Newtonian influence on Hume's methodology, it tends at least to encourage the official view. The two positions do not, however, coincide perfectly. And if they did, it would be even more difficult to account for Hume's sudden divergence from Newton's teaching upon reaching the frontier dividing natural science from natural religion. The whole weight of Hume's philosophy is set against Newton's claim that to discourse of God 'from phenomena, belongs to experimental philosophy'. Their opposition involves a crucial point of disagreement about hypotheses which the shifting unsettled sense of the term 'hypothesis' makes difficult to document. Newton's first misgivings about the term hardened into such antipathy that even when he used hypotheses he called them by another name. After Hume's initial (and rather conventional) veto on hypotheses, his aversion languished as the empirical sense of the term crystallized. Although he persisted in using the word in a pejorative sense as a polemical device,[31] he was prepared to call even such a cherished doctrine as his utility principle a 'hypothesis' ($E_2$ 285, 289). The verbal surfaces of Newton's writing and of Hume's are disturbed by the presence of a key term whose meaning is evolving. None the less, it should be possible to catch the meanings they intended. Excessive literal-mindedness will not help to fix that point of difference about hypotheses that yielded their conflicting verdicts on the limits of human knowledge.

Newton had freely admitted that he was unable to ascertain the causes of certain qualities and forces whose presence and operation were manifest in the phenomena. Those causes might be called occult, but not the qualities and forces themselves whose deducible effects were empirically verifiable. Hypotheses were permissible so long as their speculative status was acknowledged and not confused with proven results; they were to be understood as suspicions, conjectures, or hints, and were best expressed as questions

---

[30] Cf. $E_2$ app. ii 298.
[31] e.g. throughout $E_1$ XI.

for probing at theoretical possibilities which were not at the time experimentally decidable. Newton's stress on these points, if not his basic position, shifted under pressure from critics. Whenever he realized that his general conclusions were contaminated by association with speculative hypotheses in the minds of critics, he defended his confirmed laws by claiming to have altogether eliminated hypotheses from his experimental philosophy. When gravity was slandered as an occult quality, he distinguished between this manifest force and its admittedly occult cause. At other times he took the view that to certify a cause occult was to impose an arbitrary limit to scientific investigation by pronouncing the cause 'uncapable of being discovered and made manifest'.[32] Then he would refuse to pronounce the causes of gravity, attraction, and fermentation occult or unknowable, but would simply 'leave their Causes to be found out'.[33]

It is true that in the *Principia* Newton expressly contrasted hypotheses with genuine empirical propositions derived from the observation of phenomena. Unless it is realized that the distinction which Newton intended can be otherwise made between groundless speculative hypotheses ('fictions', 'philosophical romances') and empirically verifiable hypotheses ('principles', 'axioms', or 'laws'), the point of Hume's dissent will be mistaken. 'If, indeed, we take literally what Newton says about "hypotheses",' John Passmore argues, 'then Hume could not have condemned hypotheses without rejecting the whole of empirical science. Newton wrote: "whatever is not deduced from the phaenomena is to be called an hypothesis." And it is, of course, the crucial point in Hume's logic that no empirical generalization can be "deduced from the phaenomena".'[34] But did not Newton, after all, use 'deducing' synonymously with 'drawing general Conclusions from [Experiments and Observations] by Induction'? As Passmore himself remarks later 'Newton identified "induction from experience" with "deduction from phaenomena"'. Then he adds,

---

[32] *Opticks*, 401. He continues: 'Such occult Qualities put a stop to Improvement of natural Philosophy, and therefore of late years have been rejected.'
[33] Ibid. 402.
[34] *Hume's Intentions*, 46. (Newton's statement is quoted from *Principia* II. 314.)

'Hume denied that arguments from experience could ever be deductive'.[35] But Hume did not deny inductions from experience! These 'general conclusions' which are induced or deduced from experience are 'hypotheses' according to a later usage. In this reputable sense they are admitted, in fact into Newton's natural philosophy and both in fact and name into Hume's moral philosophy. Although the impropriety of Newton's using 'deduction' and 'induction' interchangeably is serious from Hume's point of view, the actual procedure for deriving general conclusions or hypotheses from experience is not in dispute. It is only when the two philosophers come to what Hume called 'the religious hypothesis' ($E_1$ 139) that they clash.

Of course, Newton would not have conceded that the Argument from Design established a hypothesis. As Koyré observed, 'Newton certainly did not mean by "metaphysical hypothesis" the existence of God and his action in the world . . . for Newton the existence of God was a certainty, and a certainty by which the phenomena, all the phenomena, had ultimately to be explained.'[36] But neither would Newton allow that gravity was a hypothesis— at least not in the sense of 'hypothesis' that would stigmatize the principle as speculative or conjectural. The same sort of evidence is claimed for God as for gravity: the effects of both are manifest in phenomena, and both are required to explain observables causally. When Newton says that to discourse of God 'from phenomena belongs to experimental philosophy', he accentuates the scientific character of the Argument from Design. He thereby arouses expectations that 'the religious hypothesis' will be made out according to his own 'Rules of Reasoning in Philosophy'. If that were not the case, there would be no apparent sense in which Newtonian science could support Newtonian theology.

But at other times Newton was equally insistent that the universe is not entirely explicable in terms of mechanical causation and that there are, therefore, theoretical limits to the experimental method. It appears on these occasions that he must resort to quite exceptional procedures in order to impose the conclusion of the Argument from Design. And then 'the religious hypothesis' looks

---

[35] *Hume's Intentions*, 51.        [36] *Newtonian Studies*, 38.

like a convenience for disposing of problems that cannot be handled in the ordinary scientific way. A concerned and eternally vigilant Deity accounts both for the initial push given the system and for the periodical spurts of energy needed to compensate for losses of impetus through resistance. The particular number, positions, orbits, and velocities of celestial bodies can be put down to 'the council and dominion of an intelligent and powerful Being'. Similarly, only the power and wisdom of this Being can account for the fixed stars holding their places in defiance of gravity.

Newton had long since passed the point where he should have elected either to advance his theological claims on the same terms as his scientific ones and to take the consequences or to declare new Rules of method to control theological speculation. He never made a clear-cut decision. On the view that religious discourse belongs to experimental philosophy, 'the religious hypothesis' must pass the same tests of verification as any other empirical hypothesis. On the other view, that natural theology begins where scientific thinking fails, 'the religious hypothesis' would have to make its own way with no accreditation from natural science. Naturally enough, Newton wanted to evade these troublesome consequences. He wanted his theology to reflect the glory of the scientific method without having to undergo the perils of verification. Therefore, he sometimes alleges that general conclusions about the existence and nature of the Deity or First Cause have been reached by analytic induction, in keeping with 'the main Business of natural Philosophy [which] is to argue from Phaenomena without feigning hypotheses, and to deduce Causes from Effects, till we come to the very first Cause . . .'.[37] At other times he speaks as if the impress of 'the divine Arm' were manifestly present in mechanically unaccountable phenomena, and that the same conclusion can be directly intuited with a certainty denied to any general conclusion reached by induction.

Newton's problem was not that he could not have it both ways, but that he could not have it either way. The price of credibility was the scientist's readiness to risk refutation by facts. It was not

[37] *Opticks*, 369 (Query 28).

enough for him to derive 'general conclusions' from the analysis of phenomena. He had to go through the synthetic movement also, checking deduced consequences against observables. Compared with the patience and caution displayed in other situations, Newton's handling of 'the religious hypothesis' was remarkably brisk and facile. Admittedly, the problem allowed no opportunities for experimental ingenuity, nor even for specialized observation. Design was as apparent a fact to a Sunday naturalist as to the foremost astronomer, even if the former's evidence was less impressive. Observable design implied a Designer, and a Designer entailed verifiable design. No argument of comparable importance could have been more logically simple nor based upon facts more readily accessible. Once the inference had been made there was nothing further to do but to return to the rapturous contemplation of nature for additional confirmation of the Deity's unlimited genius for organization. Despite its plausible air, the Argument from Design did involve some reasoning that was by ordinary scientific standards exceptionable. Hume had both the agnostic's motive and the logician's acuity to question the preferential treatment accorded 'the religious hypothesis'.

In order to qualify as scientific, the Argument from Design has to conform to the rules of causal inference. The chief point of Hume's criticism is that proponents of the argument invalidate its conclusion by violating a 'rule' or 'maxim' of causal reasoning. This 'rule', supplementing those found in the *Treatise*, and serving as the sceptic's ultimate weapon in the *Dialogues Concerning Natural Religion*, first appears in the *Enquiry Concerning Human Understanding*:

If the cause be known only by the effect, we never ought to ascribe to it any qualities beyond what are precisely requisite to produce the effect. Nor can we, by any rules of just reasoning, return back from the cause, and infer other effects from it, beyond those by which alone it is known to us. ($E_1$ 136)[38]

[38] Cf. $E_1$ 145 n. 1: 'In general, it may, I think, be established as a maxim, that where any cause is known only by its particular effects, it must be impossible to infer any new effects from that cause; since the qualities, which are requisite to produce these new effects along with the former, must either be different, or superior, or of more extensive operation, than those which simply produced the

Let us illustrate Hume's rule by considering how general conclusions about human nature might be inferred from the observation of human behaviour. Let us suppose that both mean and
generous acts are observed, kind acts and cruel ones, that there is
evidence of competition and of co-operation, of benevolence and
of malice. A theorist who drew from such mixed phenomena a
general conclusion either to the effect that all men are essentially
selfish and aggressive or that they are essentially benevolent and
altruistic should be challenged. If he then begins to interpret every
apparently altruistic act as evidence of disguised selfishness, or
every apparently selfish one as a distorted expression of self-
abnegation, he will be violating Hume's rule. He will be attributing to the cause (human nature) a quality (the capacity to disguise
motives) which was not initially inferred in order to account for
observed effects. A similar slippery tactic is the hallmark of the
design theologian's procedure. The impartial observer of the
natural order who attends to disease, famine, and earthquakes, as
well as to the starry heavens above will infer some limitation on
the Creator's power or beneficence. But the theologian does not
revise his hypothesis of an omnipotent and benevolent Creator
when confronted with the untoward evidence of natural disasters.
He saves it by inventing the subsidiary *ad hoc* hypothesis of a
future state in which those who have suffered undeservingly will
be compensated. But clearly his faith in the ultimate redress of
injustice is not supported by observing this world where evils are
scattered as carelessly as dust by the wind. Hume sees through his
attempt to palm off the Argument from Design as empirical while
reneging on the obligation to accept the results of attempting to
verify its conclusion. The shuffling of the design theologian here
illustrates the bad habit often castigated by Hume of suspending
normal procedures in order to spare a cherished doctrine.

It was Newton who first insisted that the explanatory principles
later known as hypotheses must be empirically verified to be
effect, whence alone the cause is supposed to be known to us. We can never,
therefore, have any reason to suppose the existence of these qualities', and
D 199–200: 'Whence can any cause be known but from its known effects?
Whence can any hypothesis be proved but from the apparent phenomena? To
establish one hypothesis upon another is building entirely in the air. . . .'

scientifically acceptable. But in the end it was Hume who held consistently to this basic methodological principle. Newton and his followers were prepared to relax their standards in order to accommodate 'the religious hypothesis'. Hume stubbornly refused to waive the very regulation which had set the hypothetical-deductive method of the sciences above the hypothetical imaginings of speculative metaphysics. Thus it is at the point where Newtonians move from natural science to natural religion that Hume breaks with them over the issue of hypotheses. Ironically, it is his rigid adherence to a cardinal principle of Newton's science that disqualifies him as a complete Newtonian methodologist.

## Section 4. *Analogical Reasoning*

Eventually, the concept of analogy emerged at the centre of Hume's dispute with the Newtonians. He broke with them because he could not credit their pretensions to be scientific in developing natural religion. The question was whether or not the methods of natural religion and of natural science were sufficiently analogous to allow the design theologians' conclusions scientific standing. Hume answered this great question of general principle indirectly by demonstrating that the analogical reasoning used in the Argument from Design was congenitally defective.

There was no room for argument about the legitimacy of analogical reasoning as such. It was the accepted means of inferring properties not directly observable and of generalizing beyond the limits attainable by perfect induction. Since gravity had been found to belong to all physical bodies with which Newton was acquainted, he concluded that all terrestrial bodies had this property. Observing significant resemblances between terrestrial and celestial bodies, he inferred that gravity was a property of celestial bodies also, and therefore a universal property. He also observed striking resemblances between the behaviour of material particles in chemical and physical reactions and processes and the motions of the gross bodies studied in astronomy. Reasoning by analogy, he inferred that the forces of attraction which explained planetary motion operated between the invisible atoms, and that gravity could thus be made the basis of a genuinely universal theory of attraction.

In the first *Enquiry*, Hume endorses this procedure in principle, allowing that 'experience and observation and analogy be, indeed, the only guides which we can reasonably follow in inferences of' a causal sort ($E_1$ 148). He had already admitted analogy into the *Treatise* as a 'species of probability' (T 142), i.e. as a form of induction. He recognized that the human mind is naturally disposed toward analogical reasoning. Belief in the continued, independent existence of newly perceived objects, for example, was based upon their resemblance to familiar objects whose constancy and coherence had already inspired an analogous belief (T 209). In accordance with his policy of developing methodological principles as extensions of natural principles of the understanding, he adopted analogical reasoning to his own theoretical purpose. In order to confirm his hypothesis that causes of pride and humility must be related to the self and produce pleasure or pain, he projected his explanation into the field of animal psychology, for

'Tis usual with anatomists to join their observations and experiments on human bodies to those on beasts, and from the agreement of these experiments to derive an additional argument for any particular hypothesis. . . . Let us, therefore, apply this method of enquiry, which is found so just and useful in reasonings concerning the body, to our present anatomy of the mind, and see what discoveries we can make by it. (T 325–6)

Observing resemblances between the expressions and causes of pride and humility in men and in animals, he inferred, 'According to all rules of analogy' that 'the *manner*, in which the causes operate, be also the same' (T 327). He appealed to the resemblance between his associationist theory of pride and humility and his doctrine of natural belief as confirmation of both: 'There is evidently a great analogy betwixt that hypothesis, and our present one . . . which analogy must be allow'd to be no despicable proof of both hypotheses' (T 290; cf. T 319). Again, after returning in the Appendix to the *Treatise* to strengthen his proof that belief is nothing but a peculiar feeling which accompanies the conception of a matter of fact, he then proceeded 'to examine the analogy, which there is betwixt belief, and other acts of the mind, and find the cause of the firmness and strength of conception' (T 627).

Although no formal presentation of the logic of analogy is to be found in Hume, there are incidental comments on the rules of analogy in the *Treatise*, in the first *Enquiry*, and in the *Dialogues Concerning Natural Religion*. All of these entries reaffirm the simple principles of analogical inference formulated in Newton's first three Rules of Reasoning in Philosophy. 'All of our reasonings concerning matter of fact', Hume asserts in the first *Enquiry*, 'are founded on a species of Analogy, which leads us to expect from any cause the same events, which we have observed to result from similar causes' ($E_1$ 104). He had used the case of comparative anatomy to illustrate this point in the *Treatise*: ' 'Tis indeed certain, that where the structure of parts in brutes is the same as in men, and the operation of these parts also the same. The causes of that operation cannot be different, and that whatever we discover to be true of the one species, may be concluded without hesitation to be certain of the other' (T 325).

Cogent analogical argument begins from an extensive set of significant resemblances. 'Where the causes are entirely similar,' the *Enquiry* passage continues, 'the analogy is perfect, and the inference, drawn from it, is regarded as certain and conclusive. . . . But where the objects have not so exact a similarity, the analogy is less perfect, and the inference is less conclusive; though it still has some force, in proportion to the degree of similarity and resemblance' ($E_1$ 104). Hume continued to insist upon this point, that the force of an analogy is proportional to the degree of resemblance between the analogues, first made pithily in the *Treatise*: 'In proportion as the resemblance decays, the probability diminishes . . .' (T 147).

This is the first principle which Hume invoked in the *Enquiry* and again in the *Dialogues Concerning Natural Religion* to discredit the Argument from Design. The design theologian relies upon an analogy between the created universe and works planned and

executed by men. The following speech written—or rather lifted,
as Hurlbutt³⁹ has pointed out, from Colin Maclaurin's *An Account*

³⁹ Op. cit. 42. Cf. Maclaurin: 'The plain argument for the existence of the Deity,
obvious to all and carrying irresistible conviction with it, is from the evident
contrivance and fitness of things for one another, which we meet with throughout
all parts of the universe. There is no need of nice and subtle reasonings in this
matter: a manifest contrivance immediately suggests a contriver. It strikes us
like a sensation; and artful reasonings against it may puzzle us, but it is without
shaking our belief. No person, for example, that knows the principles of optics
and the structure of the eye, can believe that it was formed without skill in that
science; or that the ear was formed without the knowledge of sounds; or that the
male and female in animals were not formed for each other, and for continuing
the species. All our accounts of nature are full of instances of this kind. The ad-
mirable and beautiful structure of things for final causes, exalt our idea of the
*Contriver*: the unity of design shew him to be *One*' (op. cit. 381) and Hume: 'The
declared profession of every reasonable sceptic is only to reject abstruse, remote
and refined arguments; to adhere to common sense and the plain instincts of
nature; and to assent, wherever any reasons strike him with so full a force, that
he cannot, without the greatest violence, prevent it. Now the arguments for
natural religion are plainly of this kind; and nothing but the most perverse,
obstinate metaphysics can reject them. Consider, anatomize the eye: Survey its
structure and contrivance; and tell me, from your own feeling, if the idea of a
contriver does not immediately flow in upon you with a force like that of sensation. The most obvious conclusion surely is in favour of design; and it requires
time, reflection and study, to summon up those frivolous, though abstruse,
objections, which can support infidelity. Who can behold the male and female of
each species, the correspondence of their parts and instincts, their passions and the
whole course of life before and after generation, but must be sensible, that the
propagation of the species is intended by nature? Millions and millions of such
instances present themselves through every part of the universe; and no language
can convey a more intelligible, irresistible meaning, than the curious adjustment
of final causes' (D 154). Cf. also Maclaurin: 'The abstruse nature of the subject
gave occasion to the later *Platonists*, particularly to *Plotinus*, to introduce the most
mystical and unintelligible notions concerning the Deity and the worship we owe
to him; as when he tells us that intellect or understanding is not to be ascribed to
the Deity, and that our most perfect worship of him consists, not in acts of
veneration, reverence, gratitude or love; but in a certain mysterious self-annihilation, or total extinction of all our faculties. These doctrines, however absurd, have
had followers, who, in this as in other cases, by aiming too high, far beyond their
reach, overstrain their faculties, and fall into folly or madness . . . (op. cit. 378–9)
and Hume: 'The ancient *Platonists*, you know, were the most religious and devout
of all the pagan philosophers: Yet many of them, particularly *Plotinus*, expressly
declare, that intellect or understanding is not to be ascribed to the Deity, and that
our most perfect worship of him consist, not in acts of veneration, reverence,
gratitude or love; but in a certain mysterious self-annihilation or total extinction of all our faculties. These ideas are, perhaps, too far stretched; but', Hume
has Philo add, as Maclaurin did not, 'still it must be acknowledged, that by

*of Sir Isaac Newton's Philosophical Discoveries*—for Cleanthes in Part II of the *Dialogues* is a compendium of the arguments in which the literature of natural religion abounded:

Look round the world: Contemplate the whole and every part of it: You will find it to be nothing but one great machine, subdivided into an infinite number of lesser machines, which again admit of sub-divisions, to a degree beyond what human senses and faculties can trace and explain. All these various machines, and even their most minute parts, are adjusted to each other with an accuracy, which ravishes into admiration all men, who have ever contemplated them. The curious adapting of means to ends, throughout all nature, resembles exactly, though it much exceeds, the productions of human contrivance; of human design, thought, wisdom, and intelligence. Since therefore the effects resemble each other, we are led to infer, by all the rules of analogy, that the causes also resemble; and that the Author of nature is somewhat similar to the mind of man; though possessed of much larger faculties, proportioned to the grandeur of the work, which he has executed. By this argument a posteriori, and by this argument alone, we do prove at once the existence of a Deity, and his similarity to human mind and intelligence. (D 143)

Philo, the sceptic, replies in part:

But whenever you depart, in the least, from the similarity of the cases, you diminish proportionately the evidence; and may at last bring it to a very weak *analogy*, which is confessedly liable to error and uncertainty.

If we see a house, CLEANTHES, we conclude with the greatest certainty, that it had an architect or builder; because this is precisely that species of effect, which we have experienced to proceed from that species of cause. But surely you will not affirm, that the universe bears such a resemblance to a house, that we can with the same certainty infer a similar cause, or that the analogy is here entire and perfect. The dissimilitude is so striking, that the utmost you can here pretend to is a guess, a conjecture, a presumption concerning a similar cause; and how that pretension will be received in the world, I leave you to consider. (D 144)

representing the Deity as so intelligible, and comprehensible, and so similar to a human mind, we are guilty of the grossest and most narrow partiality, and make our selves the model of the whole universe' (D 156).

The analogy between the universe and human constructions is
so tenuous that equally plausible alternatives leave one free to
infer, like the Brahmin, that the world had been spun from the
belly of a spider. The natural world resembles an animal much
more than a work of human art or engineering. (It is a constantly
changing, self-repairing system, for example.) Therefore, as Philo
later argues at the beginning of Part VI of the *Dialogues*, on the
principle 'that where several known circumstances are *observed*
to be similar, the unknown will also be *found* similar' (D 170),
there are firmer grounds for construing the creation of the
universe as analogous to animal generation than to the execution
of the designs of artists or artisans.

Even if this first hurdle had been cleared by establishing a
sufficiently comprehensive known positive analogy between the
natural world and the works of men, another insurmountable
obstacle stood between the theologian and his goal. The pests and
plagues, famines and floods, the deformities and diseases that beset
the world had to be squared with the infinite power, wisdom, and
goodness of its creator. The venerable sophistry used to effect this
adjustment was to argue that what appeared evil from man's
limited view of an unfinished plan was essential to the ultimate
good of the whole, and that in a future state the Creator's per-
fections would be manifestly apparent in the total design. The
sole grounds for this cosmic optimism were the attributes of God
which entailed that his created universe should realize absolute
perfection. But these attributes themselves were supposed to have
been inferred from the world as it is actually experienced. Clearly,
the theologian has gone so far beyond the evidence that he must
tamper with the effect to bring it into line with the character
gratuitously conferred upon the cause. As the Epicurean tells the
proponent of the Argument from Design in the first *Enquiry*:

You persist in imagining that if we grant that divine existence for
which you so earnestly contend, you may safely infer consequences
from it and add something to the experienced order of nature by
arguing from the attributes which you ascribe to your gods. You seem
not to remember that all your reasonings on this subject can only be
drawn from effects to causes, and that every argument deduced from

causes to effects must of necessity be a gross sophism, since it is impossible for you to know anything of the cause but what you have antecedently not inferred, but discovered to the full in the effect. ($E_1$ 140–1)

What vitiates the analogical Argument from Design is the uniqueness of the universe and its putative Designer. As in the *Dialogues*, the stock argument of natural religion is formulated and refuted: It would be reasonable for the observer of a half-finished building surrounded by the supplies and equipment needed to complete it to infer that the construction would be finished:

If you saw, for instance, a half-finished building, surrounded with heaps of brick and stone and mortar, and all the instruments of masonry; could you not *infer* from the effect, that it was a work of design and contrivance? And could you not return again, from this inferred cause, to infer new additions to the effect, and conclude, that the building would soon be finished, and receive all the further improvements, which art could bestow upon it? . . . Why then do you refuse to admit the same method of reasoning with regard to the order of nature? Consider the world and the present life only as an imperfect building, from which you can infer a superior intelligence; and arguing from that superior intelligence, which can leave nothing imperfect; why may you not infer a more finished scheme or plan, which will receive its completion in some distant point of space or time? Are not these methods of reasoning exactly similar? And under what pretence can you embrace the one, while you reject the other? ($E_1$ 143)

The sceptic's reply is that the first inference is founded upon a reliable body of information about human behaviour drawn from observation. The expectation that a half-finished building will be completed when the materials and tools are at hand is backed by numerous, almost invariable experiences. But there is no analogous source of information about the habits of the Deity to warrant an inference about his intentions and abilities: 'this method of reasoning can never have place with regard to a Being, so remote and incomprehensible, who bears much less analogy to any other being in the universe than the sun to a waxen taper, and who discovers himself only by some faint traces or outlines, beyond which we have no authority to ascribe to him any attribute or perfection' (E₁ 146). All that can be claimed on behalf of the Deity with any degree of probability must be inferred from the world as it is experienced. Every attempt to predict future effects as grounds for further attributions to the cause is 'mere conjecture and hypothesis' (E₁ 145). And every dogmatic attribution of perfection beyond what the observable evidence warrants 'savours more of flattery and panegyric, than of just reasoning and sound philosophy' (E₁ 146). The result of Hume's rigid adherence to the rules of analogy sanctioned by common sense and empirical science was that the Argument from Design yielded a pitifully weak version of the grand conclusion to which it had aspired. In the last words written for Philo in the final revision of 1776, it was simply *'that the cause or causes of order in the universe probably bear some remote analogy to human intelligence'* (D 227).

Much earlier Cleanthes had attempted to have this restriction removed by citing acceptance of the Copernican system as a precedent:

> To prove by experience the origin of the universe from mind is not more contrary to common speech than to prove the motion of the earth from the same principle. And a caviller might raise all the same objections to the COPERNICAN system, which you have urged against my reasonings. Have you other earths, might he say, which you have seen to move? Have . . .
>
> Yes! cried PHILO, interrupting him, we have other earths. Is not the moon another earth, which we see to turn round its centre? Is not Venus another earth, where we observe the same phenomenon? Are not the revolutions of the sun also a confirmation, from analogy, of the same theory? All the planets, are they not earths, which revolve about the sun? Are not the satellites moons, which move round Jupiter and Saturn, and along with these primary planets, round the sun? These analogies and resemblances, with others, which I have not mentioned, are the sole proofs of the COPERNICAN system: And to you it belongs to consider, whether you have any analogies of the same kind to support your theory. (D 150)

Continuing, Philo reminds Cleanthes of the analogical reasoning upon which 'the modern system of astronomy' was founded, especially by Galileo—'that great genius, one of the sublimest that ever existed':

But GALILEO, beginning with the moon, proved its similarity in every particular to the earth; its convex figure, its natural darkness when not illuminated, its density, its distinction into solid and liquid, the variations of its phases, the mutual illuminations of the earth and moon, their mutual eclipses, the inequalities of the lunar surface, &c. After many instances of this kind, with regard to all the planets men plainly saw, that these bodies became proper objects of experience; and that the similarity of their nature enabled us to extend the same arguments and phenomena from one to the other.

In this cautious proceeding of the astronomers, you may read your own condemnation, CLEANTHES: or rather may see, that the subject in which you are engaged exceeds all human reason and enquiry. (D 151)

No doubt religious feeling had been stirred by the mystery and splendour of the heavens since men's interest in the supernatural was first awakened. But it was since Newton that the science of astronomy had been consecrated as a chief authority for the claims of natural religion. When Hume's sceptic shows that an essential principle of the analogical reasoning upon which that science was built is and must be violated in the Argument from Design, he makes a momentous point, logically devastating for Newtonian natural religion.

## Section 5. *Hume's Methodological Problems*

Mathematical analysis and empirical observation supplied the dual sources of power of that incomparable method, admired by Hume, which Newton had inherited through Galileo from the Paduan School. The 'true and lawful marriage between the empirical and the rational faculty', for which Bacon had called in *The Great Instauration*, had been consummated in the scientific revolution which mated mathematical deductions from first principles with inductions from experience. When theorizing about the epistemological foundations of the scientific revolution, rationalistic philosophers tended to over-stress its mathematical side, and empiricists its observational aspect. Although mathematical brilliance and experimental ingenuity were not equally apportioned to each scientist, the greatest of them brought mathematical deduction to bear upon the results of experimentally controlled observations.

Edmund Halley's story of his discussion of gravitational theory with Robert Hooke and Christopher Wren in a London inn early in 1684 has often been retold. Wren offered a prize of a forty-shilling book to whoever could demonstrate that the inverse square law of attraction entailed Kepler's laws of planetary motion. Hooke, who had formulated the inverse square law ten years earlier in *An Attempt to prove the Motion of the Earth from Observations*, boasted of having found the proof, but withheld it so that others attempting it could appreciate the difficulties. When Halley's efforts came to nothing, he called on Newton at Cambridge in August and asked what curve the planets would describe if the force of gravity diminished inversely as the square of the distance. Newton, who had conceived the law of attraction nearly twenty years before, replied without hesitating, 'An ellipse'. When asked how he knew that, he said that he had calculated it, and offered Halley the demonstration. But he had mislaid it, and when a search through his papers failed to turn it up, he promised to work it out again and to send it to Halley. By making an elementary blunder in his diagram of the problem, Newton had difficulty in recapturing his proof; but in November Halley received two demonstrations and was so impressed that he returned to Cambridge where he saw the script of Newton's lectures on motion and recognized the inception of a scientific masterpiece.

Newton's proof in classical geometrical style of the fundamental principle of astronomy is a beautiful example of a mathematical demonstration which can be applied to the interpretation of physical reality. When empirical entities are substituted for undefined terms (e.g. planets for mass-points), the physical forces at work in the universe can be derived from the logical relations discovered by deductive reasoning. Resolving spheres into mass-points located at their centres where the force of attraction is assumed to be concentrated, he deduced Kepler's laws from the laws of motion. By substituting planets for mathematical points and paths of motion for curved lines, calculating gravitational pull as a physical force which varied according to the masses of the spheres and their relative positions, he was able to deduce the motions of planets as functions of the gravitational and centrifugal forces acting upon them. If the observed orbit of the moon, for example, did not conform exactly to predictions based on the earth's attraction, deviations from the mathematical ideal could be explained as the effect of another planet's action upon it which had been ignored in the interests of simplicity, but which could be accounted for by similar calculations and the same basic simple laws.

Perhaps the most impressive and puzzling of all man's intellectual feats is the mathematical deduction of empirical truths from an axiomatic system elaborated from definitions and postulates according to unprovable rules of inference. The truth of validly inferred conclusions in pure mathematics is a matter of logical necessity, the result of working out consistently the logical implications of premisses with no regard for observable objects or empirical states of affairs. As Newton advised readers of the *Principia* in the Preface, he was concerned in the first two Books with purely mathematical forces, all questions of how things went on in the physical world being suspended while he worked out the logically possible geometry of the motions and resistances of hypothetical bodies and fluids. Just how formally and unempirically he laid the foundations of his *System of the World* can be assessed by considering that his first 'Axiom, or Law of Motion' 'describes' something which not only does not exist or occur, but which, according to the chief principle of the system, could not exist or occur. And yet from certain theorems of this deductively elaborated axiomatic system he was able to infer empirical propositions which verifiably described the behaviour of natural objects.

It must, of course, be conceded to those who argue that matters of fact can never be discovered by logical deductions, even of a mathematical kind, that Newton began with massive inventories of empirical facts—with the catalogue of observations collected over the years by the first Astronomer Royal, John Flamsteed, for example—and with previously formulated laws as well, especially Kepler's laws of planetary motion and Huygens's general laws for centrifugal force. Newton's ultimate purpose was to demonstrate that such facts and laws could be mathematically deduced from the three axioms of motion and the single assumption of gravitational attraction. But it would be conceding too much to allow that discoveries about empirical reality cannot be made by the deductive elaboration of a mathematically developed system. Halley's calculation of the orbit of the comet named after him is a perfect example of the empirical relevance and predictive power of the *Principia*. Observations of the comet were of course necessary for plotting its course, but they were too infrequent to be sufficient, and it was by inference from the Newtonian system that Halley drew his conclusions. When the comet appeared as predicted on Christmas Day of 1758, Newton's cosmology received its first dramatic empirical confirmation.

There is obviously little room for experimentation in astronomy. The astronomer must simply wait for events to happen in order to see whether or not they conform to his theories. But the crucial role of verification is in no way diminished by his inability to control celestial phenomena. The function of the laboratory experiment is to isolate the phenomenon to be explained from incidental factors which obscure it under natural conditions. Whether the scientist is concerned with the motion of the earth's axis, which cannot be controlled, or with the swing of the pendulum, which can, his theories remain, at best, mere logical possibilities until their deducible consequences have passed an empirical test. Any scientific theory worthy of serious consideration entails predictions about what transpires in the physical universe. Its claim to truth must be tested by looking to see if events in the real world go on conformably to the expectations aroused by the theory.[40] Thus one finds in addition to the

---

[40] Such questions cannot, of course, always be immediately settled by observation. Observations made within an experimental situation conclusively settled the dispute between Aristotle and Galileo about whether the velocity of a falling body was a function of its weight or of the duration of its fall. The disagreement

mechanical Theorems deduced from the axioms of *Principia Mathematica* other Propositions designated 'Problems', where Newton gives directions for setting up the experiments requisite for verifying his Theorems. And in the Third Book of the treatise where, as he advertised in the Preface, 'I derive from the celestial phenomena the forces of gravity. . . . Then from these forces, by other propositions which are also mathematical, I deduce the motions of the planets, the comets, the moon, and the sea',[41] he constantly relies upon his own observations and those recorded by others to confirm his astronomical theories.

Taking up Hume's supposedly Newtonian *Treatise of Human Nature*, the reader finds neither of the chief methodological features of the *Principia* and the *Opticks*. There is not the slightest suggestion of any attempt to apply mathematics to the solution of the problems of the *Treatise*. The book is as unmathematical as Ovid's *Metamorphoses*. Nor is it experimental, except in an extremely attenuated sense, nor even observational except, at certain times, in a peculiar sense (in the sense of introspection) or, at other times, in a very loose sense (in the sense of attending to men's behaviour 'in the common course of the world').

The social sciences, which Hume called 'moral subjects', are not to this day within sight of a Newtonian-type synthesis. Even the most scientifically advanced of them, experimental psychology, is still mathematical only in a relatively primitive sense. Measurement and statistical analysis help the psychologist towards inductive generalizations expressible in quantitative terms which are, therefore, patently objective, but fragmentary, disconnected, and often pertinent to facts which Hume, I imagine, would not have found of absorbing interest. There is no immediate prospect of an axiomatic psychological system to unify the field and from which new facts and predictions could be derived. Deprived as he was of statistical procedures and of the instruments and techniques of

between Ptolemy and Copernicus was not to be so handily disposed of. For the observational data then available were equally explicable on either system. Indeed, Copernicus himself seems to have been more concerned about the in elegancies of Ptolemaic mathematics than about the system's infidelities to celestial phenomena.

[41] p. xviii.

psychometrics, it is little wonder that Hume's method did not resemble Newton's more. Taking 'experimental philosophy' in Newton's sense, in which applied mathematics was an integral, vital part, any attempt by Hume to introduce the experimental method of reasoning into moral subjects would have been premature by at least two centuries.

It is certain that Hume faced these practical difficulties, and it is at least arguable that he was further handicapped by an imperfect understanding of the very concept of applied mathematics. The theory of philosophical relations presented early in the *Treatise* distinguishes sharply between mathematical knowledge and empirical. All knowledge on Hume's view, as on Locke's, is knowledge of relations, and '*proportions in quantity or number*' (T 70) are the objects of mathematical knowledge. These belong to the class of relations which cannot change while the *relata* remain constant, in contrast to spatial relations, for example, which may alter without any change in the objects (or ideas) related. Unlike the other three relations which 'can be objects of knowledge and certainty' (T 70) (resemblance, contrariety, and degrees in quality), judgements of proportions in quantity or number are often not 'discoverable at first sight' and therefore not intuitive but demonstrative. Of the contrasting group of relations, upon which probable rather than certain judgements are grounded, the first two, identity and relations of time and place, are either matters of direct perception, rather than of reasoning, or they are dependent upon the third—causation. And it is upon the causal relation that all factual inferences are based, i.e. all empirical 'knowledge' which is not a matter of direct acquaintance. Further, causal inferences are grounded in experience, in the natural habit of associating constantly conjoined events. A cause could never be derived from the analysis of an effect, nor an effect from the analysis of a cause, as, for example, the relative magnitude of the square constructed on the hypotenuse of a right-angled triangle to the squares on the other two sides could be discovered by analysing the properties of a right-angled triangle. Clearly the reasoning involved in empirical matters is of a logical order quite different from that imbedded in the demonstrations of Geometry,

Algebra, and Arithmetic concerning proportions in quantity or number.

In the *Treatise* Geometry is denied equal standing with Algebra and Arithmetic which are said to be the only two sciences in which reasoning attains 'perfect exactness and certainty' (T 71). Hume argues 'that geometry can scarce be esteem'd a perfect and infallible science', insisting that it 'never attains a perfect precision and exactness . . . because its original and fundamental principles are deriv'd merely from appearances' (T 71) and there is no exact standard of equality for judging the proportions of extended areas. One can know with certainty that $2 + 2 = 4$ because 'the one has always a unite answering to every unite of the other' (T 71). But one cannot be quite so certain that no two straight lines have a common segment, for an inclination so slight as to be imperceptible may result in their concurring for a certain distance. At this time Hume was taking a very empirical view of geometry regarding it as a factual science descriptive of physical space. He seems not to have conceived of a geometry as an axiomatic system worked deductively from definitions and having truth value in the form of internal consistency. He will not, for example, allow that the properties of a straight line are just those conferred upon it by definition; the idea of a straight line 'is deriv'd from nothing but the senses and imagination' (T 51), he says. In the *Treatise* Hume did not construe geometry as a branch of pure mathematics. He was, indeed, making precisely the mistake which Kant supposed 'he had too much insight' to make, viz. submitting 'the axioms of pure mathematics to experience'.[42]

Hume is led by his empiricism into attempting to determine the nature of the constituents of the space which geometry is supposed to describe. He denies the reality of absolute space, pointing out that in the absence of any visible or tangible thing there would be no recognition of space. Accordingly, he identifies space and extension, and throughout Part ii of the first Book of the *Treatise* he uses the two terms synonymously, as in the following definition: '*the idea of space or extension is nothing but the idea of visible or tangible points distributed in a certain order*' (T 53). In reaching hi

42 *Prolegomena*, tr. Peter G. Lucas (Manchester U.P., 1953), 22.

conception of the constituents of space or extension (and of time
or duration), Hume starts, as Kemp Smith has shown, from the
possibilities specified by Pierre Bayle as exhaustive in his *Dictionary*
article on Zeno: 'Either they consist of mathematical points or of
physical points, or they are infinitely divisible.'[43]

Hume uses traditional arguments to dispose of the concept of
infinite divisibility, of the view that analysis can never reach an
ultimate constituent of space. But he is no better satisfied with
either of the alternatives. The view that space is composed of
physical points is unconvincingly judged untenable on the grounds
that 'A real extension, such as a physical point is suppos'd to be,
can never exist without parts, different from each other; and
wherever objects are different, they are distinguishable and
separable by the imagination' (T 40). The difficulty with
mathematical points is that they are non-entities, and extended
objects cannot be supposed to be configurations of non-entities.
Hume promptly removes this difficulty by 'bestowing a colour
or solidity on these points' (T 40). He thereby satisfies his
empiricist requirement that the ultimate constituents of space or
extension be visible or tangible and avoids the supposed logical
problem that a genuinely extended physical point would be
further divisible and therefore not ultimate. The residual problem
of how sensible qualities could be bestowed upon an unextended
point is, understandably, never resolved by Hume. When he
returns to the subject in the first *Enquiry*, he explicitly reinstates
the doctrine of physical points to which he had been logically
committed in the *Treatise* and which was most easily squared
with his empiricist theory of geometry.

Hume's unavailing struggles with space and time, his attempt
to derive their ideas from experience conformably with his first
principle that all ideas copy impressions and to elucidate geometry
as the science of spatial extension yielded the least-admired part of
the *Treatise*. It is significant that in the *Enquiry* he dropped his
attempt to distinguish the logical standing of the propositions of
geometry from those of algebra and arithmetic; all alike express
analytic truths which rest upon the law of non-contradiction.

[43] *The Philosophy of David Hume*, 285.

Here geometry appears as a branch of pure mathematics whose propositions 'are discoverable by the mere operation of thought, without dependence on what is anywhere existent in the universe. Though there never were a triangle or circle in nature, the truths demonstrated by Euclid would forever retain their certainty and evidence' ($E_1$ 25). But now the application of geometry to the interpretation of physical reality becomes an enigma. It can be demonstrated that a circle and its tangent do not concur. However, when one tries to visualize concretely the point of contact as the circle increases in diameter *in infinitum*, it becomes impossible to imagine the angle of incidence decreasing *in infinitum* and still avoid the impression of concurrence. Such a conflict between abstract reasoning and perceptual possibilities illustrates Hume's conclusion that 'the ideas of space and time . . ., when they pass through the scrutiny of the profound sciences . . . afford principles, which seem full of absurdity and contradiction' ($E_1$ 156). What Hume's final thoughts on the subject may have been we do not know, for Lord Stanhope's criticisms discouraged him from publishing his later dissertation on geometry. His recorded statements strongly suggest that he did not understand that it is logically possible, although always empirically problematic, of course, to apply the theorems of pure geometry to the explanation of physical phenomena after the names of suitable empirical entities had been substituted for undefined terms. And that is to say that he seems to have been in no position to appreciate the logical character of such a work as Newton's *Principia*.

The chief aim of Hume's Introduction to the *Treatise* is to proclaim the unparalleled merits of the experimental method which he will attempt to apply to moral subjects. That Introduction ends, prophetically, on a discordant, discouraging note. Studies of the mind are on a par with investigations of 'external bodies', he first tells us, in that 'it must be equally impossible to form any notion of its powers and qualities otherwise than from careful and exact experiments, and the observation of those particular effects, which result from its different circumstances and situations' (T xxi). But mental or moral phenomena, he quickly admits, are not subject to experimental controls. For, selfcon sciously placing himself in the appropriate 'circumstances and situations' will interfere with his normal responses and yield distorted observations. Since Hume does not consider using other human experimental subjects, he decides that 'We must therefore glean up our experiments in this science from a cautious observation of human life, and take them as they appear in the common course of the world, by men's behaviour in company, in affairs, and in their pleasures' (T xxiii).

For conducting 'experiments of this kind' (T xxiii), Hume was favoured by a sociable disposition, a humane and unsentimental interest in others, and by a shrewd but tolerant perceptiveness. But 'experiment' in this sense is a synonym for 'experience', and conforms to the usage of Thomas Hobbes[44] and of John Locke[45] rather than to that of Robert Hooke or of Robert Boyle. Observant, reflective, introspective, Hume was no experimenter in the modern sense given the term by the Royal Society. In an age when experimental work made scientific reputations, and even amateurs delighted in repeating the experiments reported by professionals, Hume remained a philosophical thinker, a stranger to the 'careful and exact experiments' which he extolled.

[44] *Human Nature*, Ch. IV, S. 6; *The English Works of Thomas Hobbes of Malmesbury*, ed. Sir William Molesworth (John Bohn; Longmans, Green, London, 1839–45), reprinted by Scientia Aalen, 1962, iv. 16: 'The *rememberance* of succession of one thing to another, that is, of what was *antecedent*, and what *consequent*, and what *concomitant*, is called an *experiment*; whether the same be made by us *voluntarily*, as when a man putteth any thing into the fire to see what effect the fire will produce upon it: or not made by us, as when we remember a fair morning after a red evening. To have had many *experiments*, is that we call *experience*, which is nothing else but *rememberance* of what antecedents have been followed by what consequents.'

[45] *An Essay Concerning Human Understanding*, ed. A. C. Fraser (Oxford, 1891/ Dover, 1959), Bk. IV, Ch. XII (ii. 349–50): 'I deny not but a man, accustomed to rational and regular experiments, shall be able to see further into the nature of bodies, and guess righter at their yet unknown properties, than one that is a stranger to them: but yet, as I have said, this is but judgement and opinion, not knowledge and certainty. This way of *getting and improving our knowledge in substances only by experience and history* . . . makes me suspect that *natural philosophy is not capable of being made a science* . . . Experiments and historical observations we may have, from which we may draw advantage of ease and health, . . . but beyond this I fear our talents reach not, nor are our faculties, as I guess, able to advance.'

It is true that Hume sometimes performs an exercise which he thinks of as conducting an experiment. As experimental confirmation of the dependence of sensible perceptions upon the percipient, Hume points out that

> When we press one eye with a finger, we immediately perceive all the objects to become double. . . . But as we do not attribute a continu'd existence to both these perceptions, and as they are both of the same nature, we clearly perceive, that all our perceptions are dependent on our organs, and the disposition of our nerves and animal spirits. (T 210–11)

One need only compare the suggested image of Hume at his desk poking his finger in his eye with the picture evoked by *New Experiments Physico-Mechanicall Touching the Spring of the Air and its Effects, Made for the most part in a New Pneumatical Engine*[46] of Robert Boyle at work with his cylinders of mercury and air-pump, his 'exact pair of Ballances' and aeolipile, to grasp the magnitude of the difference between the two men's conception of a scientific experiment. The exact nature of that difference is revealed by Hume's use of experiments in 'that most Newtonian section of the *Treatise*'[47] as John Passmore calls Book II.

In the second Section of Part ii, Hume devises eight 'Experiments to confirm this system'. In essence, the 'system' consists of a set of propositions asserting that the object of pride and humility is the self, of love and hatred another person, that the cause of the first pair of passions is some object or quality possessed by the self, and of the second an object or quality possessed by another, and, further, that such causes evoke a pleasurable or disagreeable sensation which elicits the resembling passion by association. All of Hume's eight experiments are thought experiments. We are asked to suppose the relevant factors being varied one by one in order to appreciate that the conditions for these passions have been properly specified. And then we reflect upon hypothetical situations of an everyday sort to find the entailments of the theory experientially confirmed. We suppose ourselves confronting an

---

[46] Oxford, 1660; *Works*, ed. 1772, vol. i.
[47] *Hume's Intentions*, 45.

agreeable object while in the company of another person. Despite the tendency of the pleasurable sensation to evoke the resembling passion of pride or of love, neither of these will occur, according to the theory, since the idea of the object is, *ex hypothesi*, related neither to the idea of the self nor to the idea of the other person. 'Most fortunately all this reasoning is found to be exactly conformable to experience, and the phaenomena of the passions' (T 335). In confirmation, he cites the experience of travel companions visiting a congenial foreign country for the first time. The beauty and comfort of the country will afford pleasure. 'But as we suppose that this country has no relation either to myself or friend, it can never be the immediate cause of pride or love . . .' (T 335).

As a display of certain elementary relations between the sensations and emotions which Hume has chosen to make basic, his account is not implausible. Whether or not it is very penetrating is another question. Upon being told that the self is the object of pride, a passion caused by an object or quality which affords pleasure and is related to the self, one is entitled to ask whether this theory reveals anything about a psychological process beyond what is implicit in the meaning of the word 'pride'. Putting this question of superficiality aside, the fact remains that his 'experiments', which he allows to be 'reasoning *a priori*' (T 334), are deductive elaborations of what he calls (falling in line with Newton's inconsistency) 'my hypothesis' (T 337). The verifying experiments to which Hume's conclusions are submitted when put on 'trial', to use his term, are devised for confirmation, and it would have been astounding had he contrived one which could not have been reconciled with his hypothesis. An unfriendly critic, however, could easily invent counter-examples, imagining the pride of a traveller who 'adopts' a country which his companion is incapable of appreciating. The game is only too easy to play. Once the literary imagination is made the agent of research, science is restricted only to the realm of logical possibility.

The point is not that Hume's stories are improbable. The point is that stories are not experiments. It is one thing to devise an experiment which allows one to observe whether or not events actually occur as predicted by a hypothesis. It is quite a different procedure, and an unscientific one, to illustrate a hypothesis by fictitious events. An illustration, however apt and ·imaginative, can never amount to an *experimentum crucis*.

It is not in the least surprising that Hume's 'attempt to introduce the experimental method of reasoning into moral subjects' did not succeed. If one understands 'experimental' in the sense it had for Galileo and Huygens and for the physicists of the Royal Society, the attempt was never made. Hume faced all the technical and ethical problems which still hinder experimental research in human psychology. And he foresaw the difficulty that responses would be distorted when artificially elicited under experimental conditions. Given his interest in man's social, political, and aesthetic experience, he showed good sense in his time in relying upon 'a cautious observation of human life, . . . of . . . men's behaviour in company, in affairs, and in their pleasures' (T xxiii) rather than upon the laboratory experiment. Hume did not turn to historical writing in later life because, as is often said, he had lost interest in the problems which had first drawn him to philosophy. All of his working life, Hume remained interested in the fundamental principles underlying human behaviour. When he wrote the *Treatise*, he hoped to derive passion and action, love, pride, compassion, benevolence, hatred, malice, resentment, and the sense of justice, obligation, law, and property from the elemental forces of pleasure and pain and the principle of association taken to be analogous to the axioms of motion and the force of gravity. Apparently he emerged from that strenuous and disappointing exercise with the realization that in the human sciences the time was not yet ripe for a Newtonian synthesis. Something less ambitious, but of value for understanding the forces that move men, could be accomplished by an attentive observer favourably placed, as Hume later was by his diplomatic appointments, and by a psychologically reflective student of the past, which Hume also was, who read history as the record of human nature displayed in action.

Applied to psychology, Hume's experimental method amounted to reliance upon observation for the raw material that went into his theoretical construction and upon appeals to ordinary experience for confirming the theory. In laying the epistemological foundations of his projected system, Hume ran into special difficulties in the way of satisfying even these minimal requirements of the empirical method. He announces in the Introduction to the *Treatise* that 'the only solid foundation we can give to this science itself must be laid on experience and observation' (T xx). But it appears at the outset of Hume's investigation 'Of The Understanding' that what there is to be observed is not a bit like the public objects which the statements of physical scientists describe. It is true that scientists may speak of atoms and corpuscles, of aetherial fluids and animal spirits, which are never objects of sense experience. But these theoretical entities are invented to account for the behaviour of publicly observable objects, and their conceptual value is assessed with reference to such objects. By contrast, the perceptions with which Hume's theory is concerned are all strictly private, and so are the mental events which they are introduced to explain. The external world enters his account only as an insoluble problem. Perceptions may be accessible to introspection, but they are not, in any ordinary sense of the word, 'observable'. Impressions of sensation and ideas need never, as impressions of reflection (passions) often do, show any overt sign of occurring.

The logical structure of Hume's theory of the understanding reflects its Newtonian model. From a few simple principles, analogous to Newton's Axioms or Laws of Motion, and a principle of association as the counterpart of the principle of universal attraction, Hume attempts to derive the phenomena of the mental world. The data with which he had to contend was immune to mathematical analysis, and thus his theory could not be developed by mathematical deduction, nor could it be subjected to such verifying tests as are acceptable in experimental science.

Hume's problem at this point is simple, inevitable, and insoluble. His mental psychology has to do with phenomena which are inherently private, and statements descriptive of them are not publicly verifiable in the straightforward sense that statements about pendulums, planets, and projectiles are. Admittedly it may be argued from the very metaphysical position which Hume adopts that observations of such physical objects occur as sense data and therefore are, as experienced, quite as private as memories, desires, or beliefs. However, even from this standpoint, some provision must be made for distinguishing between mental events which are the objects of introspective psychology and physical events which are the objects of observational physical science. In the former case, certain mental entities and acts constitute the phenomena which are to be explained, in the latter they provide the data for explaining events in the external world. The claim for the objectivity of empirical science need not depend upon a false denial of the subjectivity of sense experience, but may be based upon the use made of sense data as a basis for inferences to the external world. Such inferences may be instinctively determined, matters of animal faith, amenable to no stronger sense of rational justification than their standing as natural belief entitles them to. But this metaphysical problem about the reality of the external world may be set aside when considering Hume's purely practical, insuperable problem of verifying his theories about strictly private mental phenomena. Whatever ontology a scientist may incline toward in off-duty metaphysical moments, he will acknowledge that the familiar procedures for testing physical theories are inapplicable to Hume's theory of the understanding.

It may seem an ironical paradox that Hume's defence of the verification requirement in natural science is made by way of an epistemological theory which is itself unverifiable. But this outcome is more properly considered inevitable than paradoxical. When sense experience and thinking are used for acquainting oneself with objects in the external world and for understanding events there, certain predicted experiences confirming hypotheses are accepted as experiences of public objects and events. Whatever metaphysical questions may be raised about the location of these verifying events, the assumption of their externality is pragmatically justified within the context of methodology. When, on the other hand, sense experience and thinking, which normally serve for understanding the world, are made the objects of investigation, verifying instances are one and all internal, private events. The impressions and ideas acquired in an investigation of human understanding are perceptions of impressions and ideas and of mental events, not of tangible things and of physical events. And there is no possibility of going beyond these private data to confirm explanatory principles based upon introspection. The epistemologist may, like Hume, request others to consult their own inner experiences, but he cannot, like Galileo or Guericke, require them to recognize the objective evidence displayed by a telescope or an air-pump.

# PART IV

## Philosophical Analysis and Psychological Explanation

### Section 1. *The Trouble with Dualism*

HUME's science of man developed along lines which are historically explicable, but which were not, I should say, historically inevitable. Newtonian science appealed to Hume as a paradigm of method upon which to model inquiries into man's intellectual and social life. Following Locke's lead, he detaches moral phenomena—events involving human agency—from events in the natural world, treating thinking and feeling in isolation from physical processes. His theory of human nature is thus constructed parallel to the theories of the physical world which were being elaborated in his own time, but independently of them. Given the efforts of Newtonian scientists to extend the principles of the so-called mechanical philosophy into new areas of investigation, it might have been expected that philosophers interested in human understanding, passion, and behaviour would attempt to devise theories as extensions of the mechanical principles by which physical phenomena were being explained. Such in fact had been the programme which Hobbes had laid out for himself, but which the turbulent events of the previous century had prevented him from adhering to. In the eighteenth century only David Hartley conceived of a mental science constructed in tandem with physical science, the connection between them being effected by a theory of sensation, just as, in fact, contact between the inner and the outer world is made through sensation. With the other writers of his time, Hume proceeded on the dualistic assumption that the mental realm differs totally from the physical. From a study of physical science one became acquainted with methodological principles, which, it was hoped, would serve for exploring the inner world. But the facts encountered there differed in kind from physical facts, and the laws which explained mental facts were not derivable, even in principle, from the laws governing events in the external world. On this view, even the thinker's body is relegated to the external world, and the functioning of sense organs, of nerves and brain is as irrelevant to a theory of mind as the phases of the moon or the precession of the equinoxes.

When Descartes had become oppressed by objections to his attempt to explain the relations between mind and body, he retorted irritably, in a letter to Arnauld, that 'we are not in a position to understand . . . how the mind, which is incorporeal, can move the body. . . . This is one of those things which are known in and by themselves and which we obscure if we seek to explain them by way of other things.'[1] Locke inherited Cartesian dualism gratefully; the inability of matter to think supplied a premiss for his proof of the existence of God, and he wrote, complacently, in answer to John Norris's objection that he had not explained the 'causes and manner of production' of ideas, that 'no man can tell . . . because no man can give any account of any alteration made in any simple substance whatsoever; all the alteration we can conceive being only of the alteration of compounded substances, and that only by a transposition of parts'. Locke does admit that 'it seems probable that in us ideas depend on and are some way or other the effect of motion', but this was not a clue that he was prepared to follow, for he concerned himself, on principle, with ideas 'only so far as experience and observation lead me; wherein my dim sight went not beyond sensation and reflection'.[2]

Despite his scepticism about the validity of any metaphysical solution to the problems created by divorcing mind from body, Hume commits himself to dualism. Very early in the *Treatise* he

[1] *Descartes' Philosophical Writings*, tr. Norman Kemp Smith (Macmillan, London, 1952), 280-1.
[2] *Locke Selections*, ed. Stirling Lamprech (Scribners, New York, 1928-56), pp. 321-2.

observes that sensation 'arises in the soul originally, from un-known causes' (T 7) and adds 'The examination of our sensations belongs more to anatomists and natural philosophers than to moral; and therefore shall not at present be enter'd upon' (T 8). In other words, a philosophy of mind must be worked out quite independently of any scientific investigation of the physical con-ditions which make perceptual and cognitive experiences possible. The findings of anatomy, physiology, optics, and of other similar disciplines are strictly irrelevant to a philosophical concern with sense experience, as Hume confirms in this well-known passage:

> As to those *impressions*, which arise from the *senses*, their ultimate cause is, in my opinion, perfectly inexplicable by human reason, and 'twill always be impossible to decide with certainty, whether they arise immediately from the object, or are produc'd by the creative power of the mind, or are deriv'd from the author of our being. Nor is such a question any way material to our present purpose. We may draw inferences from the coherence of our perceptions, whether they be true or false; whether they represent nature justly, or be mere illusions of the senses. (T 84)

In developing his theory of knowledge, Hume's attention, like Locke's and Berkeley's, is fixed upon what occurs in conscious-ness, upon psychic entities and processes which constitute a distinct class of phenomena called mental.

How could an explanation of these phenomena emerge from a procedure which isolates them from both the external, impersonal world and the body of the person? If a human infant were trans-ported to the far side of a distant star and miraculously survived, living in total darkness and in absolute silence, the sense ex-periences which interested Hume would not occur—at least not without further miracles. Nor would they occur if a human being's sensory and cerebral organs were reduced by surgery to the efficacy of an oyster's or a newt's. If certain conditions in both the natural environment and in the physical constitution of the person are necessary for the occurrence of the mental phenomena which Hume investigates, an explanation of those phenomena depends absolutely upon an understanding of those conditions.

Since Hume is content to ignore both sets of conditions on principle, he is clearly in no position to present a theory amounting to a genuinely scientific explanation of mental phenomena. If this is what he intended to claim when he said, just before the Conclusion of Book I of the *Treatise*, that he had 'fully explain'd the nature of our judgement and understanding' (T 263), his whole epistemology can be shown to rest upon a mistake about what such a full explanation requires. In the main philosophical tradition from Descartes to the phenomenologists of the present day, epistemologists have isolated the data of consciousness from their necessary physical conditions in the external world and in the body. If explanation of mental phenomena is the aim of epistemology, then an analysis of the disabling error so frequently made at the very first step would be relevant not only to the criticism of Hume's philosophy but to the reappraisal of a very long and difficult stretch of intellectual history. A momentary digression will suffice for outlining my own diagnosis.

In the situation to be examined there are three classes of events which must be distinguished and their relations to one another determined. There are the events which occur in the inanimate material universe which are to be classified as physical phenomena. There are events which occur within the bodies of sentient creatures which may be classified as physiological phenomena. And there are events which occur within consciousness which we shall call mental phenomena. Physical phenomena include those which concern astronomers, chemists, geologists, and other physical scientists as well as those observed by laymen who look at the world around them. Physiological phenomena, which interest anatomists, neurologists, physiologists, and certain experimental psychologists, include those involving sense receptors, nervous tissue, neural pathways in the brain, and so on. Mental phenomena include sensations, perceptions, ideas, inferences, decisions, etc., of which there is immediate awareness only on the part of the person in whose consciousness they occur, and which have preoccupied introspective psychologists and philosophers interested in problems of knowledge.

For present purposes the relations between these three classes of events can be specified in terms of an order of dependency. It is clear that many physical phenomena do not depend for their occurrence upon either of the other two. There is no reason to suppose that if all conscious beings, or even all animate life, should perish the physical universe would thereby be destroyed. Stars could continue to reflect their suns and satellites to orbit their planets when no creature was left alive to observe them. But this relationship is obviously asymmetrical. Physiological and mental phenomena depend upon certain physical conditions, and if the physical universe returns to chaos, all animate and conscious life will go down to destruction with it. Similarly, mental phenomena depend upon physiological; but the converse does not hold. Without a brain in his body, a man cannot think; but it is not necessary to think in order to grow hair on one's head—and if it is not growing there, no amount of thinking will help. Regarding phenomena, then, in the order of dependency physical events are fundamental; physiological events depend upon them, and mental events upon physiological and thus, ultimately, upon physical ones also. Of course it does not follow that physiological events can have no effects in the physical world, nor mental events no physiological effects. But these considerations are irrelevant for the purposes of my argument.

There is another series to be considered, consisting not of sets of events but of explanations of events. Pertaining to physical phenomena, there are the descriptions, generalizations, hypotheses, laws, and theories found in physical and allied sciences. There is also a group of biological sciences in which a roughly similar method is applied to the investigation of physiological phenomena. This leaves mental phenomena to be dealt with by philosophers and—although we shall not further consider them—by psychologists of a certain sort.

The order of dependency amongst these three classes of explanation appear at first glance to reverse the order specified for the phenomena themselves. Theories of physics clearly depend upon mental phenomena: the observations recorded in descriptive statements and generalizations depend upon some physicist's perceptions, hypotheses upon conceptions which he has entertained, and so on. And explanations in physiology have the same sort of dependency upon mental events. In this series, it might appear, mental events rather than physical ones are fundamental. And, of course, mental *events* are fundamental, for, unless they occur, there can be no physiological or physical explanations of anything at all. But this fact is at the moment irrelevant, for we are not now concerned with events but with explanations of events. Therefore, the relevant question at this point is not whether explanations in physics and physiology depend upon mental phenomena, which they do, but whether they depend upon explanations of mental phenomena, which they do not. The illusion that mental phenomena can be explained independently of physics and physiology, of our knowledge of the external world and of the body, arises from supposing that because mental events are fundamental to all other forms of explanations, being presupposed by them, explanations of mental events are fundamental and presuppose explanations of no other types of events. But the actual order of dependency of classes of theories or explanations is the reverse of this.

The physicist has no need of any theories that might be put forth to explain physiological and mental events in order to conduct his experimental investigations of the material world. The physiologist can afford to ignore philosophical explanations of mental phenomena, but not the theories of physical science, of optics and acoustics, for example, which bear directly upon his investigations of two important sensory processes. The philosopher can afford to ignore neither the physicist nor the physiologist, if his aim is to explain the events which take place in consciousness. From this we must conclude that either the history of epistemology traces the course of a misbegotten venture, or that it aims at something quite different from explanations of the type found in the natural sciences. It is, of course, possible that in aiming at what could never be realized because of the procedural error just reviewed, Hume and his predecessors constituted epistemology as a discipline with legitimate ends quite different in kind from those sought in empirical science. The origins of chemistry and astronomy provide precedents too striking for us to rule out, *a priori*, this conjecture about modern epistemology having issued from a felicitous mistake.


## Section 2. *Psychological Fact and Psychological Theory*

Hume's dissatisfaction with current trends in moral philosophy and natural religion prompted him to attempt to determine the limits of human understanding. It seemed to him appropriate that he should set about discovering how knowledge is acquired and beliefs are formed. He supposed that the means and limits to knowledge and tenable belief are matters of natural fact discoverable by empirical investigation, and he therefore introduced himself on the title-page of his first book as an experimental philosopher. This reputation he rested upon constant appeals to experience—upon introspecting the data of consciousness, and upon occasional sets of rather desperate thought experiments. But it is not at all clear how Hume expected to realize his sceptical intentions by making himself a master of mental mechanics. For even if he had overcome the methodological problems which we have been considering throughout this book, the way from a scientific explanation of mental phenomena to the determination of the theoretical limits of human understanding is blocked by two further obstacles which appear insurmountable. The first is raised by the key role played by language in human knowledge, and the second concerns Hume's alleged practice of adducing psychological theories in support of logical standards.

Long before Hume, many philosophers had sensed that the key to certain problems in epistemology was to be found through a study of language. It appeared that language served not only for recording and communicating knowledge but also for acquiring it beyond the rudimentary level attainable by dumb animals. It would eventually appear, also, that linguistic phenomena were unique, without parallel elsewhere in nature, and that whatever the origin of language, very early in its evolution it became autonomous, emancipated from purely physical and biological determinants. The rules governing linguistic behaviour, unlike the laws governing natural processes, codify human decisions, customs, and conventions, and have no apparent basis other than tacit agreements amongst members of a linguistic group. Speech, which is not acquired involuntarily, but must be learned through imitation, practice, and correction, is a cultural rather than a natural phenomenon. Although certain physical conditions necessary for using a language may interest the anatomist and physiologist, their scientific investigations of these conditions would not help the epistemologist to solve his semantic and logical problems. There is no distinction to be drawn in terms of anatomy and physiology between the liar and the man who speaks the truth. And even if one supposes, for example, that there is, in principle, a distinguishable and describable difference between the cerebral processes involved in speaking or listening to nonsense and in using language meaningfully, not only would the practical difficulty of detecting them be formidable even now, and in Hume's time overwhelming, but also the distinction between nonsensical and significant assertion would have to be drawn prior to the scientific investigation of its underlying conditions in the nervous system. In short, criteria of meaning must be derived from studies of the use of language, and not from empirical investigations of natural facts.

Analogous difficulties would have blocked any attempt on Hume's part to derive logical standards from the facts of experimental psychology. Rules of evidence and principles of inference, like grammatical rules and semantic principles, are conventions which have evolved during the course of man's intellectual history. Standards for assessing the relevance of evidence and the accuracy of descriptions, the strength of generalizations, the force of analogies, the validity of deductions, techniques of verification, and so on, can be formulated, but only at a late stage, after they have already come into play as implicit controls upon reasoning and argument. At any time an accepted standard may be challenged, and another which is operative in a particular discipline recommended as generally reliable. But there can be no proof of the principles upon which all proof depends, except in an older sense of the term which makes 'to prove' synonymous with 'to test'; and the test will be a pragmatic one. If a form of argument consistently fails to resolve disagreement, or a method of investigation to discover what is sought, then one would be pragmatically justified in replacing old standards by new ones. Legislation of this sort can be based only upon an analysis of arguments and theories conducted in the light of what the reasoner aimed to accomplish. A scientific explanation of mental processes will be quite irrelevant to this critical purpose. The psychologist or physiologist must not only assume certain methodological principles which the epistemologist may wish to question, but he must also remain indifferent to the reliability and validity of the reasoning processes which he investigates. Fallacious reasoning is as acceptable grist for his mill as cogent reasoning, and it is not in terms of brain chemistry that the distinction between the two is to be expressed.

No one now can tell whether or not Hume suspected these difficulties when he began the *Treatise*, sensed them while he was writing this book, or understood them after he had finished it. If, despite his own stricture against drawing normative conclusions from factual premises, he really intended to derive criteria of meaning, knowledge, and belief from an empirical theory of mental events, the logic of the situation took over. Hume the philosophical analyst and Hume the 'experimental' psychologist are not really very compatible throughout most of Book I of the *Treatise*. It is true that they sometimes collaborate, the analyst detecting an error (the imputation of necessary connection to causally related events, for instance), the psychologist explaining it (in this case by the natural disposition of men to project features and qualities of their inner experiences on to the external world). But each has his own work to do and goes about it independently of the other, the analyst relying upon the copy principle, the psychologist upon the principle of association. Even at the Conclusion of Book I of the *Treatise* the psychologist, with most of his work still before him, appears intimidated and discouraged. And it is the analyst who dominates the proceedings in *An Enquiry Concerning Human Understanding*.

When introducing his second study Hume stresses his critical aims, specifying religiously inspired metaphysics as his chief target. He still regards the human mind as an intrinsically interesting object of impartial research, even if one can go no further than 'mental geography'—the distinguishing and classifying of mental entities and functions. However, he does consider the discovery of general laws governing mental phenomena to be, at least in principle, possible, but now, scaling down his former pretentious claim to have 'fully explained the nature of our judgement and understanding' (T 263), he offers his first *Enquiry* as a contribution to mental sciences which 'longer time, greater accuracy, and more ardent application may bring . . . still nearer their perfection' ($E_1$ 15).

It is very significant that although Hume does not here promise a complete system of mental mechanics as a foundation for the moral and natural sciences, he still has hopes that he 'can undermine the foundations of an abstruse philosophy, which seems to have hitherto served only as a shelter to superstition, and a cover to absurdity and error' ($E_1$ 16). It appears from this that in the interval between the *Treatise* and the first *Enquiry*, Hume had decided that his attempt to determine the limits of human understanding did not depend upon a Newtonian synthesis in the field of mental psychology. Even in the *Treatise*, the principles upon which Hume relied for philosophical analysis were not derived from the explanations of mental processes which he supplied as an associationist psychologist. The alleged dependence of Hume's logical theories upon a shaky psychological footing is a criticism most easily sustained by using the terms 'logic' and 'psychology' in senses as vague as possible. What appears in contemporary literature as Hume's confusion between logic and psychology amounts, in my opinion, to no more than the critics' confusion between two senses of the term 'psychology'.

It is one thing to advance a psychological theory to explain certain facts of behaviour and quite another to appeal to psychological facts to ground a theory which defines the meaning of a concept. Hume's analysis of causation inevitably involves references to the experiences in which this concept plays a key role. It is to be expected that the meaning of 'cause' will become

manifest in those situations in which causal inferences, generalizations and predictions are made and causal expectations aroused.
To ask what it means to say that certain events are the causes of
others is, therefore, to ask about the constitutive features of the
perceptual and cognitive experiences which underlie such judgements. Consequently, Hume proposes that we 'cast our eye on
any two objects, which we call cause and effect' (T 75) in order
to determine the properties of the causal relationship. These are
discovered by reflection on the relevant experiences to be
temporal and spatial contiguity and the priority of the cause. But
'causation' conventionally bears the connotation of 'necessary
connexion' in addition to contiguity and succession, and it is not
possible to locate the source of this third constituent of the term's
meaning in the experience of 'any two objects, which we call
cause and effect'. It is well known that Hume resolves necessary
connexion into constant conjunction; the idea of a necessary connexion between a pair of objects or events does not arise from
witnessing a single instance of their contiguity and succession but
from observing an invariable series of such conjunctions. Since,
so far as the objects or events themselves are concerned, there is
nothing in the repetition not present in a single instance to account
for the idea of necessary connexion, its source must be located in
the mind, where expectations are based upon the association of
ideas conjoined in recurrent resembling instances.

   Now Hume is aware that when people say that one type of
event is the cause of another they usually suppose that the two
are necessarily connected—that unless the first occurred the
second would not, and that if the first occurred, the second must.
Thus part of what they mean by saying that two sorts of events
are causally related is that the two are necessarily connected, and
therefore 'necessary connexion' is part (a defining term) of the
meaning of 'causation' as ordinarily used. But Hume is no
ordinary language philosopher. Because he believes that many
'words, as commonly used, have very loose meanings annexed to
them; and their ideas are very uncertain and confused' ($E_1$ 77 n),
a clarification of the meaning a term has acquired in 'common
conversation, as well as in philosophy' (ibid.) constitutes the

initial, not the terminal, stage in the analysis of a term. Furthermore, Hume says nothing to indicate that he is interested in elucidating the meaning of 'necessary connexion' as this expression is used in ordinary discourse—if, indeed, it is ever used there at all. On the contrary, he makes it very clear that he is concerned with a 'philosophical term', with a fundamental concept of metaphysics and science (T 156, E₁ 61–2), and with the faulty analyses ('vulgar definitions' (T 157)) of it offered by 'antient and modern philosophers' (T 156–62, E₁ 64–73). What Hume offers is a redefinition of the concept of causation which excludes from the *definiens* all terms for which there is no experiential warrant. How else could Hume show that there is no warrant for attributing necessary connection to causally related events—that the expression is 'wrong apply'd' (T 162) to objects—than by showing that in the relevant situations we have no acquaintance with such a relation? And how could he do that otherwise than by directing our attention to those experiences in which the idea of necessary connexion has its genesis? What we attend to when so directed are certain psychological facts, but we are surely not at this stage of the analysis being offered psychological theory. And therefore Kemp Smith's criticism of 'Hume's tendency to substitute psychological for logical analysis'[3] seems to me fundamentally misleading, as is John Passmore's account of Hume's 'reduction of philosophy to psychology'.[4]

It is pretty obvious that the theory of association which Hume invokes to explain the feeling of necessity which attaches to constantly conjoined events is no part of the analysis of causation construed as a philosophical relation. Hume would surely have seen that any attempt to define 'causation' psychologically in terms of 'causality' as a principle of association would have been open to the same objection of circularity that he brought against the 'vulgar definitions' (T 157) of 'necessity' in 'terms of *efficacy, agency, power, energy* etc.'. Once Hume has resolved the complex idea of causality into the objectively observable constituents of contiguity and succession and defined the third, necessary connexion, in terms of constant conjunction, his analysis is complete.

---

[3] *The Philosophy of David Hume*, 561.      [4] *Hume's Intentions*, 83.

And the validity of that analysis does not depend upon the subsidiary psychological theories of association and projection by
which Hume explains the feeling of necessity and its imposition
on objects and events.

What was the ultimate purpose of Hume's meticulous analysis
of causality in the *Treatise*, to which he returns in the first *Enquiry*?
From his premiss that ' 'Tis evident, that all reasonings concerning *matter of fact* are founded on the relation of cause and effect'
(A 11; cf. T 74, $E_1$ 26, 76), it follows that an appraisal of the
grounds upon which empirical knowledge rests depends upon an
understanding of that relation. Some writers, A. E. Taylor and John
Randall, for instance, have been stalled at this point and supposed
that the subjective construction put upon necessity was motivated
by Hume's desire to undermine empirical science—a perverse
ambition for a philosopher setting out to apply the experimental
method to the social sciences! In order to read such a self-defeating
manœuvre into Hume's strategy one must ignore his preoccupation with metaphysical theories devised to explain causal necessity.
It is against Locke, Descartes, Malebranche, and other Cartesians
that Hume writes (T 157–61; $E_1$ 64–73), not against natural
philosophers, not, for example, against Sir Isaac Newton, whom
he extolls above 'our modern metaphysicians' ($E_1$ 73 n). Hume
intends to show that speculative hypotheses invented to explain
causal efficacy in nature are gratuitous. Since experience provides
no idea of power in objects, we have no need of a metaphysical
theory to account for it. The idea of necessity arises from 'that
determination of the thought, acquir'd by habit, to pass from the
cause to its usual effect' (A 23), and it therefore calls for a psychogenetic explanation. Thus Hume's 'reduction of philosophy to
psychology', of which Passmore speaks, takes place only after
philosophical analysis has shown that necessary connection calls
for psychological rather than for cosmological theorizing.

It is astonishing to find some of Hume's most illustrious commentators ignoring the bearing of his analysis of causation upon
metaphysics, classical and modern, the full significance of which
Kant was the first to appreciate.[5] There is not a word in Kemp

---

[5] *Prolegomena*, tr. Peter G. Lucas (Manchester U.P., 1953), 5–6: 'Hume

Smith's discussion 'Of the idea of necessary connexion' to suggest that the philosophical point of Hume's analysis is to eliminate a collection of metaphysical theories by obviating the need for them.[6] Nor is the point explicitly stated by Charles Hendel, not even in the long chapter on causation, where Hume's comments on the Cartesians are paraphrased.[7] The point is again obscured in A. H. Basson's otherwise illuminating account, for there Hume's disagreements with the metaphysicians are characterized as purely epistemological and not, as they also are, ontological.[8] As usual, D. G. C. MacNabb[9] sees the point clearly and states it incisively, and in the first respect at least he is followed by Antony Flew.[10]

started in the main from a single but important concept in metaphysics, namely that of the *connection of cause and effect* (together with its consequential concept of force and action etc.). He challenged Reason, who pretends to have conceived this concept in her womb, to give an account of herself and say with what right she thinks: that anything can be of such a nature, that if it is posited, something else must thereby also be posited necessarily; for that is what the concept of cause says. He proved irrefutably: that it is wholly impossible for reason to think such a conjunction *a priori* and out of concepts. For this conjunction contains necessity; but it is quite impossible to see how, because something is, something else must also necessarily be, and how therefore the concept of such an *a priori* connection can be introduced. From this he inferred that Reason completely deceives herself with this concept, in falsely taking it for her own child, whereas it is nothing but a bastard of the imagination fathered by experience. The imagination, having by experience brought certain representations under the law of association, passes off a subjective necessity arising out of this, namely custom, for an objective necessity from insight. From this he inferred: reason has no power to think such connections, not even only to think them universally, because its concepts would then be mere fictions, and all its ostensibly *a priori* knowledge is nothing but falsely stamped ordinary experiences; which is as much as to say that there is no metaphysics at all, and cannot be any.'

[6] *The Philosophy of David Hume*, Ch. xvii, 'Belief in Causality: The Origin of the Idea of Necessity', 271–403.

[7] *Studies in the Philosophy of David Hume*, Ch. v, 'The Nature and Meaning of Causation', 136–76.

[8] *Hume* (Penguin, Harmondsworth, 1958), Ch. 4, 'The Understanding', 56–85.

[9] *David Hume, His Theory of Knowledge and Morality* (Hutchinson's University Library, London, 1951), Ch. vii, 'Necessary Connexion', 103–17.

[10] *Hume's Philosophy of Belief*, Ch. vi, 70.

## Section 3. *Logical Status of the Copy Principle*

It is not always by realizing first intentions that a thinker makes contributions of permanent value to philosophy. It is not surprising that in the beginning Hume was attracted by the idea of a science of man which would determine the limits of human understanding and explain the compulsion to transcend them. However, criteria of meaning, knowledge, and rational belief are not matters of fact, and any attempt to derive them from theories of empirical psychology is bound to fail. The psychologist is committed to explaining communication, judgement and inference, opinion and belief; he has no means within his own discipline for discriminating between sense and nonsense, truth and falsity, validity and invalidity, between views which are well founded and views which are groundless, reasonable beliefs and unreasonable ones. If Hume had used his copy principle as an empirical generalization for purposes of psychological explanation, it would not have helped him in the least to dispose of metaphysical theories woven around fictions. But he does not use it in that way, however he may have conceived it originally. He uses it as an instrument for analysing philosophical terms, for elucidating basic concepts, and that is why in the first *Enquiry* he calls his first principle 'a new microscope or species of optics' ($E_1$ 62). Once conceptual confusion about existence, space, time, causality, substance, identity, and so on, has been removed, the need for metaphysical constructions vanishes with the fictions, making room for psychological explanations of the errors and illusions which generate pseudo-problems. And this, I take it, is what Hume meant in the Conclusion to Book I of the *Treatise* where he spoke of 'giving in some particulars a different turn to the speculations of philosophers' (T 273). The explanations are derived from the theory of the association of ideas, which is a genuine psychological theory or hypothesis essential to Hume's constructive purposes but quite distinct in kind from the copy principle upon which he relies for the critical analysis of philosophical theories. The most insidious criticisms of Hume's philosophy in contemporary literature betray insensitivity to this vital distinction between the roles played by the copy principle and the principle of association.

From the time that Hume's literary reputation made his neglected philosophical opinions appear worthy of being reckoned with, the sceptical conclusions to which his method of analysis leads have provoked hostility. Writers who, like James Beattie, regarded Humean scepticism as an affront to common sense and Christian belief were not over-scrupulous in their choice of means to make it appear ridiculous. In our own time, the most destructive attacks have been made by logical empiricists who have arrived by other logical conveyances at Hume's final position on the limits of human understanding. They are at odds, then, not with Hume's conclusions but with his method of reaching them.

Hume presents his 'first principle . . . in the science of human nature' (T 7), the copy principle, as an empirical proposition. He professes to have discovered the near universal resemblance of impressions and ideas by observing his own perceptions. He requests his readers to confirm his conclusion by consulting their own experience, and challenges anyone who disputes it to produce an idea which has no corresponding impression or an impression with no corresponding idea. In order to confirm the next part of his principle, that impressions are causes and ideas their effects, he cites as evidence the inevitable sequence followed in teaching children ideas of colours, which is first to present them with various coloured objects in order to evoke the relevant impressions. Further allegedly empirical evidence is provided by persons congenitally blind or deaf who have no visual or auditory ideas because they have had no corresponding impressions to copy. The argument is clinched by a shop-worn example long cherished by philosophers: 'We cannot form to ourselves a just idea of the taste of a pineapple, without having actually tasted it' (T 5).

Hume does admit one exception to his 'general maxim'. Suppose a man is presented with a graduated series of colour samples, running from the darkest shade of blue to the lightest. If one sample were removed, the subject might notice the greater-than-average difference between the samples on either side; and he would be able to imagine the idea of the missing shade of blue without ever having had an impression of it. This counter-example is dismissed on the grounds that it is 'so particular and singular, that 'tis scarce worth our observing' (T 6). Hume's nonchalance in the face of this exception is at first sight curious. But it will later prove to be instructive for determining the true logical character of his first principle.

It will be remembered that Hume's science of man is expected not only to 'explain the nature of the ideas we employ, and of the operations we perform in our reasonings' but also, according to the preceding clause, to make us 'thoroughly acquainted with the extent and force of human understanding' (T xix). Human understanding cannot extend beyond the range of available ideas, as Locke had taught, and it was therefore important to determine at the beginning the conditions required for ideas to occur. These conditions are identical with those upon which philosophical terms acquire meaning. Although Hume's empiricist criterion of meaning is clearly implicit and repeatedly used in the *Treatise*, a precise, formal statement of it is first made in the *Enquiry*:

When we entertain, therefore, any suspicion that a philosophical term is employed without any meaning or idea (as is but too frequent), we need but enquire, *from what impression is that supposed idea derived?* And if it be impossible to assign any, this will serve to confirm our suspicion. By bringing ideas into so clear a light we may reasonably hope to remove all dispute, which may arise, concerning their nature and reality. (E₁ 22)

A. H. Basson warns us that Hume's first principle ('Hume's chief analytical tool') is not an empirical proposition at all but a definition. 'No matter how he purports to prove his principle, the use he makes of it shows that for him an idea is *by definition* a copy of an impression.'[11] Noting the conspicuous point that 'Hume describes his method as an experimental method, involving careful and accurate experiments', Basson 'warned the reader that this is not a fair description of his actual procedure'.[12] His remark that Hume 'cannot show the limitations of the human understanding simply by making a definition'[13] seems to have been put

[11] *Hume*, 37.    [12] Ibid. 24.    [13] Ibid. 35.

into the mouth of some anonymous opponent of Hume—'Some-one who is metaphysically inclined'. Basson himself is not greatly perturbed by Hume's betrayal of the empirical method at his very first and quite crucial step. For he does not believe that the limits of human understanding is an empirical problem to be solved by scientific investigation. And about that I believe he is right. Whatever 'opinion Hume himself may have had about the absolute validity of his scheme',[14] his only realistic prospect was to persuade others that their efforts to answer certain questions would be wasted because the ideas needed to ground their think-ing in experience would not be forthcoming. Hume could not establish a verifiable conclusion about the limits of human know-ledge on the basis of observation and experiment. At most, he could offer one logically possible analysis of the conditions of common sense and scientific knowledge, and show that these con-ditions could not be satisfied in certain metaphysical, ethical, and theological contexts. 'We have seen that Hume's theory of im-pressions and ideas, and of the connexion between them, is not so much a psychological theory to be verified by observation, as an attempt to provide a framework for analysis.'[15] 'If Hume's works are seen in this light,' he advised earlier, 'they make great philo-sophy and good sense. If they are taken the other way, they look like poor psychology and poor sense.'[16]

Detaching the copy principle from the psychological theory elaborated in Hume's work, particularly in the *Treatise*, is one great merit of Basson's commentary. Recognizing that the philosophical value of this principle of analysis is not to be assessed by criteria and tests appropriate to empirical theories is another. None the less, Basson's interpretation illustrates my earlier point that the distinction between a psychological theory propounded to explain facts and psychological facts adduced to support epistemological theories is commonly overlooked. Hav-ing recognized that the copy principle is not the first principle of an empirical psychological theory, Basson sees no alternative to construing it as a definition of 'idea'. It would be hopeless to attempt to defend Hume against a charge of dogmatism if he

14 Ibid. 44.    15 Ibid. 24.    16 Ibid. 26.

had based his philosophical analysis upon a perfectly arbitrary definition of this key term. The way to disarm such opponents is by construing the copy principle neither as an empirical generalization nor as a definition but as a third type which I shall soon explain.

Antony Flew is more puritanical than Basson. He accuses Hume of converting his first principle, first presented as a contingent generalization, into a 'pretentious tautology'. He charges Hume with dogmatically rejecting any suggested counter-instance as failing to qualify by the terms of his own definition as a real idea. Hume's 'armchair psychology', he says,

. . . leaves the doctrine a contingent generalization, open to falsification by the production of a recalcitrant negative instance. But Hume wants also to base a method of challenge on precisely the same proposition, taking the absence of any appropriate antecedent impressions as a sufficient reason for saying of any supposed idea that there really is no such idea.[17]

Hume's 'intellectual misdemeanour', he explains,

. . . consists in: first presenting a generalization as a matter of universal but contingent fact, . . . and then refusing to accept as authentic any counter example suggested, and this on the sole ground that, as the original generalization is true, what is offered cannot possibly be a genuine case of whatever it is which would falsify it.[18]

Flew concludes this phase of his critique with a tidy formulation of a common and quite destructive objection to Hume's statements of his first principle:

. . . most of the time they are taken to express a contingent generalization; but at some moments of crisis he apparently construes them as embodying a necessary proposition. Such manœuvres have the effect of making it look as if the immunity to falsification of a necessary truth had been gloriously combined with the substantial assertiveness of a contingent generalization. But this, as Hume himself is going soon most clearly and unequivocally to insist, is impossible.

The ground which Hume tried to defend is thus manifestly untenable.[19]

---

[17] *Hume's Philosophy of Belief*, 25.    [18] Ibid. 26.    [19] Ibid.

The same point is scored against Hume's first principle by Vere Chappell in his Introduction to the Modern Library anthology of Hume's writings:

Resting as it does on empirical premises, this conclusion itself must have empirical force. Hume often uses it, however, as if it were a necessary truth, for he employs it to show the impossibility or unintelligibility of many of the favorite ideas, or alleged ideas, of other philosophers. The idea of substance, for example, is held to be no proper idea, since there is (and can be) no resembling impression which precedes it—as if ideas were not just in fact regularly preceded by resembling impressions but necessarily had to be. This, it seems clear, is one of the places at which Hume abandons empiricism.[20]

Lazerowitz joins the chorus in *The Structure of Metaphysics*:

When it is claimed that none of our senses acquaints us with substance, that they all fail to reveal to us a support of such experienced qualities as shape, colour, and taste, what this claim has to be construed as coming to is that it is *logically impossible* to perceive in any way the subject of attributes.[21]

The copy principle is vitiated by the construction put upon it by these critics. If it is taken to be an empirical generalization or hypothesis, then Hume cannot legitimately dismiss an exception (the missing shade of blue) as 'scarce worth our observing' (T 6). In addition to violating a fundamental principle of the experimental method, he would be allowing for the reprieve of the metaphysical ideas which he condemns, a reprieve solicited on the basis of this precedent. If, on the other hand, it were correct to say that Hume uses this principle as if it expressed a logically necessary

---

[20] *The Philosophy of David Hume* (Random House, New York, 1963).

[21] (Routledge and Kegan Paul, London, 1955), 153–4. Previously, Lazerowitz had written (p. 153): 'Consider again what Hume appears to have done, namely, to have looked for something by means of a series of careful observations. . . . The search was only a sham. For when Hume points out that the supposed idea of substance derives neither from sensation nor reflection, . . . it in effect tells us, not that it, like the idea of a centaur, is *fictitious*, but that there is *no such idea*. He tells us that the phrases "substance in which attributes inhere", "owner of attributes", "support of qualities" describe nothing actual or imaginable and are literally empty phrases to which no application has been given. Of course, then, there can be no looking for a bearer of properties . . . any more than there can be a search for binomial scarlet or for a "slithy tove".'

proposition, true by definition, then clearly his procedure throughout runs counter to the chief logical thesis of his entire system. His first principle formulates an inductive conclusion, based, like all inductions, upon the causal relation. ('The constant conjunction of our resembling perceptions, is a convincing proof, that the one are the causes of the other; and this priority of the impressions is an equal proof, that our impressions are the causes of our ideas, not our ideas of our impressions' (T 5).) According to the theory of philosophical relations expounded in the *Treatise* (Book I, Part iii, Section 1), or the distinction between Relations of Ideas and Matters of Fact, drawn in the first *Enquiry* (Section IV, Part i), this 'general proposition', 'maxim', or 'first principle' cannot be regarded as intuitively or demonstratively certain. Since the contrary of every matter of fact is possible, Hume has no logical warrant for denying the existence of any idea not derived from an impression. Thus Hume is depicted by his critics as setting out in the painfully awkward position of being impaled on the horns of a dilemma. If his first principle is accepted, as he presents it, as an empirical proposition, not only does he admit at the start that it has been falsified, but in any case it would lack the logical force needed for his analyses. If it is taken as a definition, his use of it is quite arbitrary, and his claim to have 'proved' it (T 5; $E_1$ 19, 62) violates his own distinction between analytic and synthetic propositions.

In my view, the copy principle is neither a 'contingent generalization' nor a 'pretentious tautology'. Nor is it a logical bastard born of miscegenation between these two distinct breeds of propositions. The copy principle is a rule of procedure. It pre-scribes a technique for investigating terms which are suspected of not having the meanings imputed to them in philosophical theories. It is a methodological instrument devised for semantic analysis. It is, as Hume says, a 'maxim', which means, in one acceptable sense of the term, 'a general principle serving as a rule or guide'—in this case, a rule or guide for testing terms by attempting to locate their referents amongst experienced ideas.

The question of whether or not a man has actually experienced the ideas required to ground his terms empirically is a question about his mental biography. It is inconvenient that no one but himself has access to the historical evidence needed to answer the question. No one can falsify his claims by adducing contrary empirical evidence, much less demonstrate their absurdity. But we are entitled to demand some information about the experiences from which his alleged ideas could have been derived. If the man suspected of talking nonsense is unable to indicate any imaginable experience to the content of which his terms might be related, 'this will serve to confirm our suspicion' (E₁ 22). It is important to notice how modest is Hume's claim for the result of any such analysis. Contrary to Thomas Reid and other critics down to our own time, philosophical terms are not condemned by Hume for their failure to pass his test. Suspicion that they may be meaningless is merely 'confirmed' by it.

The critical picture of Hume dismissing philosophical terms as meaningless (or ideas as fictions) by an automatic application of his copy principle is so gross an over-simplification that it bears almost no resemblance to his practice as an analyst. He feels compelled to explain how terms which are, in the sense intended, empirically vacuous found their way into the philosophical vocabulary. His aim is not the merely negative one of eliminating ⎤ ideas, but rather of removing conceptual confusion by clarifying ⎦ ideas. He does not, for example, simply discard the idea of necessary connexion after failing to ground it in causally related objects. He persists in his reflective analysis until he has elucidated the idea by discovering its source in a mental habit or propensity. Speaking of 'power', 'force', and 'necessary connexion', he says, revealingly:

... in all expression, *so apply'd*, we have really no distinct meaning, and make use only of common words, without any clear and determinate ideas. But as 'tis more probable, that these expressions do here lose their true meaning by being *wrong apply'd*, than that they never have any meaning; 'twill be proper to bestow another consideration on this subject, to see if possibly we can discover the nature and origin of those ideas, we annex to them. (T 162; Hume's italics)

There is no evidence that Hume came to regard his copy principle as a logically certain truth. His use of it implies the contrary. If Hume had wielded his first principle as a logically necessary one, as his critics allege, he would have condemned terms which violated the principle as absurdities. He never does this. He does not, for example, dismiss the idea of a simple, unchanging self as a self-contradiction, but as a fiction for which introspection discovers no source in experience.

Unfortunately, Hume was not always over-careful about making the purport of his arguments plain, and a less-than-careful reading usually ensures misunderstanding. Regarding the self of whose 'perfect identity and simplicity' some philosophers claim to be 'intimately conscious', he asks,

> For from what impression cou'd this idea be deriv'd? This question 'tis impossible to answer without a manifest contradiction and absurdity; and yet 'tis a question, which must necessarily be answer'd, if we would have the idea of self pass for clear and intelligible. It must be some one impression, that gives rise to every real idea. (T 251)

What Hume means is not that the idea of a simple, unchanging self is *per se* 'a manifest contradiction and absurdity', but that the attempt to locate 'some one impression' to which *all* of an individual's impressions 'are suppos'd to have a reference' would be self-contradictory and absurd. Even then he does not rest his cause upon logical grounds. He adduces the alleged fact that 'there is no impression constant and invariable' which could give rise to the sort of idea of the self which he contests. Any false impression arising here from Hume's speaking of contradiction and absurdity should have been corrected by his concluding remark:

> If any one upon serious and unprejudic'd reflexion, thinks he has a different notion of *himself*, I must confess I can reason no longer with him. All I can allow him is that he may be in the right as well as I, and that we are essentially different in this particular. He may, perhaps, perceive something simple and continu'd, which he calls *himself*; tho' I am certain there is no such principle in me. (T 252)

According to Hume's own account of the matter, he arrived at his copy principle by induction. The observed resemblance of simple ideas to prior impressions could not logically guarantee a universal law or axiom from which the exclusion of metaphysical fictions could be deduced. What Hume's introspection could quite legitimately, and actually did, yield was a methodological principle to guide him in the analysis of dubious terms. When the copy principle is construed as a rule of procedure, rather than as an empirical law, Hume's lack of concern about that missing shade of blue and other 'very rare . . . exceptions' (T 7) is understandable and does not, I think, contrary to Passmore, illustrate 'that insensitivity to consistency which Hume shares with Locke'.[22] Since the principle is not an empirical hypothesis threatened by negative instances, there is no more reason for Laird to extoll Hume's 'candour'[23] than for Prichard to deplore his 'effrontery'.[24] Hume's first principle must be assessed for its instrumental value in detecting the empirical content of key philosophical terms. If it really helps him to show that certain ideas which have been supposed to have given sources in experience have in fact others, and that the related terms must be redefined accordingly, the principle is pragmatically justified. The fact that a man may have the idea of a particular shade of blue of which he has had no prior impression shows only that in certain 'very rare' cases Hume's 'new microscope' (E$_1$ 62) will not work. We do not scrap our microscopes upon realizing their limitations. But neither do we claim that nothing can exist except what they reveal. But this, as I have argued, Hume never does. His 'new microscope' is not a magical device for making ideas vanish, but an instrument for tracing philosophical conceptions to their sources in experience.

In order to confirm this 'instrumentalist' interpretation it should be sufficient to consider only one other familiar objection to Hume's first principle which is thereby answerable but not otherwise. It is obvious that the distinction between impressions and ideas is absolutely fundamental to Hume's philosophy. The distinction is drawn in the very first sentence of the first Book of the *Treatise* and Hume invokes it repeatedly throughout that work and the first *Enquiry*. Unless there were a real difference between

[22] *Hume's Intentions*, 93.
[23] *Hume's Philosophy of Human Nature*, 36.
[24] Quoted in Passmore, op. cit. 93.

impressions and ideas, such that they could actually be distinguished in experience, there would be no warrant whatsoever for saying '*That all our simple ideas in their first appearance are deriv'd from simple impressions, which are correspondent to them, and which they exactly represent*' (T 4). Relations between indiscernibles cannot be determined. And yet Hume does admit that in certain exceptional circumstances it will be impossible to discriminate between them: 'Thus in sleep, in a fever, in madness, or in any very violent emotions of the soul, our ideas may approach to our impressions: As on the other hand it sometimes happens, that our impressions are so faint and low, that we cannot distinguish them from our ideas' (T 2). Construed as a psychological law from which explanations of mental processes are to be derived, the copy principle would be crippled by these occasional breakdowns in the distinction upon which it is based. No experimental philosopher could afford to base a psychological theory upon a first principle which might at any time be rendered inoperable. Taken as a guiding principle, or rule of procedure for analysis, Hume's copy principle can survive these lapses. For it is then understood simply as a technique to be consciously applied whenever possible by a philosopher reflecting upon the source of his ideas. Given the state of critical awareness assumed for such introspection, the philosopher, unlike the dreamer, the fevered, insane, over-wrought, or languid person, would not be likely to confuse what he sees with what he remembers, for example, or what he feels with what he imagines.

## Section 4. *Psychologism: A Parting Shot at Hume's Accusers*

It is time to sum up, and to take a parting shot at the critics of Hume's 'psychologism'. The copy principle is not a psychological law, but a methodological rule. It does not serve, as the principles of association do, as an axiom of the science of man. Its function is to provide clarifications of philosophical concepts, not explanations of psychological events. It is neither a definition nor a hypothesis used in the construction of psychological theories. It is a maxim to be followed in the course of philosophical analysis. It is true that Hume's first principle was derived from a reported observation of psychological facts, and its use does entail appeals to psychological facts. But it is no part of a psychological theory advanced to explain those or other facts. The psychological facts to which Hume appeals in the course of analysis are not adduced in order to verify the principle, for it is not put forth as an empirical hypothesis. The role of the principle is to direct Hume to the facts of immediate experience from which the meanings of key terms have been derived. Hume's first principle does not belong to the domain of descriptive psychology at all. Its force is prescriptive; it is a directive, a recommendation: 'Produce the impressions or original sentiments, from which the ideas are copied' ($E_1$ 62), he advises.

Antony Flew's patronizing comment about the success of Hume's analysis of necessary connection, 'notwithstanding that Hume is still thinking and writing within a cramping and distorting psychological framework',[25] seems to me 'distorted'. It presupposes that questions of meaning (problems of conceptual vagueness and confusion) can be resolved at a verbal level, without reference to the experiences of people who use language. Of this same analysis Flew later remarks, 'The contention which he was supposed to be supporting there was psychological. The thesis which the arguments he actually deploys in fact succeed in establishing is philosophical.'[26] Apparently Flew either maintains that psychological facts are irrelevant to philosophical theses, which strikes me as a pernicious dogma,[27] or he makes no distinction between psychological facts and psychological theories, which, I have been arguing, is a vicious confusion.

One may agree that what Flew calls the 'psychogenetic framework'[28] within which Hume fits his theory is unworkable. That

---

[25] *Hume's Philosophy of Belief*, 115.                    [26] Ibid. 117.
[27] See Donald S. Lee, 'The Pernicious Distinction Between Logic and Psychology', *Tulane Studies in Philosophy*, 13 (1964), 44–9. Cf. J. A. Robinson, 'Hume's Two Definitions of "Cause" Reconsidered', *Hume*, ed. V. C. Chappell, 167: 'Systematic evasion of empirical questions is an affectation philosophers have acquired in the twentieth century, and it is a very silly one.'
[28] *Hume's Philosophy of Belief*, 115.

much had been said before, by Basson,[29] for example, and, even earlier, by H. H. Price.[30] Strictly speaking, one cannot 'produce the impressions . . . from which the ideas are copied'. Sense impressions are not the sort of thing that can be publicly displayed, even if they could be retrieved. But, of course, they cannot be retrieved *as* impressions, but only in the form of ideas. Only a very literal-minded or contentious reader would interpret Hume's proposed technique of analysis as an operation which could never, on his own account of perception and memory, be performed. What he recommends is obviously the very sort of hypothetical reconstruction of the experiences with which controverted terms are associated that he devises for his own analyses. The modernization of Hume's empiricist criterion of meaning can be effected automatically by redirecting the testing procedure, by making it predictive rather than retrospective. Instead of asking a historical question about the experience out of which the alleged idea is supposed to have originated, one requests directions for setting up an experimental or experiential situation in which the authenticating sense experience should be forthcoming. This innovation represents merely an improvement on Hume's formulation of his technique by bringing it into line with practical possibility and with his own actual procedure. But it does not, I think, warrant the logical positivist's treatment of Hume as a superannuated precursor who muddled psychology and logic.

In *Language, Truth and Logic*, with explicit reference to Hume, A. J. Ayer proclaims that

the discussion of psychological questions is out of place in a philosophical inquiry. For the empiricist doctrine to which we are committed is a logical doctrine concerning the distinction between analytic propositions, synthetic propositions, and metaphysical verbiage; and as such it has no bearing on any psychological question of fact.[1]

Ayer may be right in thinking that definitions of 'analytic

---

[29] *Hume*, 36.

[30] 'The Permanent Significance of Hume's Philosophy', *Philosophy*, 15 (1940), 10–34; reprinted in Alexander Sesonke and Noel Fleming, edd. *Human Understanding: Studies in the Philosophy of David Hume* (Wadsworth, Belmont, California, 1965), 6.

[31] Gollancz, London, 1954, pp. 121–2.

proposition', 'synthetic proposition', and 'metaphysical verbiage' need not include any psychological terms. But is he right in thinking that one could arrive at the point of defining these logical types without any consideration of the mental experiences in which they are involved? Is it true to say that his version of the verifiability principle, in contrast with Hume's, has 'no bearing on any psychological question of fact'?

The criterion which we use to test the genuineness of apparent statements of fact is the criterion of verifiability. We say that a sentence is factually significant to any given person, if, and only if, he knows how to verify the proposition which it purports to express—that is, if he knows what observations would lead him, under certain conditions, to accept the proposition as being true, or reject it as being false.[32]

For a philosopher who distinguishes his own doctrine from classical empiricism, chiefly on the grounds of excluding 'irrelevant' psychological issues, Ayer's lapses into traditional patterns are strikingly frequent. One example may suffice to illustrate:

To say that an observation increases the probability of a hypothesis ... is equivalent to saying that it increases the degree of confidence with which it is rational to entertain the hypothesis. And here we may repeat that the rationality of a belief is defined, not by reference to any absolute standard, but by reference to part of our own actual practice.[33]

[32] Ibid. 35.
[33] Ibid. 101. Cf. Donald S. Lee, op. cit. 48–9: 'We can see the positivists condemning "psychologism" of any kind when it creeps into philosophy.

' "Epistemology used to be, by and large, a confused mixture of psychological and logical investigation. . . . Psychological investigations belong to the domain of factual knowledge, and must be conducted by using the methods of empirical science. Thus, they do not belong in epistemology. The latter can be nothing else but the logical analysis of knowledge . . ." (Kraft, Victor, *The Vienna Circle* (New York, 1953), p. 24.)

'If the early positivists were sure of what they meant by "psychology" then the above dichotomy would be very clear, but they themselves find answers to some questions in psychological terms and so fall into a pit they had dug for others. For the following quote contains more doubtful psychology than most behavioristic psychologists would allow:

' "But what occurs in the process of understanding the designation [of anything] is that each one of us substitutes for these variables qualitative contents from his own experience which are determined by these relationships. The designation is thus connected for each person individually with a subjective quality content, not

How can one account for this discrepancy between official policy and actual practice except by recognizing that the wholesale exclusion of psychological considerations from epistemology is impractical? That is a point which Hume recognized and upon which he stands in need of no correction.

just with a structure. The designation, then, has an individual subjective meaning over and above its intersubjective meaning; for each individual it also designates a qualitative content known to him from his own experience." (Ibid. p. 44.)

'I would hardly go so far as to say that this is a logical analysis of knowledge.'

# PART V

## Beliefs, Reasonable and Otherwise: New Grounds for Discrimination

### Section 1. *The Earlier and the Later Hume*

HUME formed his opinions in epistemology and metaphysics, in ethics and politics, and upon human nature and religion when very young, and during forty years of philosophical thinking he found no sufficient reason for altering them materially. Despite this stability of conviction, after the indifferent reception of *A Treatise of Human Nature*, he was able to make a new departure in his treatment of those subjects. His grand design for a comprehensive, integrated system was shelved, and thereafter his writings appeared independently of one another. They are all, of course, expressions of a single, coherent philosophical point of view, recognizably Hume's own. But unlike the three Books of his first prodigy, each later essay, treatise, and dialogue could have made its own way alone in the world.

The first decisive move in this new deployment of forces is made by exploiting the analytical or critical value of his theory of knowledge independently of its role in a general theory of human nature. In the *Treatise*, Hume's theory 'Of the Understanding' takes its place alongside theories 'Of the Passions' and 'Of Morals' as part of a systematic explanation of man's intellectual, emotional, and social life. It is also intended to vindicate the method used throughout and, along with the psychology of the emotions, to stand as the foundation of work in politics and criticism as well as in ethics. But this is not the end of the various and exacting demands which Hume makes upon his epistemology, or 'Logic', as he calls it. It is also expected to control later examinations of the foundations of natural science, mathematics, and natural religion, and it is applied to the critical analysis of a number of meta-physical concepts, principles, and doctrines. Given this diversity of assignments, and Hume's policy of following his analyses of conceptual errors with psychological explanations of them, it is not surprising that the distinction between philosophical analysis and psychological theory was obscured in the *Treatise*. In *An Enquiry Concerning Human Understanding* Hume displays this 'Logic' essentially *as* a theory of philosophical analysis, and it appears much more clearly in this book that the validity of his sceptical critique of metaphysics and theology does not depend upon psychological theories introduced to explain thought processes.

It was not difficult to show that Hume's original intention of basing his logic upon the science of human nature (i.e. his philosophical analysis upon a psychology of the understanding) was misconceived and aborted by natural causes. It would be more difficult to conclude how he diagnosed the disorders of the *Treatise*. In an oft-quoted passage of his autobiography, Hume remarks that he 'had always entertained a notion, that my want of success in publishing the Treatise of Human Nature, had pro-ceeded more from the manner than the matter, and that I had been guilty of a very usual indiscretion, in going to the press too early. I therefore cast the first part of that work anew in the enquiry concerning Human Understanding. . . .'[1] And in the 'Advertisement' prefixed to the 1777 edition of *Essays and Treatises on Several Subjects*, written, like 'My Own Life', a few months before his death, he admitted 'some negligences in his former reasoning', but again insisted that the defects of the *Treatise* were more a matter of the 'expression'. He does not advertise any significant changes or additions to the philosophical content of the *Treatise*; on the contrary, he begins by saying that 'Most of the principles, and reasonings, contained in this volume, were published in a work in three volumes, called A Treatise of Human Nature.' Although Hume's claim to have 'cast the whole [of the *Treatise*] anew in the following pieces' is surely an over-statement, omissions of earlier material from the recastings are not

---

[1] 'My Own Life', prefixed to *The History of England*, dated 18 Apr. 1776.

reliable signs of changes in his 'philosophical sentiments and principles'. In his own judgement, the Enquiries present 'the same Doctrines, better illustrated & expresst' (L I 187).

Not all of Hume's commentators agree with his own estimate of the consistency between his earliest and later writings. The chief aim of Selby-Bigge's Introduction to his edition of Hume's Enquiries is to document changes, especially deletions from the recastings of the first two Books of the *Treatise* into the *Enquiry Concerning Human Understanding* and the *Dissertation on the Passions*, and changes of emphasis, as well as omissions, in the rewriting of Book III as the *Enquiry Concerning the Principles of Morals*. A subsidiary purpose is to display most of these alterations as symptomatic of 'the lower philosophical standard of the later work' (E xiv), which, it is insinuated, is attributable to Hume's having sacrificed philosophical rigour, profundity, and completeness to literary 'elegance, lucidity and proportion' (E x). Antony Flew, who deplores Selby-Bigge's imputation of unworthy motives to Hume, regards the first *Enquiry* as 'a substantially different book'[2] rather than a pared and polished version of Book I of the *Treatise* redesigned for popular consumption. By contrast, whereas Selby-Bigge is led to suppose 'that the system of Morals in the Enquiry is really and essentially different from that in the Treatise' (E xiii), John Stewart argues at length that 'there is nothing in the *Enquiry* that requires that a theory attributed to Hume on the basis of what he says in the *Treatise* be modified'.[3]

I shall not attempt to arbitrate between these conflicting accounts of the relations between Hume's first book and its successors, much less to mediate in the dispute about their comparative merits. All must agree upon the factual issue of what material differences there are between the original and later versions. The contentious question is what interpretation is to be put upon these differences in order to give an illuminating account

[2] *Hume's Philosophy of Belief*, 7. Flew stresses the point that almost a third of the first *Enquiry* consists of entirely new material.
[3] *The Moral and Political Philosophy of David Hume*, Appendix: The Recastings, 337.

of Hume's philosophical development. Consequently, I am here concerned with these changes only as signs of the fundamental redirection of Hume's approach to philosophical problems which took place after the publication of the *Treatise*.

There are two reasons for attempting to work out my version of these differences with reference to Hume's theory of belief. One has to do with the importance of the theory, the other with certain difficulties which make it a test case for my interpretation. Most commentators would, I think, concur with John Stewart's judgement that Hume's 'great and central aim in the first book of the *Treatise* is to reveal the importance and nature of belief'.[4] And most readers would consider Antony Flew's study of the first *Enquiry* appropriately entitled *Hume's Philosophy of Belief*. The problem of belief, of discovering the grounds upon which men base their beliefs, and of discriminating between ground which is tenable and that which is not concerned Hume, as it should any serious philosopher, from the beginning, and, as his last work shows, it held his interest to the end. Hume makes such a prolific display of psychological ingenuity in investigating belief that it becomes increasingly difficult to defend him against the charge of burying philosophical issues beneath an avalanche of psychological theory. From a philosophical theory of belief one expects a criterion for distinguishing between rational beliefs and irrational ones, and undoubtedly it was this that Hume aimed to provide. But how could any such criterion be derived from a psychological explanation of how beliefs are, in fact, acquired? If the problem of belief is construed as an empirical one, the appropriate solution consists in specifying the conditions under which beliefs of all sorts come to be held. It seems pretty obvious that an investigation conducted with such indifference to normative distinctions could yield no standard by which to separate justifiable beliefs from superstitions or prejudices. Even more threatening to the construction which I have been putting on the history of Hume's thought is the reappearance of a distinctly psychological treatment of belief in the first *Enquiry*.

---

[4] *The Moral and Political Philosophy of David Hume*, Appendix: The Recastings, 325.

Any reader coming to Section V, Part ii of the *Enquiry* from Book I, Pt. iii of the *Treatise* will find himself on familiar, although greatly contracted, ground. He will meet some of the same illustrations, and even several paragraphs transplanted intact; and he will find nothing to cast doubt on Hume's own statement to Gilbert Elliot that 'The philosophical principles are the same in both' (L I 158). But he will also notice how drastically Hume has pruned his original text. The question is whether these deletions are merely a case of 'shortening and simplifying', as Hume explained in this same letter, or reliable signs of the change of tactics which I have been attributing to the later Hume. I believe that a comparison of Hume's two presentations of his doctrine of belief will confirm my view that the critical function of his 'Logic' (epistemology) is performed independently of the explanatory role of his empirical psychology. The actual independence of logic and theoretical psychology, which was obscured in Hume's fated attempt to integrate philosophical analysis with the science of human nature in the *Treatise*, shows itself plainly in the first *Enquiry*, where Hume's aims are essentially critical, not constructive.

## Section 2. *Hume's Theory of Natural Belief: the* Treatise *and* First Enquiry *Compared*

Hume did not overtax himself in rewriting his theory of natural belief for the first *Enquiry*. He simply culled passages from Sections 7 and 8 of Book I, Part iii of the *Treatise*, and from the Appendix, and rearranged them. Some he rephrased; others are set down verbatim. Apart from lines inserted to stitch this patchwork together, no new material of any interest shows up until the last two paragraphs of Section V, Part ii ($E_1$ 54–5). Since men can imagine many things which they cannot believe, Hume asks, 'Wherein, therefore, consists the difference between such a fiction and belief?' ($E_1$ 47; cf. T 95). It does not consist in a 'peculiar idea' (of reality or existence, Hume presumably means) being connected with credible ideas, for then the freedom of the imagination to associate ideas would make believing purely voluntary, which it is not ($E_1$ 47–8; cf. T 624). The difference, Hume concludes, is a matter of feeling determined by natural causes ($E_1$ 48; cf. T 96). One object or event, perceived or remembered, evokes the idea of another which has been experienced in conjunction with it ($E_1$ 48; cf. T 97). One is free to imagine unlikely objects and implausible events, but to believe only those ideas which are called up in accordance with principles of association: 'I say, then, that belief is nothing but a more vivid, lively, forcible, firm, steady conception of an object, than what the imagination alone is ever able to attain' ($E_1$ 49; cf. T 97, 629). Hume stresses the pragmatic difference between fictions and beliefs; belief in ideas 'gives them more weight and influence . . . and renders them the governing principle of our actions' ($E_1$ 49–50; cf. T 629).

This description of belief is followed by an explanation derived from the theory of association. The vivid and steady conception typical of belief is analogous to the manner of entertaining ideas evoked by association through resemblance, contiguity, or causation ($E_1$ 50–1; cf. T 98–101). In four paragraphs copied straight from the *Treatise* Hume illustrates this point ($E_1$ 51–3; cf. T 99–101). The idea of an absent friend is enlivened by a picture of him. The returning traveller's idea of his home is vivified by contiguity as he enters his own neighbourhood. The devotee's idea of a saint is intensified by handling some artefact produced by him. Whereas in the *Treatise* Hume devoted one Section (Book I, Part iii, Section 9) to showing the subordinate role of resemblance and contiguity, here in the *Enquiry* he merely observes that their efficacy in enlivening ideas presupposes belief ($E_1$ 53–4). (A portrait would not enhance the idea of a subject in whose reality the viewer did not already believe.) Beliefs in matters which transcend present sense experience and memory are founded on the causal relation. Our belief that a dry log thrown on the fire will burn derives from our invariable experience of past conjunctions.

The metaphysical complacency of Hume's concluding note strikes a dramatic contrast with the scepticism of the *Treatise*:

Here, then, is a kind of preestablished harmony between the course of nature and the succession of our ideas; and though the powers and forces, by which the former is governed, be wholly unknown to us; yet our thoughts and conceptions have still, we find, gone on in the same train with the other works of nature. (E$_1$ 54–5)

In the *Treatise* Hume had said,

'Tis evident, that however that object, which is present to my senses, and that other, whose existence I infer by reasoning, may be thought to influence each other by their particular powers or qualities; yet as the phaenomenon of belief, which we at present examine, is merely internal, these powers and qualities, being entirely unknown, can have no hand in producing it. (T 102)

If so, how can we '*find*' that mental sequences correspond to the course of nature? Hume's reply is pragmatic and naturalistic. We find that we must posit such a correspondence in order to account for our success in predicting and controlling events and thus for our ability to profit from experience. Man's adaptation to his environment is not an achievement of reason, but must be attributed to 'some instinct or mechanical tendency' (E$_1$ 55; cf. T 103–4). The dualism between events in the mind and those in the external world is retained. We can understand neither the 'powers and forces' which determine physical events, nor the means by which they are harmonized with mental ones. We can only wonder, and admire the orchestration. Hume has not relinquished his former scepticism. He has learned to accept it with equanimity.

However, it is differences, rather than similarities, between the first and the revised version of the theory of belief that concern us. In the *Treatise* Hume leaves no doubt that his 'new hypothesis' (T 107) advanced to explain belief is of crucial importance. After meticulously exploring the same ground later sketchily surveyed in the *Enquiry*, he begins a new Section (9) to 'confirm such extraordinary, and such fundamental principles' (T 106–7). In the course of answering anticipated objections, he applies his theory to the explanation of credulity and self-deception and of beliefs attributable to conditioning and education. Hume always had a consuming interest in the pathology of error, and he obviously valued his theory as a basis for explaining aberrant beliefs. In the

*Enquiry*, however, his theory is introduced on very different terms. Having in Part i of Section V shown that inductive inferences are grounded in habits formed by observing constant conjunctions, not in rational insight into causal properties, he concludes by remarking, 'At this point, it would be very allowable for us to stop our philosophical researches' ($E_1$ 47). He suggests that readers who find abstract speculation entertaining, despite 'a degree of doubt and uncertainty', proceed with Part ii. 'As to readers of a different taste; the remaining part of this section is not calculated for them, and the following enquiries may well be understood, though it be neglected' ($E_1$ 47). This contrast reflects a profound change in Hume's conception of the role to be played in his philosophy by his psychological explanation of belief. Since Hume nowhere comments on his change of tactics, it is impossible to say how calculated it was. But if one reflects on the differing uses actually made of the theory of belief in the two works, it appears that Hume's sceptical critique of metaphysics and religion has settled itself on a new basis in the first *Enquiry*.

Part iv of Book I of the *Treatise*, 'Of the Sceptical and other Systems of Philosophy', is not short nor easy, and its connections with earlier parts are numerous and complicated. Fortunately, it is not necessary to examine it in detail in order to compare the method of criticism used there with that adopted in the first *Enquiry*. A few remarks on the general purport of Part iv will suffice to introduce the main point about Hume's style of philosophical criticism in the *Treatise* and the modifications of it made in the first *Enquiry*.

In his critique of philosophical systems, Hume deals with representative positions and doctrines, often without identifying their contenders. He usually begins by probing at some vulnerable assumption shared by unreflective men. He next introduces a philosophical theory which has been devised to remove the perplexities inherent in the presuppositions of common sense. Then he examines the theory in order to show that it involves even greater difficulties than the naïve view that it was supposed to improve upon, and furthermore lacks the natural authority of a spontaneous belief. The logical sequence of Hume's procedure duplicates the stages in the history of all attempts to rationalize such instinctually based beliefs as that a world of physical objects exists independently of mind and its perceptions. The result of the metaphysician's failure to validate the fundamental beliefs upon which men are required by nature to act is philosophical scepticism about the possibility of rationally reconstructing the foundations of thought and action. The sceptic adopts, as a matter of conscious and enlightened policy, the same attitude of 'Carelessness and in-attention' (T 218) toward the inconsistencies inherent in prag-matically justified beliefs as the plain man takes unreflectively.

It is taken for granted by 'the generality of mankind' (T 202) that sense perception is a matter of immediate acquaintance with objects. It never occurs to the plain man to distinguish between perceptions in his mind and objects in the external world. It is, however, easy for philosophers to show that his naïvely realistic assumption is untenable. A few references to experience are enough to convince him that his perceptions are dependent upon his sense organs. But no one could convince him that objects are so dependent. He experiences the discontinuity of his perceptions and believes in the continuity of objects which, on the assumption that perceptions and objects are identical, leaves him with a pair of incompatible convictions. In order to take account of the fleeting character of perceptions and the permanence of physical objects, philosophers distinguish between perceptions and objects.

When this dualistic system becomes in turn a subject of philosophical scrutiny, it fares no better than the unreflective view which it replaced. The objects in question would have to be inferred from perceptions, the only entities with which a mind has immediate acquaintance. Such an inference, from a present impression to an object beyond the limits of sense experience, could only be based upon causality. But the idea of a causal relation between perceptions and objects could never be acquired; since perceptions alone are experienced, constant conjunctions between them and objects could never, in principle, be observed. The philosophers' objects are metaphysical fictions in whose reality experience provides no grounds for belief and whose re-lation to perceptions cannot be explained. Since only perceptions are ever present in consciousness, it is impossible to conceive of objects distinctly in contrast to them.

Although Hume is bent upon discrediting perception/object dualism, he is not sceptical of men's natural belief in the independent existence of objects, despite its self-contradictory entailments. The metaphysical hypothesis is expendable. It cures old problems by creating new ones. It commits the philosopher to a speculative opinion which is set aside in the affairs of everyday life. It opens up a line of questioning which would undermine the belief that it aims to validate, were that belief not unshakeable by nature, neither needing nor admitting rational justification. Although there is no way to prove that the objects in whose reality men believe actually exist, it should be possible to discover the causes of the belief. And it is with this problem of psychological explanation that Hume is mainly preoccupied in the *Treatise*.

It is otherwise in the first *Enquiry*, where, in Section XII, Hume restricts himself to making the purely sceptical point that philosophers are unable to supply a rational basis for natural belief. Part i of that Section is a compendium of those passages of Sections 2 and 4 of Book I, Part iv of the *Treatise* in which Hume examines the plain man's tacit assumptions and the philosophers' assertions about the perceptual world in order to bring out the internal contradictions in both. No psychological explanation of the natural belief in the external world is attempted in the *Enquiry*. It is simply put down to a 'blind and powerful instinct of nature' ($E_1$ 151). When introducing his discussion in the *Treatise*, Hume wrote, 'The subject, then, of our present enquiry is concerning the *causes* which induce us to believe in the existence of body' (T 187–8); and he devoted twenty-three of the thirty-one pages of Section 2 to that subject, relying constantly upon his doctrine of belief and, therefore, ultimately, upon the theory of association. The perplexities latent in the natural belief of the unreflective man, and the futility of metaphysical devices to remove them, which in the *Treatise* is a derivative theme developed in the last eight pages, becomes the exclusive subject of Section XII, Part i, of the *Enquiry*. In other words, Hume has divorced his philosophical analyses of common-sense assumptions and metaphysical speculation about the external world from his doctrine of belief. Far from providing a psychological theory from which the analysis is supposedly derived, his psychological explanation of belief is offered earlier (Section V, Part ii) as speculation which 'though it be neglected', as he says, 'the following enquiries may well be understood' ($E_1$ 47).

What seems to me to have happened is that the actual logical independence of Hume's psychological theory and his philosophical analysis, which was sometimes obscured in the presentation of the *Treatise*, has been tacitly recognized in the procedure adopted in the first *Enquiry*. Nowhere in his published writings, as I have mentioned, nor in the letters which have survived, does Hume expressly acknowledge that in the *Enquiry* philosophical analysis is put on a new footing. Although Hume's own conception of this change of policy is therefore a subject for speculation, the actual nature and importance of the change itself is evident in the texts. The substitution of a distinction between types of propositions ($E_1$ 25–6), based on the concept of logical possibility, for the theory of relations (T 13–15; 69–70), which distinguished intuitive and demonstrative reasoning from empirical on the basis of a describable difference in the mental operations involved, is the most obvious instance of a quasi-psychological doctrine being replaced by a logical one. But even more interesting than this generally recognized case is the detaching of Hume's psychology of belief from his philosophical analysis of the natural belief in the reality of the external world and of the attempt by metaphysicians to rationally justify it. For this move was forced by Hume's inevitable failure in the *Treatise* to integrate his science of man with his analytical philosophy, and it shows that more than 'shortening and simplifying' was required of the *Enquiry* to establish his credentials as a critic of metaphysics independently of his merits as a psychologist.

Epistemological questions about belief are mainly normative, to be answered in terms of tests of significance, rules of evidence, principles of inference, standards of testimony, and the like. The epistemologist aims at formulating criteria by which to distinguish rationally justified beliefs from groundless opinions, from

superstition and prejudice. Psychological questions about belief
are factual, to be answered by empirical investigations of the
temperamental and cultural factors which influence belief and of
the behaviour which is motivated by it, of the experiences through
which beliefs are reinforced and weakened, and so on. In searching
for general principles by which to explain belief, the psychologist
reserves judgement on which beliefs are reasonable, impartially
taking all those which men actually hold as data. He may, of
course, acknowledge a distinction between reasoned belief and
prejudice, for example, and search out the differing underlying
conditions; but the distinction itself must be given prior to his
investigation, not derived from it. The neutrality of the psychologist and the bias of the epistemologist are oddly mixed in
Hume's writing about belief in the *Treatise*; and it is instructive
for understanding his dilemma to consider the incongruity.

   Hume's discussion 'Of the causes of belief' in Section 8 of Part
iii, Book I, of the *Treatise* begins with a statement of 'a general
maxim in the science of human nature, *that when any impression
becomes present to us, it not only transports the mind to such ideas as are
related to it, but likewise communicates to them a share of its force and
vivacity*' (T 98). Among the 'experiments' which he cites in confirmation of this maxim are the 'mummeries' of Roman Catholics
('devotees of that strange superstition' (T 99; cf. $E_1$ 51)) who
strengthen their belief by the use of 'sensible types and images'
(T 100; cf. $E_1$ 51–2), and the fondness of 'superstitious people' for
'reliques of saints and holy men' (T 101; cf. $E_1$ 53). Hume's
pejorative language makes it abundantly clear that he gives no
credence to these beliefs. He is none the less quite prepared to use
them as verifying evidence for his theory. Similarly, in the next
Section, he finds in credulity—the 'remarkable propensity to
believe whatever is reported, . . . however contrary to daily experience and observation' (T 113)—and in beliefs induced by education, whose 'maxims are frequently contrary to reason' (T 117),
'additional confirmation' for 'the present hypothesis' (T 115).
Evidently Hume did not suppose that strength of conviction was
an index to the probable truth of a belief. Indeed, in Section 13,
'Of unphilosophical probability,' he concedes that it would be

unphilosophical to suppose that an argument is weakened because the belief induced by it diminishes with time. It is in this same section that Hume describes the natural tendency to mistake accidental associations for causal relations and anticipates the need for 'Rules by which to judge of causes and effects' (S. 15). The need for such rules is genuine, and as I argued earlier, extracting them from procedures which have proved reliable is legitimate. But neither the rules nor even the need of them can be inferred solely from the descriptive account of the vagaries of the imagination which sometimes produce belief.

Since philosophical analysis reveals the contradictions inherent even in universal and invulnerable beliefs—that an external world exists and is perceived, for example, or that men preserve their identities throughout their lifetimes—no standard of rationality can be derived from a psychological explanation of how beliefs are actually acquired. At this point either one becomes utterly sceptical about all beliefs and therefore either entirely permissive or quite dogmatic, or new ground upon which to make discriminations must be found. In my view, it was because Hume recognized or, at the very least, sensed this requirement that he so drastically scaled down his psychological theory of belief and declared it irrelevant to the critical analyses of metaphysics and religion which followed.


## Section 3. *Hume's Thinking About Religious Belief*

The once prevalent view that Hume's treatment of religious belief is 'wanting in high seriousness', as A. E. Taylor complained,[5] is now, I trust, superannuated, along with Selby-Bigge's verdict that Sections X and XI of *An Enquiry Concerning Human Understanding*, 'Of Miracles' and 'Of a particular Providence and of a future State', are 'quite superfluous' (E viii). Judgements such as Randall's, that Hume 'had no real interest in either science or

[5] 'Symposium: The Present-Day Relevance of Hume's *Dialogues Concerning Natural Religion*', *Proceedings of the Aristotelian Society*, Supp. Vol. 18 (1939), 179.

religion',[6] or Taylor's, that 'he did not "care" in any vital sense'
about the issue 'between theism and atheism',[7] admit of no
decisive refutation simply because they are gratuitous. Where no
reasons are offered for such aspersions, there is no point toward
which a counter-argument can be directed. If a writer were
sufficiently perverse to declare that Newton had no real interest in
either astronomy or optics, or that Gibbon did not really care
about history, it is unlikely that he would be dissuaded by a
dispassionate review of the scientist's or the historian's career.
Critics who appreciate Hume's quality as a man and as a thinker
would no doubt have ignored such bigoted nonsense had not a
tradition of disparagement grown up around his work. However,
since such basically sympathetic luminaries as John Stuart Mill and
T. H. Huxley, as well as Hume's own major editors, have affected
the abusive tone adopted in the eighteenth century by John
Brown, William Warburton, James Beattie, and many others, a
number of Hume's admirers have rallied to his defence.

Norman Kemp Smith's inaugural address[8] to a joint meeting of
the Aristotelian Society, the Scots Philosophical Club, and the
Mind Association in the bicentenary year of the publication of the
*Treatise* and, seventeen years later, Ernest Campbell Mossner's
paper, 'Philosophy and Biography: the Case of David Hume',[9]
are, I suppose, the best known of these apologies. The conventional picture of Hume as an opportunist who quit the straight
path of philosophy early in life for an easier road to literary fame
and fortune was already discredited by 1961 when Antony Flew
published *Hume's Philosophy of Belief*. The main contribution of
this book to the reappraisal of Hume's reputation consisted in
defending *An Enquiry Concerning Human Understanding* against the

[6] 'David Hume: Radical Empiricist and Pragmatist', quoted by E. C. Mossner,
'Philosophy and Biography: The Case of David Hume', in *Hume*, ed. V. C.
Chappell, p. 11.
[7] 'Symposium: The Present-Day Relevance of Hume's *Dialogues Concerning
Natural Religion*', 180.
[8] In 'Hume and Present-Day Problems', *Proceedings of the Aristotelian Society*,
Supp. Vol. 18 (1939). The address appears as ch. xxiv, 'The Relation of the
*Treatise* to the *Enquiries*', of *The Philosophy of David Hume*.
[9] *The Philosophical Review*, 59 (1950); reprinted in V. C. Chappell, ed. *Hume*
(Doubleday Anchor, New York, 1966).

current view expressed by Green and Grose in the Preface to their edition of Hume's works: 'Anyone who will be at the pains to read the "Inquiries" alongside of the original "Treatise" will find that their only essential difference from it is in the way of omission. They consist in the main of excerpts from the "Treatise", re-written in a lighter style, and with the more difficult parts of it left out' (G & G I vi)—a reading quite in keeping with Grose's opinion that after the publication of the *Treatise* Hume 'wrote little that was new' (G & G III 75).

Another conventional and moralistic judgement, that Hume irrelevantly inserted offensive discussions of miracles and the design argument into the first *Enquiry* as a bid for notoriety—with 'habituées of coffee-houses', as Selby-Bigge put it (E xii)—is challenged by Flew's chapters (viii and ix) on Sections X and XI. It is astonishing that a quarter of a century after the publication of Kemp Smith's critical edition of *Dialogues Concerning Natural Religion*, with its introductory review of Hume's life-long and deeply felt preoccupation with religious belief and its associated irrationality, bigotry, and cruelty, Flew still felt the need to con-tend against the charge that Hume's concern with religious belief was superficial and his discussion of its grounds in the first *Enquiry* superfluous. However, if further stragglers flying Taylor's colours turn up at the arena, they will find Antony Flew there, admirably fit to joust with them in order to prove the 'high seriousness' and relevance of the religious content of the first *Enquiry*. Unfortun-ately, Flew is in no position to defend his author against the philosophically more interesting and important charge that Hume's psychological theory of belief provides no grounds for distinguishing between the reasoned beliefs of the wise man and the 'sophistry and illusion' of the superstitious. I shall return to consider this objection after reviewing the main points of Hume's critique of religion, both natural and revealed.

It appears from Hume's letters that a discussion of miracles had been intended for the *Treatise* but was withdrawn out of deference to Joseph Butler whose opinion of the manuscript Hume hoped to solicit before publication. By its inclusion in the first *Enquiry*, whether in original or revised form is not certain, Hume made public his enmity to revealed religion. Natural religion is served with less contempt but equal stringency in the following Section, 'Of a particular Providence and of a future State'. It has been suggested that 'Of the Practical Consequences of Natural Theology', as this Section was called on its first appearance, may also have been prepared for the *Treatise*; but it seems to me more likely that it represents work in progress toward *Dialogues Concerning Natural Religion*, about which Hume was corresponding within three years.

Hume's eleventh-hour pruning—'castrating', he called it—did not strip his first work of all its obvious religious implications. For example, he concludes from his analysis of immaterial substance that 'the question concerning the substance of the soul is absolutely unintelligible' and whether one holds a materialist or immaterialist doctrine of mind 'In both cases the metaphysical arguments for the immortality of the soul are equally inconclusive' (T 250). His analysis of the idea of existence in the closing Section of Part ii, Book I exposes the fallacy of treating existence as a predicate (i.e. a specific idea derived from a distinct impression), as required by the ontological argument. The cosmological proof of God's existence, which turns upon the necessity of every being having a cause, is undermined by his analysis of causality, which construes causal necessity as a psychological rather than as a cosmological force (T 159–60; 248–9; cf. D 188–9). Of the three traditional proofs of God's existence recognized by Kant, the argument from design (the physico-theological proof) remained; and because natural theology had come to rest almost entirely upon it in the Newtonian age, Hume dealt with it exhaustively in later works.

Whereas his refutation of the first two arguments depends upon analysis of a central concept, his criticism of the design argument involves elaborating and applying rules of inductive logic which have been extracted from scientific procedures to which theologians pretend to conform their speculations. The moral argument for God's existence and for the immortality of the soul, to which Kant resorted, also becomes a casualty in Hume's campaign against the argument from design. From the natural inequities amongst men one might infer the indifference or even the malice of the author of nature. Against this verdict the theologian keeps ready a convertible argument, the vicious circularity of which he hides by never displaying both of its advantages on the same day. On one day he argues from the premiss of God's perfect justice to an after-life in which the inequities of this world will be redressed; on another day he uses the rectifying after-life as a premiss from which to reach a conclusion about God's perfect justice. The sequence is reversible, of course, but Hume will concede neither argument, for he sees that both premisses are groundless. In his suppressed essay 'On the Immortality of the Soul' he puts the same question as is raised by the spokesman for Epicurus in the *Enquiry* (E₁ 141) and by Philo in the *Dialogues* (D 166, 199):

> Let us now consider the *moral* arguments, chiefly those derived from the justice of God, which is supposed to be further interested in the further punishment of the vicious and reward of the virtuous.
>
> But these arguments are grounded on the supposition, that God has attributes beyond what he has exerted in this universe, with which alone we are acquainted. Whence do we infer the existence of these attributes? (G & G IV 400)

In the *Enquiry* Hume shows that the inference violates a rule of causal reasoning tacitly honoured by scientists:

> If the cause be known only by the effect, we never ought to ascribe to it any qualities, beyond what are precisely requisite to produce the effect: Nor can we, by any rules of just reasoning, return back from the cause, and infer other effects from it, beyond those by which alone it is known to us. (E₁ 130)

Hume then applies his rule to the design argument, by which God's moral perfection is established on the supposition of a future state:

> And if you affirm, that, while a divine providence is allowed, and a supreme distributive justice in the universe, I ought to expect some more particular reward of the good, and punishment of the bad, beyond the ordinary course of events; I here find the same fallacy, which I have before endeavoured to detect. You persist in imagining, that, if we grant that divine existence, for which you so earnestly

contend, you may safely infer consequences from it, and add something to the experienced order of nature, by arguing from the attributes which you ascribe to your gods. You seem not to remember, that all your reasonings on this subject can only be drawn from effects to causes; and that every argument, deducted from causes to effects, must of necessity be a gross sophism; since it is impossible for you to know anything of the cause, but what you have antecedently, not inferred, but discovered to the full, in the effect.

But what must a philosopher think of those vain reasoners, who, instead of regarding the present scene of things as the sole object of their contemplation, so far reverse the whole course of nature, as to render this life merely a passage to something further; a porch, which leads to a greater and vastly different building; a prologue, which serves only to introduce the piece, and give it more grace and propriety? Whence, do you think, can such philosophers derive their idea of the gods? From their own conceit and imagination surely. For if they derived it from the present phenomena, it would never point to anything farther, but must be exactly adjusted to them. ($E_1$ 140–1)

The attempt 'to save the honour of the gods' must fail without the doctrine of immortality, to which Hume's objections are, I find, quite irresistible. After disposing of the metaphysical arguments in the *Treatise*, Hume added that 'the moral arguments and those deriv'd from the analogy of nature are equally strong and convincing' (T 250). In the essay 'On the Immortality of the Soul' all three go down together. Hume argues that since the permanence of immaterial substance is compatible with total loss of memory or consciousness, the concept of substance is useless for the doctrine of personal immortality. Physical arguments from the analogy of nature are pressed to a conclusion contradicting Butler's. Speaking of body and soul, Hume writes,

Where any two objects are so closely connected, that all alterations, which we have ever seen in the one, are attended with proportionable alterations in the other: we ought to conclude, by all rules of analogy, that, when there are still greater alterations produced in the former, and it is totally dissolved, there follows a total dissolution of the latter. (G & G IV 403)

So far as moral arguments are concerned, Hume finds them vindictive and inhumane. Eternal rewards and punishments are socially useless and incommensurate with man's frailty and the brevity of his earthly life. 'Punishment, without any proper end or purpose, is inconsistent with *our* ideas of goodness and justice and no end can be served by it after the whole scene is closed. Punishment, according to *our* conception, should bear some proportion to the offence. Why then eternal punishment for the temporary offences of so frail a creature as man?' (G & G IV 402).

Although the spokesman for Epicurus in the *Enquiry* claims that his own morality is based solely upon his experience of the natural and social consequences of virtuous and vicious behaviour, the question of whether or not belief in eternal rewards and punishments does have a salutary effect upon the conduct of unphilosophical men is left hanging. It is answered negatively in Part XII of the *Dialogues*, where Philo expresses Hume's animus toward religious influences upon morality. Hume considered religious belief psychologically debilitating (D 225-6), morally ineffectual at best (D 220-1), but often pernicious (D 222), and socially disastrous (D 220). The aim of his ethical work, described in very general terms, is to give a humanistic interpretation of moral experience. The genesis of moral feelings, distinctions, and judgements he finds in human nature and the exigencies of social life. Specifically religious virtues make no appeal to a man's natural sympathy for other men, nor do religious sanctions promote the interests of the artificial virtues in regulating communal life. 'To suppose measures of approbation and blame different from the human', Hume observes, 'confounds everything' (G & G IV 402). His first purely religious publication, 'Of Superstition and Enthusiasm', concerns 'the pernicious effects of *superstition* and *enthusiasm*, the corrupters of true religion . . . on government and society' (G & G III 144). Since by 'true religion' Hume means a philosopher's rational assent to '*one simple, though somewhat ambiguous, at least undefined proposition, that the cause or causes of order in the universe probably bear some remote analogy to human intelligence*' (D 227)—a proposition with no practical (moral) consequences whatever—he obviously intends his strictures to apply to 'religion, as it has commonly been found in the world' (D 223). The indictment is pressed outspokenly in *The Natural*

172 Beliefs, Reasonable and Otherwise

*History of Religion* where Hume castigates theism for its 'sacred zeal and rancour, the most furious and implacable of all human passions' (G & G IV 337), whose evil consequences are copiously documented in *The History of England.*[10]

[10] For example, commenting on events in Britain prior to the Civil War, Hume observes that '. . . the grievances which tended chiefly to inflame the Parliament and nation, especially the latter, were the surplice, the rails placed about the altar, the bows exacted on approaching it, the liturgy, the breach of the sabbath, embroidered copes, lawn sleeves, the use of the ring in marriage, and of the cross in baptism. On account of these, were the popular leaders content to throw the government into such violent convulsions; and, to the disgrace of that age and of this island, it must be acknowledged that the disorders in Scotland entirely, and those in England mostly, proceeded from so mean and contemptible an origin' (H LIV). Writing of the Protectorate, he recalls '. . . that Cromwell thought it requisite to establish something which might bear the face of a commonwealth. He supposed that God, in his providence, had thrown the whole right, as well as power, of government into his hands; and without any more ceremony, by the advice of his council of officers, he sent summons to a hundred and twenty-eight persons of different towns and counties of England, to five of Scotland, to six of Ireland. He pretended, by his sole act and deed, to devolve upon these the whole authority of the state. . . .

'There were great numbers at that time who made it a principle always to adhere to any power which was uppermost, and to support the established government. This maxim is not peculiar to the people of that age; but what may be esteemed peculiar to them is, that there prevailed a hypocritical phrase for expressing so prudential a conduct: it was called a waiting upon Providence. When Providence, therefore, was so kind as to bestow on these men, now assembled together, the supreme authority, they must have been very ungrateful, if, in their turn, they had been wanting in complaisance towards her. . . .

'In this notable assembly were some persons of the rank of gentlemen; but the far greater part were low mechanics; fifth monarchy men, anabaptists, antinomians, independents; the very dregs of the fanatics. They began with seeking God by prayer. This office was performed by eight or ten *gifted* men of the assembly; and with so much success that, according to the confession of all, they had never before, in any of their devotional exercises, enjoyed so much of the Holy Spirit as was then communicated to them' (H LXI). In concluding this treatment of the Commonwealth, Hume remarks, 'At this era, it may be proper to stop a moment, and take a general survey of the age, so far as regards manners, finances, arms, commerce, arts, and sciences. The chief use of history is, that it affords materials for disquisitions of this nature; and it seems the duty of an historian to point out the proper inferences and conclusions.

'No people could undergo a change more sudden and entire in their manners, than did the English nation during this period. From tranquillity, concord, submission, sobriety, they passed in an instant to a state of faction, fanaticism, rebellion, and almost frenzy. . . .

'The gloomy enthusiasm which prevailed among the parliamentary party is

In order to vent his religious scepticism without convicting himself of blasphemy, Hume adopted several traditional stratagems and devised a few of his own. The dialogue form allowed him to assign risky opinions to an interlocutor and safe ones to himself, as in Section XI of the *Enquiry*, or to disappear behind the scenes altogether, as in *Dialogues Concerning Natural Religion*. By removing his discussions to an earlier time or another place, Hume shifted responsibility to readers who chose to apply these lessons to local doctrines and controversies. One may disparage the mental and moral capacities of Jupiter without offending the children of Jehovah. One is permitted to scorn superstition and enthusiasm so long as 'true religion' is spared. It is also fairly safe to kick one of the props from under a religious dogma so long as allegedly stronger ones are left in place. These may be removed at a later date; the diligent philosophical reader will appreciate the net result of the several arguments; the censor, sniffing at each publication as it appears for taints of heresy, may miss the connection. (The only work in which all acknowledged arguments for a religious doctrine are attacked at once, 'Of the Immortality of the Soul', and the only one in which an act proscribed by Christianity is condoned, 'Of Suicide', were both menaced after circulation in manuscript and suppressed by Hume before publication.)

The reservations which many commentators on the *Dialogues* have felt about identifying Philo's position as Hume's are mainly owing to the difficulty of reconciling the sceptic's damaging analysis of the design argument with Hume's own endorsement

surely the most curious spectacle presented by any history; and the most instructive, as well as entertaining, to a philosophical mind. All recreations were, in a manner, suspended by the rigid severity of the presbyterians and independents. . . . Though the English nation be naturally candid and sincere, hypocrisy prevailed among them beyond any example in ancient or modern times. The religious hypocrisy, it may be remarked, is of a peculiar nature; and being generally unknown to the person himself, though more dangerous, it implies less falsehood than any other species of insincerity' (H LXII). To give only one other statement characteristic of Hume's appraisal of the social effects of religion ('enthusiasm'): 'It must, however, be confessed, that the wretched fanaticism which so much infected the parliamentary party was no less destructive of taste and science, than of all law and order. Gaiety and wit were proscribed; human learning despised; freedom of inquiry detested; cant and hypocrisy alone encouraged' (ibid.).

of it elsewhere. On the opening page of *The Natural History of Religion*, for example, he writes, 'The whole frame of nature bespeaks an intelligent author; and no rational enquirer can, after serious reflection, suspend his belief a moment with regard to the primary principles of genuine Theism and Religion' (G & G LV 309).[11] Even without asking what Hume withholds by his qualifier, 'genuine', this apparently erratic proposal of a doctrine elsewhere undermined can be explained in terms of Hume's strategy of limited offensives. Here, in the *Natural History*, the question of religion's 'foundation in reason' is set aside in favour of a question 'concerning its foundation in human nature'. Having traced popular religion to its source in ignorance, duplicity, perversity, and the least estimable passions, Hume can return later to the purely rational foundation of philosophical theism. His condemnation of superstition and fanaticism ('religion, as it has commonly been found in the world') on the evidence of an unsavoury historical record will not offend a thinking man who prides himself on the reasonableness of his religious beliefs and practices. He would, no doubt, be less receptive of Hume's arguments if he were shown in the same volume that the rational foundation of his religion was too insubstantial to support any theological system or religious institution.

Hume's chief defensive manoeuvre after demolishing arguments for a religious dogma is to issue a call to faith. It is a mocking call, no doubt; but who could prove it? His essay, 'Of the Immortality of the Soul', ends on this sanctimonious note: 'Nothing could set in a fuller light the infinite obligation which mankind have to Divine revelation, since we find that no other medium could ascertain this great and important truth' (G & G IV 406).

The famous last words of Philo in the *Dialogues* are these:

But believe me, Cleanthes, the most natural sentiment, which a

---

[11] Cf. the essay, 'Of Suicide', where the major premiss of Hume's argument 'To prove that suicide is no transgression of our duty to God' is stated as follows: '. . . from the mixture, union and contrast of all the various powers of inanimate bodies and living creatures, arises that surprising harmony and proportion which affords the surest argument of supreme wisdom' (G & G IV 408).

well-disposed mind will feel on this occasion, is a longing desire and expectation, that Heaven would be pleased to dissipate, at least alleviate, this profound ignorance, by affording some more particular revelation to mankind, and making discoveries of the nature, attributes, and operations of the divine object of our Faith. A person, seasoned with a just sense of the imperfections of natural reason, will fly to revealed truth with the greatest avidity: While the haughty dogmatist, persuaded that he can erect a complete system of theology by the mere help of philosophy, disdains any farther aid, and rejects this adventitious instructor. To be a philosophical sceptic is, in a man of letters, the first and most essential step towards being a sound, believing Christian. . . . (D 228)

Proving the failure and folly of attempts rationally to justify religious beliefs accords with Hume's general philosophical programme. Natural belief in the uniformity of nature, for example, or in the independent existence of objects of perception, is grounded in instinct and enforced by habit. The initial result of efforts to vindicate such beliefs is scepticism about them. The final result is scepticism of reason itself for contesting beliefs upon which men are determined by nature to act as a condition of survival. The final result, in other words, is that the philosopher who begins with the aim of rationalizing natural beliefs ends as 'a person, seasoned with a just sense of the imperfections of natural reason'. Hume never intended to discredit these beliefs simply because the rational arguments advanced in their defence were specious. What then did he think of this 'longing desire and expectation' of a revelation from Heaven which he (or rather Philo) says is 'the most natural sentiment, which a well-disposed man will feel on this occasion'? Did he consider religious belief a species of natural belief, or sufficiently analogous to it, that a man would be justified in flying 'to revealed truth with the greatest avidity' upon being disappointed by natural theology?

Hume's answer to that question, prepared well in advance, is set down in Section X of *An Enquiry Concerning Human Understanding*, 'Of Miracles', where Hume mischievously declares, 'Our most holy religion is founded on *Faith*, not on reason; and it is a sure method of exposing it to put it to such a trial as it is, by no means, fitted to endure' ($E_1$ 130). This piece is essentially (but not openly) an assessment of the historical evidence for the miracle of the Resurrection, upon which beleaguered theologians could regroup forces when the bulwark of natural religion began to crumble. The alliance between natural and revealed religion which many writers, notably Joseph Butler, had laboured to bring about was inherently unstable; the one relied upon the inviolable reign of divinely legislated natural law, the other upon divine transgressions of it. The harassed Christian who flew to Revelation would find Hume waiting with an established 'maxim, that no human testimony can have such force as to prove a miracle, and make it a just foundation for any such system of religion' ($E_1$ 127).

As Sir Leslie Stephen pointed out seventy-five years ago,[12] and as Antony Flew has had again to remind excited critics twice recently,[13] Hume is concerned with the evidence that must be weighed before deciding whether or not to believe in an alleged miracle. 'A wise man, therefore [who] proportions his belief to the evidence' ($E_1$ 110), must ask himself whether it is more or less probable that a witness is deluded or lying than that 'a violation of the laws of nature' ($E_1$ 114) has taken place. On the one side of the balance there is the uniform experience and, therefore, 'a direct and full *proof*' ($E_1$ 115) of natural sequences—dead men stay dead, for example; on the other side is the variable experience of human veracity. As a historian, Hume was professionally interested and repeatedly engaged in the evaluation of testimony;[14] as a

[12] *History of English Thought in the Eighteenth Century*, (Harbinger, New York, 1962), i. 287.

[13] 'Hume's Check', *Philosophical Quarterly* Vol. 9, no. 34 (Jan. 1959), 2; *Hume's Philosophy of Belief*, Ch. 8, *passim*.

[14] See, for example, Notes G and H to Ch. XLII of *The History of England* in which Hume considers whether the conspiratorial letters by which Mary, Queen of Scots was convicted of high treason were genuine or forgeries. Although Hume (naturally) was much more sympathetic toward Mary ('the most amiable of women') than toward Elizabeth ('an excellent hypocrite'), his scrupulous sifting of circumstantial evidence and sensitive probing of the behaviour of the chief personages involved led him to conclude 'that all the suppositions of . . . forgery . . . fall to the ground'. It is interesting to consider the perfect objectivity of this verdict in the light of Hume's insistence (to which David Fate Norton, cited below, has perceptively called attention) that every man must rely upon his own personal experience of human nature in evaluating testimony. For the

philosopher, he was concerned with articulating general rules by which judicious decisions could be made. 'Of Miracles' is not only an irreligious polemic; it is also a study in historical methodology —'his most extended treatment of the problem of conflicting evidence',[15] as David Fate Norton has observed.

Since every man's first-hand experience is limited, he must often rely upon testimony, 'the reports of eyewitnesses and spectators' ($E_1$ 111). Hume allows that no other means of acquiring beliefs is 'more common, more useful, and even necessary to human life' ($E_1$ 111), and for a historian, obviously, almost no other means are available. The degree of confidence which a man is generally disposed to place in witnesses is a function of his personal experience of the conformity of testimony to fact. If events had proved all of a man's witnesses to be perfectly reliable, he would be justified in accepting future testimony as proof; if all his witnesses had proved to be liars, he would be right to reject all new reports as false. Since experience teaches him that some performances are directed by 'an inclination to truth and a principle of probity' ($E_1$ 112) and others by human susceptibility to prejudice, deceit, and credulity, he must evaluate the probability of each account in the light of the sort of event reported and, so far as he can assess it, the capability and integrity of the witness. When the alleged occurrence is contrary to his invariable experience of natural events, and the witness open to suspicion on other grounds, the wise man will conclude that it is more probable that his witness is deluded or lying than that the miracle actually took place:

It is experience only, which gives authority to human testimony; and it is the same experience, which assures us of the laws of nature. When, therefore, these two kinds of experience are contrary, we have

benefit of those who might consider it paradoxical to admit a subjective ground of historical objectivity, Norton quotes from a letter of Hume's to Hugh Blair: 'No man can have any other experience but his own. The experience of others becomes his only by the credit which he gives to their testimony, which proceeds from his own experience of human nature' (L I 349).

[15] 'History and Philosophy in Hume's Thought', introductory essay to *David Hume: Philosophical Historian*, edd. David Fate Norton and Richard H. Popkin (L.L.A., Bobbs-Merrill, 1965), p. xliv.

nothing to do but subtract the one from the other, and embrace an opinion, either on one side or the other, with that assurance which arises from the remainder. But according to the principle here explained, this subtraction, with regard to all popular religions, amounts to an entire annihilation: and therefore we may establish it as a maxim, that no human testimony can have such force as to prove a miracle, and make it a just foundation for any such system of religion. ($E_1$ 127)

So that, upon the whole, we may conclude, that the *Christian Religion* not only was at first attended with miracles, but even at this day cannot be believed by any reasonable person without one. Mere reason is insufficient to convince us of its veracity: And whoever is moved by *Faith* to assent to it, is conscious of a continued miracle in his own person, which subverts all the principles of his understanding, and gives him a determination to believe what is most contrary to custom and experience. ($E_1$ 130)

Whether one regards this finale as a 'volte-face',[16] as did Taylor, or, like Flew, as 'blisteringly sardonic',[17] it implies a very odd conclusion about religious belief. If Christian faith is a miraculous event, then no wise man would believe anyone who claimed to believe in Christianity. Whether this cryptic flourish of double talk was inspired by caution or by irony, it seems to have landed Hume in a dilemma. For now, apparently, he must either admit that miracles occur by the millions, or that millions of witnesses to their own beliefs are deluded or lying. In other words, he must either admit that beliefs are so frequently acquired in contravention of 'all the principles of [human] understanding' that his theory of the understanding has been disconfirmed, or he must autocratically reject the evidence of countless people who came forth testifying to their own beliefs.

The second line of defence might appear to offer a staggeringly dogmatic expedient. None the less, Hume had frequently adopted it in the past. Readers of the *Treatise* will remember his scepticism about professions of belief in a future state. The indifference to their future condition manifest in most men's conduct Hume attributed to its 'want of resemblance to the present life' (T 114) and consequent weakness of the idea. He remarks that most

---

[16] *Philosophical Studies*, 341.          [17] *Hume's Philosophy of Belief*, 210.

Roman Catholics deplore 'the massacre of St. Bartholomew, as cruel and barbarous, tho' projected or executed against those very people, whom without any scruple they condemn to eternal and infinite punishments. All we can say in excuse for this inconsistency is, that they really do not believe what they affirm concerning a future state . . .' (T 115). The 'studious' and the 'pious', who are here exempted from the charge of hypocrisy, are dealt with elsewhere. In the light of Hume's examination of the doctrine in 'Of the Immortality of the Soul' one need not suppose that he seriously intended to 'except those few, who . . . imprint in their minds the arguments for a future state' (T 114). The case of the pious, the divines and preachers, is also tactfully reserved for later disposal in the essay on immortality:

> There arise, indeed, in some minds, some unaccountable terrors with regard to futurity: But these would quickly vanish, were they not artificially fostered by precept and education. And those, who foster them: what is their motive? Only to gain a livelihood, and to acquire power and riches in this world. Their very zeal and industry, therefore, are an argument against them. (G & G IV 401)

It seems to me very likely that Hume's immediate response to many reports and confessions of religious belief was incredulity. It is not unusual to suspect the sincerity of a man who professes to believe what strikes one as preposterous. But if these notions endure and are propagated, one must, Hume realized, acknowledge that they command some form of assent and come to terms with them. He attempted to do this in *The Natural History of Religion* by constructing an anthropological museum of religious absurdities where he could search in the dark recesses of human nature for the sources of superstition and fanaticism. Here the historical and pyschological sides of Hume's genius worked brilliantly in equipoise upon the problem which constantly fascinated him, aberrant belief, and the result is a richly learned, imaginative, penetrating vision of the primitive origins of religious experience. Once free of the Newtonian machinery with which he had laboured in the *Treatise*, Hume found in history his natural ally. Human nature reveals itself to the man who contemplates its history, and no aspect of that history is more revealing than the delusive beliefs which men have entertained. And no delusions are so deeply rooted as those which infest the religious life. However, in presenting himself as historian and psychopathologist of irrational belief, Hume presupposes the validity of a distinction between rational and irrational belief. The question is how he can justify this distinction on his own principles and, by somehow accommodating legions of exceptions to his theory of how beliefs are acquired, avoid the second of the fatal alternatives mentioned above.

## Section 4. *Critique of Religion, Natural and Revealed: The Principle of Methodological Consistency*

No satisfactory answer to that question can be expected from 'those dangerous friends or disguised enemies' of Hume's philosophy who assume that its critical analysis of religious teaching depends upon a psychological theory of belief. After an obsessive struggle with Taylor, Flew, at the last crucial moment, concedes the match. Taylor had argued that since many people do believe the 'incredible' ('what is most contrary to custom and experience' $(E_1 \ 131)$), Hume was driven to acknowledge these miraculous exceptions. Flew is disarmed by this thrust simply because he has adopted throughout Passmore's generally accepted view of Hume's 'identification of logical with psychological problems':[18]

Taylor here certainly has a point. We have ourselves argued both at the beginning of the present chapter and earlier that insofar as Hume really does want to insist on reducing all questions about the reasonableness or unreasonableness of beliefs about matters of fact and real existence to questions merely about the psychological mechanisms which produce these beliefs, he does indeed leave himself no room to make any evaluative distinction between the reasonable beliefs entertained by the wise and learned and the bigotries and superstitions with which others delude themselves.[19]

[18] *Hume's Intentions*, 18.

[19] *Hume's Philosophy of Belief*, 211–12. Admittedly Flew immediately quotes from *Hume's Intentions* the concession that such criticism ignores ' "an important tendency in Hume's thinking" (Passmore, p. 57)', viz., to distinguish between

Quite so; 'insofar' as Hume really does want to insist upon this sort of psychological reductionism, he is to that extent powerless to defend a distinction between reasonable belief and superstitious delusion. But how far does he really wish to go, or (substituting a question in principle decidable by textual evidence), how far does he actually go up this blind alley? Even in the *Treatise*, where logic is consigned to the empirical science of human nature at the start, a distinction between the critical analysis of defective concepts and theories and the psychological explanation of their prevalence soon emerged. Confused concepts and illicit doctrines were not indicted on the grounds of 'the psychological mechanisms which produce these beliefs'; the 'mechanisms' were introduced only subsequently to explain how such mistaken beliefs had been acquired. Rather than depending upon psychological theories, the philosophical analyses were presupposed by psychology as detecting errors which called for explanation. If Hume originally intended to base a norm of rationality upon his psychology of the understanding, his practice in the *Treatise* persistently departed from that policy, and in the first *Enquiry* his policy was decisively altered.

Perhaps even more indicative of Hume's firmer grasp of his own strategy than the actual reduction of psychological content in the first *Enquiry* is his explicit declaration there that his psychological theory of belief is immaterial to the philosophical investigations which follow ($E_1$ 47). It would never occur to a reader who approached Sections X and XI of the *Enquiry* without preconceptions instilled by commentators to say that Hume is here 'reducing all questions about the reasonableness or unreasonableness of beliefs to questions merely about the psychological mechanisms which produce these beliefs'. It is certainly not upon psychological theory that Hume's critique of revealed and natural

groundless fancies and beliefs authorized by experience, while allowing that all beliefs are in another (rationalistic) sense unjustified. Although Flew thus acknowledges the tendency, he finds no justification for it; on the contrary, he decides that Hume means to say what on his own principles he is not, just as Taylor had argued, entitled to say: 'It is also a critical policy radically unsound to argue, as Taylor does, from [his view of] what "Hume is entitled, on his own principles, to mean" [*Philosophical Studies*, 348] to what in fact he did mean' (ibid. 212).

religion is grounded. It is by reference to rules of historical and judicial evidence and testimony, principles of causal inference, the computation of relative degrees of probability, and estimates of the strength of analogies that Hume makes his assessment of the reasonableness of believing reports of miracles and conclusions about the nature of God. There is a single instance of distinctly psychological theorizing in the whole of these two sections. Early in Part ii of Section X, when considering factors which should diminish confidence in witnesses who testify to miracles, Hume mentions man's 'love of wonder' ($E_1$ 117), his predilection for marvellous and mysterious tales. One may willingly suspend disbelief in a story too fantastic to fall anywhere within the range of probability, and later find some motive or other for relating it as true. Even here the question of the reasonableness of believing purveyors of such phantasies is not reduced to the question of the psychological mechanisms which produce their beliefs, real or affected. They are disbelieved because they report 'facts' which appear physically impossible by contradicting one's own invariable experience. For that reason the wise man who has some acquaintance with human credulity and duplicity, but perhaps no theory of psychological mechanisms at all, will feel justified in dismissing their evidence.

But is he—for that matter, is Hume (who no doubt considered himself a wise man)—really justified in making of his own experience a standard of reasonable belief? In one sense, a strictly rationalistic sense, he is not justified; nor could he ever have claimed to be without renouncing a basic tenet of his teaching. His most distinctive doctrine, and in many ways his most historically important and still most interesting one, is that there can be no rational proof, no ultimate intellectual justification, of any of the beliefs which men hold, nor of their ways of acquiring them. Against this background of epistemological insecurity, however, decisions must be made, and, of course, they are constantly made without demur by men whose souls are untroubled by metaphysical scruples. But these decisions are not all equally wise, and some ground for distinguishing between them must be found. Hume found it in those elementary beliefs which men acquire unreflectively in the course of ordinary experience and upon which they become conditioned by natural consequences to act spontaneously. It would make no sense outside a metaphysical argument to tell a man that he was not justified in believing what he was determined by his nature to believe (that objects exist independently of his perceptions, for example) or what intelligent behaviour in the affairs of everyday life requires him to believe (that the future will resemble the past, for example). There is, therefore, a non-rationalistic sense, a naturalistic and pragmatic sense, in which these universal and biologically indispensable beliefs are justified. Their characteristics, both subjective and objective, are the marks of reasonableness; they are 'more vivid, lively, forcible, firm, steady'; they 'weigh more in the thought' and have 'a superior influence on the passions and imagination' ($E_1$ 49), and they are 'essential to the subsistence of all human creatures' ($E_1$ 55). It is the inconstancy of religious belief or superstition, so dependent upon changes of mood and the caprice and artifice of teachers, and their ineffectualness in governing conduct that arouses Hume's scepticism about them.

Now it is possible to answer the incriminating question which Flew poses in common with so many other critics.

For if belief, considered as a psychological phenomenon, were indeed, as Hume maintains that it is, the automatic result of the operation of a sort of experiential computing machine, then how are we to account for the undoubted fact that people sometimes have 'a determination to believe what is most contrary to custom and experience'?[20]

Part of the 'account' demanded is supplied by the psychological exploration of superstition in *The Natural History of Religion*; but of course the real point of Flew's question is not to ask for an account, but to insinuate that no psychological explanation of the mechanics of acquiring beliefs 'essential to the subsistence of all human creatures' provides any basis for dismissing beliefs acquired through some other process. And that is perfectly true. Since there is no way to demonstrate the rational validity of empirical principles, there is, conversely, no way to prove *a priori* the

[20] *Hume's Philosophy of Belief*, 212.

absurdity of alternative principles. The answer to Flew, however, is that the 'experiential computing machine' does not operate automatically above the level of mental activity which men share with animals. Superstitious thinking, which 'opens a world of its own, and presents us with scenes, and beings, and objects, which are altogether new' (T 271), is well beyond the range of adaptive mental processes governed by instinct and habit. But so, for that matter, are history and natural science and all other theoretical disciplines which engage the minds of men. Obviously, therefore, the tests of reasonableness which a man must pass on the basic practical questions which decide his sagacity cannot be applied directly to his speculative beliefs. When thinking is diverted from its original end of action towards contemplation, it becomes sub-ject to new rules. These rules (like the social virtues) are not natural, but artificial, codifying the tacit decisions of men about how best to regulate theoretical pursuits. At this point questions about what it is reasonable to believe cease to be psychological questions and become methodological questions. And it is upon methodological grounds strictly that Hume discredits belief in reports of miracles in Section X of the first *Enquiry* and disables the argument from design in Section XI.

Methods of science develop out of techniques devised for solving the practical problems of everyday life, and they bear the marks of their ancestry ('. . . philosophical decisions are nothing but the reflections of common life, methodized and corrected' ($E_1$ 162).) The laboratory experiment, as a verification device, is an artificial substitute for the actual events which confirm or disprove judgements in an intellectual state of nature. As a means of discovery, it is a refinement upon the tedious method of accumulating observations of conjoined events as a basis for prediction and explanation. The calculation of probabilities is an adaptation of the natural tendency to base expectation upon relative frequency of occurrence. The principle of parsimony reflects the need in practical tasks to eliminate superfluous opera-tions. And so on. Although the rules of method to which empirical scientists subscribe acquire no absolute authority by virtue of their lineage, they are relatively immune to challenge by those who choose to work by other rules or, perhaps, not consistently by any rules at all. No one is likely to parade his own inconsistency by demanding that the consistency of a method with the natural principles of intelligent behaviour be justified. He is much more likely to cloak his own erratic procedures with the trappings of a respectable discipline. For the Newtonian theologian of the eighteenth century this was a fatal pretence. Now Hume had only to show him that proceedings in natural religion violated certain basic rules honoured in the science from which he was claiming to borrow credit.

Hume's treatment 'Of Miracles' is similar in kind but rather more difficult to execute. What is to be examined here is a historical claim, and the rules for assessing historical testimony were (and still are) less precise and generally recognized than those governing causal inferences in natural science. It is not a matter of invoking an accepted rule, but of having first to articulate implicit rules which conscientious historians impose upon themselves. A suspect document creates for the historian in acute form the sort of problem which everyone faces almost every day. All but the most gullible people acquire certain rules of thumb which they use automatically when they do not feel certain of the veracity of an informant. His manner, coherence, intelligence, motives, reputation, access to fact, concurrence with other informants, and many other considerations (often including some irrelevant ones, no doubt) come into play without any realization that rules are being applied. Historical witnesses are no longer available for questioning and often very little is known about them. None the less the historian must make decisions and be prepared to defend them. His rules of evidence—those 'of common life, methodized and corrected'—will be manifest in the arguments he offers, and the next step, taken by Hume, is to begin to codify them. I am inclined to agree with David Norton when he points out, after cataloguing Hume's rules, that the experience upon which one must ultimately rely when evaluating testimony is one's own '*personal* or *individual* experience'[21] of human nature and the ways of the world. Nevertheless, it seems to me that even from this

---

[21] Op. cit. xlvi.

subjective position Hume scores the decisive point by putting a
most disarming question to Christians who believe witnesses to
the miracle of the Resurrection. According to the rules of evidence
upon which you customarily rely, he in effect asks, would you,
in any matter of secular history, credit the testimony of such
witnesses to so extraordinary an event? Since I cannot suppose
that they could candidly answer 'yes', and yet see no reason for
suspending the rules of historical evidence in this particular case,
I am driven to conclude that Hume was justified in his disbelief.

The potentially verifiable theories of empirical disciplines derive
what authority they have from the natural principles of the understanding. For the theologian, whose metaphysical speculations
are neither grounded in sense experience nor subject to correction
by it, everything is possible but nothing is in the least more
probable than anything else. Hume's conception of the difference
between an empirical hypothesis and a 'philosophical romance'
was clearly explained by Philo in Part I of *Dialogues Concerning
Natural Religion*:

. . . from our earliest infancy we make continual advances in forming
more general principles of conduct and reasoning; . . . the larger
experience we acquire, and the stronger reason we are endowed with,
we always render our principles the more general and comprehensive;
and . . . what we call *philosophy* is nothing but a more regular and
methodical operation of the same kind. To philosophize on such
subjects is nothing essentially different from reasoning on common
life; and we may only expect greater stability, if not greater truth, from
our philosophy, on account of its exacter and more scrupulous method
of proceeding.

But when we look beyond human affairs and the properties of the
surrounding bodies: When we carry our speculations into the two
eternities, before and after the present state of things; into the creation
and formation of the universe; the existence and properties of spirits;
the powers and operations of one universal spirit, existing without
beginning and without end; omnipotent, omniscient, immutable,
infinite, and uncomprehensible: We must be far removed from the
smallest tendency to scepticism not to be apprehensive, that we have
here got quite beyond the reach of our faculties. So long as we confine
our speculations to trade, or morals, or politics, or criticism, we make

appeals, every moment to common sense and experience, which strengthen our philosophical conclusions, and remove (at least, in part) the suspicion, which we so justly entertain with regard to every reasoning that is very subtle and refined. But in theological reasonings, we have not this advantage; while at the same time we are employed upon objects, which, we must be sensible, are too large for our grasp, and of all others, require most to be familiarized to our apprehension. We are like foreigners in a strange country; to whom everything must seem suspicious, and who are in danger every moment of transgressing against the laws and customs of the people with whom they live and converse. We know not how far we ought to trust our vulgar methods of reasoning in such a subject; since, even in common life and in that province which is peculiarly appropriated to them, we cannot account for them, and are entirely guided by a kind of instinct or necessity in employing them. (D 134–5)

# CONCLUSION

HUME's projected philosophical system inspired by Newton was a most improbable venture. Overwhelming technical difficulties stood in the way of applying the experimental method to human thought, feeling, and action. An insoluble problem created by the metaphysical dualism which Hume presupposed vitiated his attempt to explain mental events scientifically. Even if these methodological and metaphysical problems had been overcome, Hume would have arrived at the impassable gulf dividing the descriptive theories by which empirical scientists explain thought processes from the rules of method by which logicians evaluate the products of thought. Moreover, any intention of fixing the limits of human knowledge *a priori*, by deduction from a theory of mind, is alien to Hume's empiricist instincts, a prospect likely to attract him only when dazzled by the glamour of Newton and still unclear and unsure about himself. The sceptical side of Hume's nature found its effective means of expression in a demand for methodological consistency. If Hume could not demonstrate that the answers to certain metaphysical and religious questions are 'utterly inaccessible to the understanding' (E$_1$ 11), he could show that they have been reached by violating rules of evidence and principles of inference tacitly accepted in the affairs of everyday life and endorsed in history and natural science. Thus the onus is put upon the theologians and metaphysicians to justify their sudden departures from accepted practices when factors of intellectual vanity, fear, acquired prejudice, and self-interest are at stake. While the world waits for a satisfactory defence, one may say, in the meantime, that Hume's critical aims have been realized.

Hume's constructive aims underwent a comparable change. At first he thought that his moral, political, and aesthetic philosophy should be firmly grounded in a comprehensive theory of human nature. In Book II of the *Treatise* he produced an elaborate psychology of the emotions from which, in conjunction with his theory of mind, explanations of social behaviour were to be derived. Sympathy is the prime example of an associationist mechanism to which he reduces a wide range of behaviour involving the ethics of personal relationships, social responsibility, and aesthetic experience. The recastings of his psychological, moral, and political theories give notice of the dissolution of the original system. The psychology of the passions is withdrawn as a basis for ethical theory—*A Dissertation on the Passions*, his only perfectly monotonous and uninspired book, is a sparse, dry abstract of Book II of the *Treatise*, and it appears only when Hume's second and final ethical work has already been in print for nine years. No suggestion is made that the *Dissertation* might be of any use for grounding a system of the moral sciences. Its purpose, Hume concludes by saying, is simply to show that the experimental method can be applied to the psychology of the emotions, an enterprise in which, to judge by this perfunctory performance, he had lost interest.

*An Enquiry Concerning the Principles of Morals* depends upon no psychological theory of mind or emotion. It is written on the supposition that moral feelings, attitudes, and judgements constitute a distinct class of phenomena open to independent investigation. 'Sympathy' resumes its ordinary meaning of 'humanity and benevolence' ($E_2$ 220) and no longer functions as a prime technical concept of psychology for unifying the explanations of natural (personal) and artificial (social) virtues. No more compelling evidence of Hume's waning interest in theoretical psychology could be found than by comparing his theory of sympathy in the *Treatise* with the cursory use he makes of the notion in the second *Enquiry*. In the *Treatise* he wrote, 'No quality of human nature is more remarkable, both in itself and in its consequences, than the propensity we have to sympathize with others, and to receive by communication their inclinations and sentiments, however different from, or even contrary to our own' (T 316). After exemplifying this, he added, 'So remarkable a phaenomenon merits our attention, and must be trac'd up to its first principles'

(T 317). In the second *Enquiry*, apparently discarding his earlier intricate psychological explanation, he writes:

> It is needless to push our researches so far as to ask, why we have humanity or a fellow-feeling with others. It is sufficient, that this is experienced to be a principle in human nature. We must stop somewhere in our examination of causes; and there are, in every science, some general principles, beyond which we cannot hope to find any principle more general. . . . It is not probable, that these principles can be resolved into principles more simple and universal, whatever attempts have been made to that purpose. But if it were possible, it belongs not to the present subject; and we may here safely consider these principles as original: happy, if we can render all the consequences sufficiently plain and perspicuous. ($E_2$ 219 n; quoted above, pp. 93–4.)

Only once in *An Enquiry Concerning the Principles of Morals* does Hume appeal directly to the doctrine of a previous work of his own, and that is when he returns in Appendix 1 to consider further the question discussed in the opening Section: 'concerning the general foundation of Morals; whether they be derived from Reason, or from Sentiment?' ($E_2$ 170). Having conceded the need of reason to devise means to moral ends, he still insists that the choice of ends is not based upon rational decision but upon preference governed by feeling. Recalling the logical distinction drawn in the first *Enquiry* between types of propositions (synthetic and analytic)—'Reason judges either of *matter of fact* or of *relations*' ($E_2$ 287; cf. $E_1$ 25)—he enjoins the rationalists to show that the moral offence of ingratitude is a particular sensible fact or an intelligible logical relation. It is indicative of the change of interest and method which I have been documenting that the doctrine to which he appeals to support his criticism of rationalist ethics is a logical one, and that he does not renew the attempt made in the *Treatise* to explain confusion on this point psychologically in terms of fluctuations in the intensity of impressions and ideas which sometimes obscure their distinction (T 470).

Hume's Introduction to *A Treatise of Human Nature* ended on a discordant but prophetic note. He had just declared that his experimental science of human nature would provide the basis for rapid advances in the social sciences. Almost immediately he was brought up short by the realization that phenomena involving human agency is distorted by experimental manipulation (essentially, for Hume, introspection), and that knowledge of human nature and society must be attained by another means: 'We must therefore glean up our experiments in this science from a cautious observation of human life, and take them as they appear in the common course of the world, by men's behaviour in company, in affairs, and in their pleasures' (T xxiii). Although Hume suppressed his awareness of the methodological problem and proceeded throughout the *Treatise* to conduct his 'experiments', it was obvious that what he knew about human nature he had learned from his own observation and the records of history and not from experimental psychology.

Hume's mature work as a political philosopher, the *Political Discourses*, borrows nothing from the science of psychology. Of course it owes a great deal to psychological insight cultivated through a reflective search for the meaning of human history. Hume discerns the motive of self-aggrandizement behind the Whigs' advocacy of the social contract as grounds for limiting the prerogatives of monarchy. He relies entirely upon historical evidence to refute this doctrine which, since Locke, had become the mainstay of liberal ideology both at home and abroad. He takes no notice of the psychological considerations from which Hobbes had derived his hypothetical reconstruction of the origin of government. As in *The History of England*, the social-contract theory is rejected in his essay 'Of the Original Contract' because 'it is not justified by history or experience in any age or country of the world. Almost all the governments, which exist at present, or of which there remains any record in story, have been founded originally, either on usurpation or conquest, or both, without any pretence of a fair consent, or voluntary subjection of the people' (G & G III 447).

Step by step Hume's science of human nature was transformed into a history of human acts. Perhaps some day the truths about man to be learned from the Book of Deeds will be made intelligible within the system of some Newton of the moral sciences. That was an honour to which Hume no longer aspired after he

failed to attain it in *A Treatise of Human Nature*. Probably he
realized that the time was not ripe for a grand synthesis in
psychology. Perhaps he concluded that in order to make wise
decisions in the affairs of everyday life and of politics it is enough
to know the truth about men even if one doesn't understand it.
What seems to me certain is that mid-way in his career, when
writing *An Enquiry Concerning Human Understanding*, Hume
decided that the student of human nature has more to learn from
history than from the experimental method:

> Mankind are so much the same, in all times and places, that history
> informs us of nothing new or strange in this particular. Its chief use is
> only to discover the constant and universal principles of human nature,
> by showing men in all varieties of circumstances and situations, and
> furnishing us with materials from which we may form our observations
> and become acquainted with the regular springs of human action and
> behaviour. These records of wars, intrigues, factions, and revolutions,
> are so many collections of experiments, by which the politician or
> moral philosopher fixes the principles of his science, in the same
> manner as the physician or natural philosopher becomes acquainted
> with the nature of plants, minerals, and other external objects, by the
> experiments which he forms concerning them. Nor are the earth,
> water, and other elements, examined by Aristotle, and Hippocrates,
> more like to those which at present lie under our observation than the
> men described by Polybius and Tacitus are to those who now govern
> the world. ($E_1$ 83–4)

# Index of Names

D'Alembert, Jean de Rond, 74
Alexander, G. H., 51 n.
Anaxagoras, 67
Aquinas, Saint Thomas, 67
Aristotle, 111 n., 192
Arnauld, Antoine, 125
Ayer, Sir Alfred Jules, 150

Bacon, Sir Francis, 31, 32, 68 n., 75, 108
Balguy, John, 65
Basson, A. H., 137, 140–2, 150
Bayle, Pierre, 69–70, 115
Beattie, James, 17 n., 139, 166
Bentley, Richard, 45, 45 n., 46, 49, 51 n., 65, 66
Berkeley, George, 12, 51 n., 52, 75, 79 n., 126
Bernoulli, John, 51 n.
Birch, Dr. Thomas, 74, 75
Black, Joseph, 64, 75, 75 n.
Boyle, Sir Robert, 41, 45, 63, 64, 65, 73, 117, 118
Brewster, Sir David, 43 n.
Brown, John, 166
Buffon, Georges Louis Leclerc, Comte de, 74
Butler, Joseph, 77, 77 n., 167, 170, 176

Cajori, Florian, 27 n., 41 n., 52
Caroline, Princess of Wales, 51 n.
Cavendish, Henry, 64
Chappell, V. C., 29, 30, 79 n., 143, 149 n.
Cherbury, Lord Herbert of, 66
Cheyne, Dr. George, 65, 68, 68 n., 80
Cicero, 79 n.
Clarke, Samuel, 51 n., 57, 65, 68, 68 n., 70 n.
Clephane, John, 74
Cohen, I. Bernard, 34 n., 37, 38 n., 39, 40, 42, 50, 57, 63, 69
Collins, Anthony, 66

Copernicus, Nicolas, 27, 40, 107, 111 n.
Cotes, Roger, 27 n., 46, 48–9, 51 n., 52, 83
Craig, John, 65
Cromwell, Oliver, 172 n.
Cudworth, Ralph, 70 n.

Descartes, René, 1–2, 9–11, 32, 39, 41, 43, 46, 48, 49, 58–60, 63, 64, 65, 70 n., 71, 75, 125, 127, 136
Diderot, Denis, 69, 74

Edelston, J., 49 n.
Elizabeth I, Queen, 176 n.
Elliot, Gilbert, 157
Epicurus, 46 n., 169, 171
Euclid, 116

Flamsteed, John, 111
Flew, Antony, 18 n., 29, 79 n., 137, 142, 149, 155, 156, 166–7, 176, 178, 180, 180 n., 183–4
Fontenelle, Bernard le Bovier de, 59 n.
Franklin, Benjamin, 28, 64, 74

Galileo, 27, 30–1, 34, 108, 111 n., 120, 123
Gardiner, P. L., 29 n.
Gay, John, 75
Gibbon, Edward, 166
Green, T. H., xi, 65, 78, 167
Greig, J. Y. T., xii, 68 n.
Grose, T. H., xi, 65, 78, 167
Guericke, Otto von, 123
Guerlac, Henry, 75 n.

Hall, Marie Boas, 60 n.
Hall, Rupert A., 60 n.
Halley, Edmund, 39, 43, 64, 109, 111
Hartley, David, 75, 124
Hartsoecker, Nicolas, 49, 52
Helmer, Olaf, 42 n.

Taylor, A. E., 79, 79 n., 136, 165–7, 178, 180, 180 n.
Tindal, Mathew, 66
Toland, John, 66
Tonson, 59 n.

Voltaire, 69

Warburton, William, 66, 78, 166

Weyl, Hermann, 42
Whiston, William, 65, 68
Wittgenstein, Ludwig, 88
Wolheim, Richard, 78 n.
Woolaston, William, 65
Woolston, Thomas, 66
Wren, Christopher, 109

Zeno of Elea, 69, 115

# Index of Subjects